IMAGES
*of America*

# JEWS OF RHODE ISLAND

1658–1958

Seven individuals had the vision to found an organization dedicated to procuring, collecting, and preserving historical material relating to the Jews of Rhode Island. From their early efforts, our organization grew. The association publishes an annual journal, *The Rhode Island Jewish Historical Notes*, which records this history and maintains an archive.

IMAGES
*of America*

# JEWS OF RHODE ISLAND
## 1658–1958

Geraldine S. Foster, Eleanor F. Horvitz, and Judith Weiss Cohen
From the Archives of the Rhode Island Jewish Historical Association

ARCADIA
PUBLISHING

ISBN 978-0-7385-9015-8

Published by Arcadia Publishing
Charleston, South Carolina

Printed in the United States of America

For all general information contact Arcadia Publishing at:
Telephone 843-853-2070
Fax 843-853-0044
E-mail sales@arcadiapublishing.com
For customer service and orders:
Toll-Free 1-888-313-2665

Visit us on the Internet at www.arcadiapublishing.com

*Dedicated to Judith Weiss Cohen,*
*our co-author, editor, and friend*
*who died during the preparation of this book,*
*November 17, 1997*

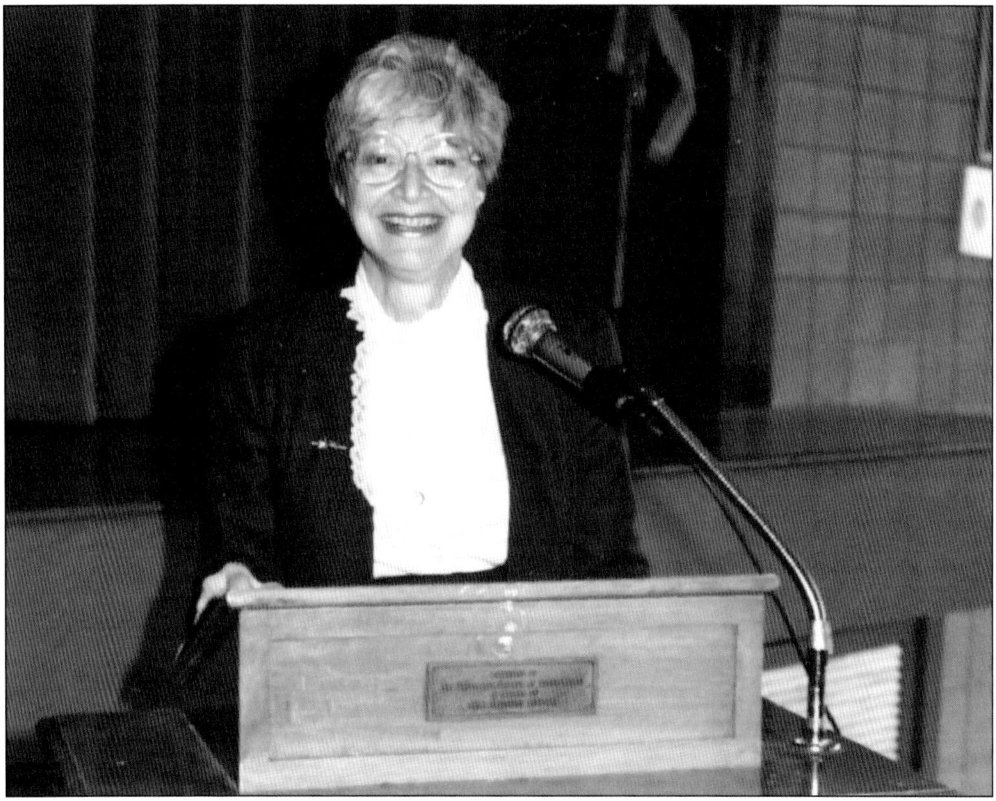

Judith Weiss Cohen at the podium of the 1991 Annual Meeting of the Rhode Island Jewish Historical Association.

# Contents

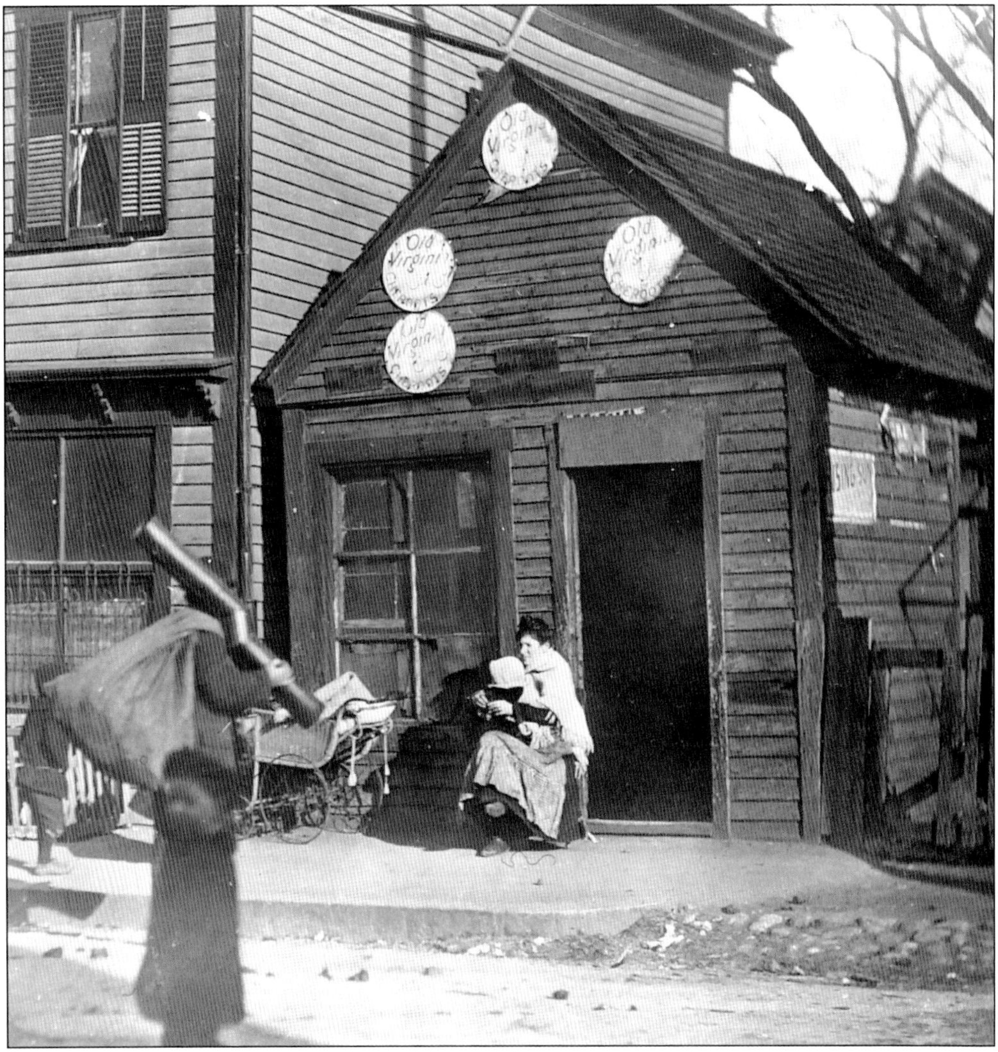

"Jewtown," Lower Chalkstone Avenue, *c.* 1903. (Courtesy of Rhode Island Historical Society.)

# Introduction

Jews have been a part of the American experience since early colonial days. Although a tiny minority, they have contributed in important ways to this country's social, economic, scientific, and cultural fabric.

The first Jews came to America, to New Amsterdam, in 1654. They were not welcomed but were finally permitted to remain, with restrictions.

Four years later other Jewish settlers arrived on these shores, this time in Rhode Island. Word of Roger Williams's "lively experiment" had spread quickly, even to the islands of the Caribbean. Many Jews had found their way to the Caribbean after their expulsion from the Iberian Peninsula. Attracted by the promise of religious toleration and economic opportunity, a small group left Barbados for Newport. This time their reception was more welcoming. With their coming begins the history of the Jews in Rhode Island.

This history is both colorful and rich in its variety. It speaks of the interaction of generations of Jews with their home in America. It chronicles the experiences of the immigrants and their descendants in Rhode Island. *Jews in America: 1658–1958* offers vignettes of that history, moments captured in photographs and ephemera collected in the archives of the Rhode Island Jewish Historical Association. It is by no means definitive, but rather a sampling of persons, places, and happenings during the first three hundred years of the Jewish experience in Rhode Island.

Eleanor F. Horvitz
Librarian/Archivist
Rhode Island Jewish Historical Association
130 Sessions Street
Providence, RI 02906

*One*

# The First Jews in Rhode Island: Newport

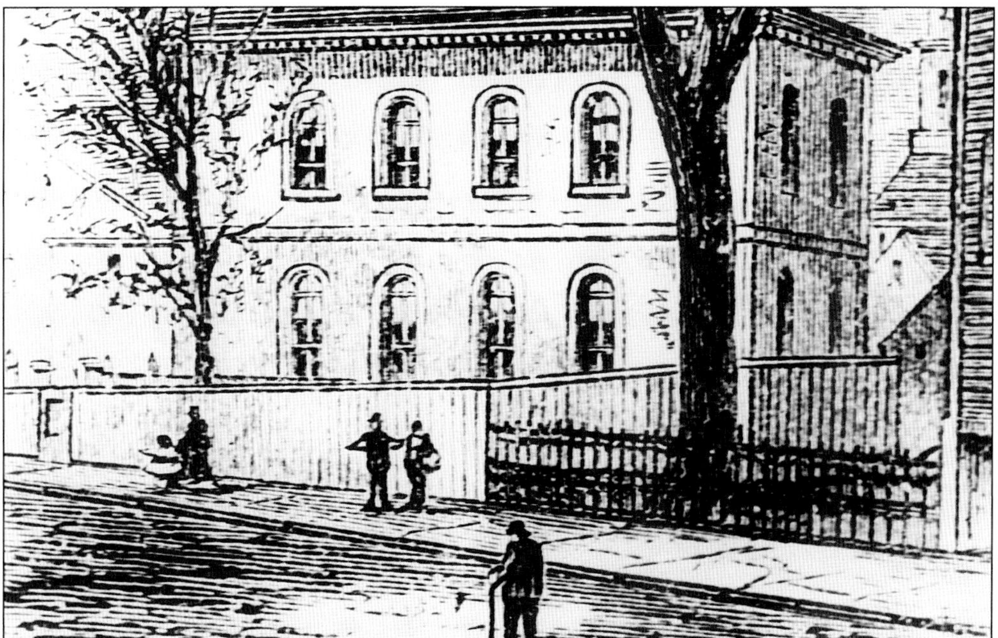

A woodcut of the Touro Synagogue from *Harper's New Monthly Magazine*, August 1874, vol. 49. This edifice, completed in 1763 for Congregation Yeshuat Israel, was designed by renown architect Peter Harrison. The synagogue stands at an acute angle to the street in order to have the Holy Ark facing east toward Jerusalem as is customary in Jewish houses of worship. It is believed that the synagogue was called Touro because of a bequest, the Touro Jewish Synagogue Fund, made by Abraham Touro, which saved the building from ruin. (Courtesy of Friends of Touro Synagogue.)

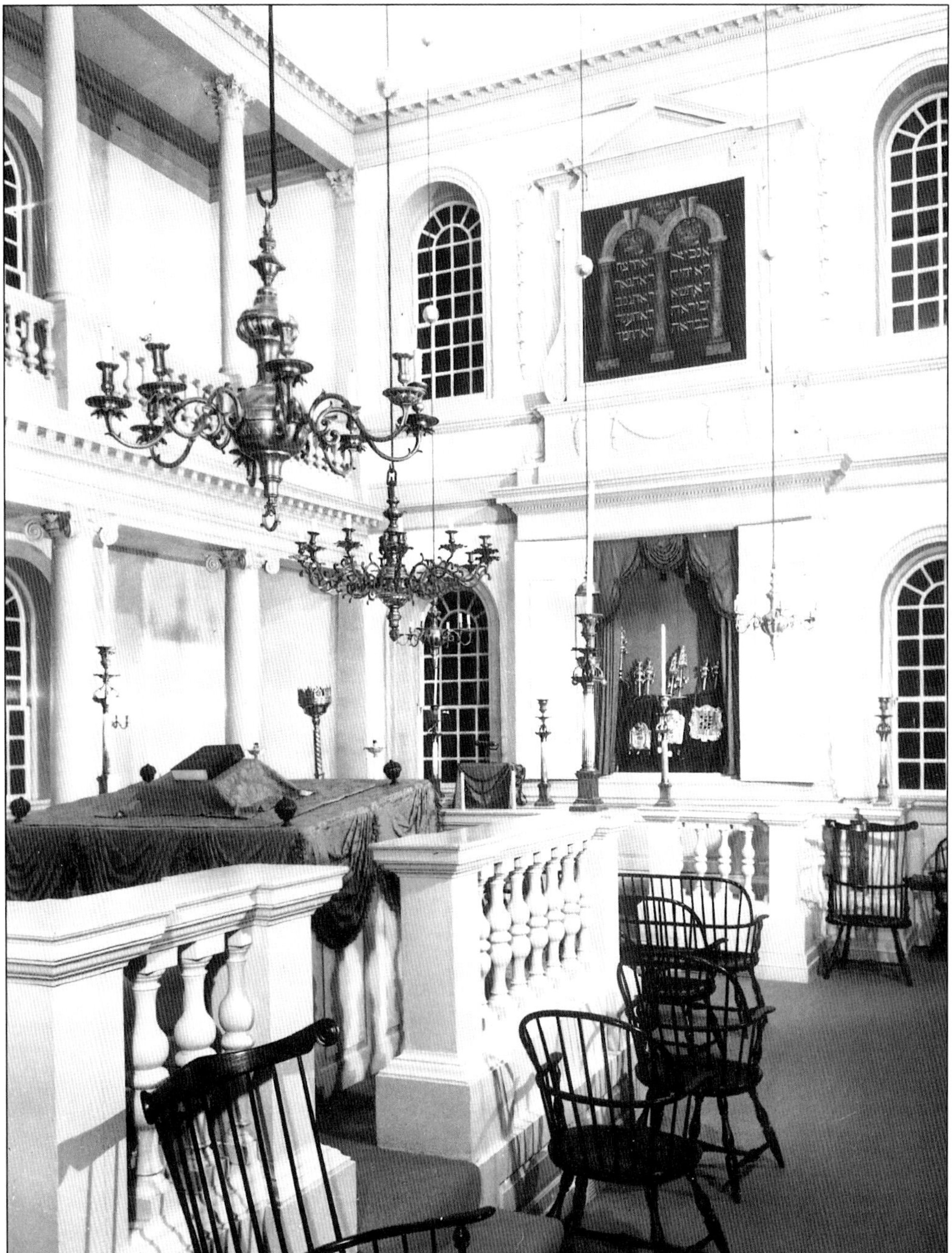

The interior of the Touro Synagogue. The interior of the synagogue resembles in miniature the design of the Sephardic Synagogue in Amsterdam. One tradition holds that Isaac Touro described the original building in great detail to his friend Peter Harrison, who then copied many of its details. (Photograph by John Hopf.)

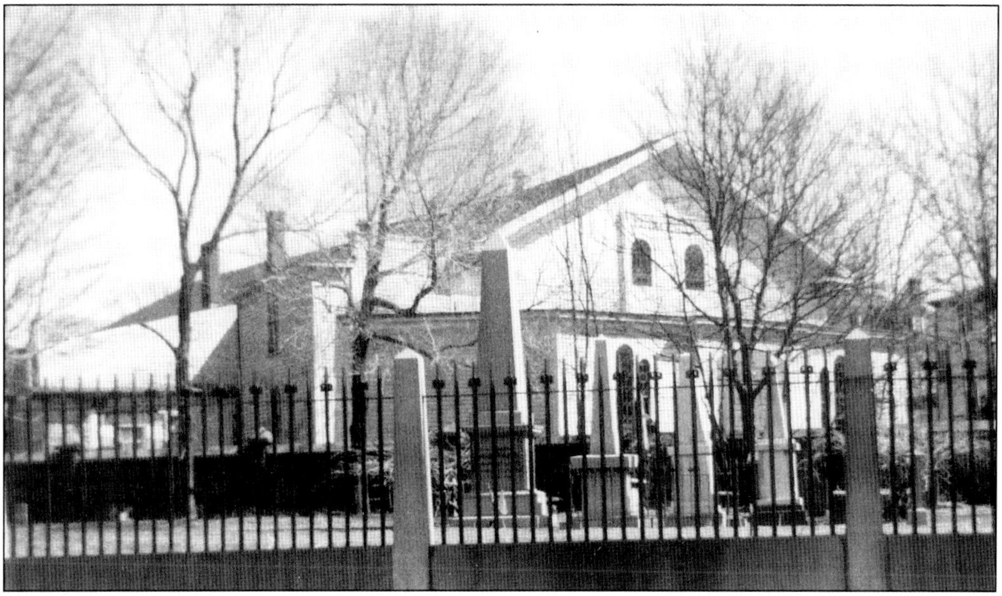

The Old Cemetery. The first Jews to settle in Newport arrived in 1658 from Barbados and immediately entered the commercial life of the colony. Among the few bits of evidence of their settlement is a copy of a deed dated February of 1678 to land at Kay Street and Bellevue Avenue for use as a cemetery, which indicated their intent to remain in Newport. Charges of trade law violations discouraged many of them, and although vindicated, many returned to Barbados. (Photograph by Francine Helfner.)

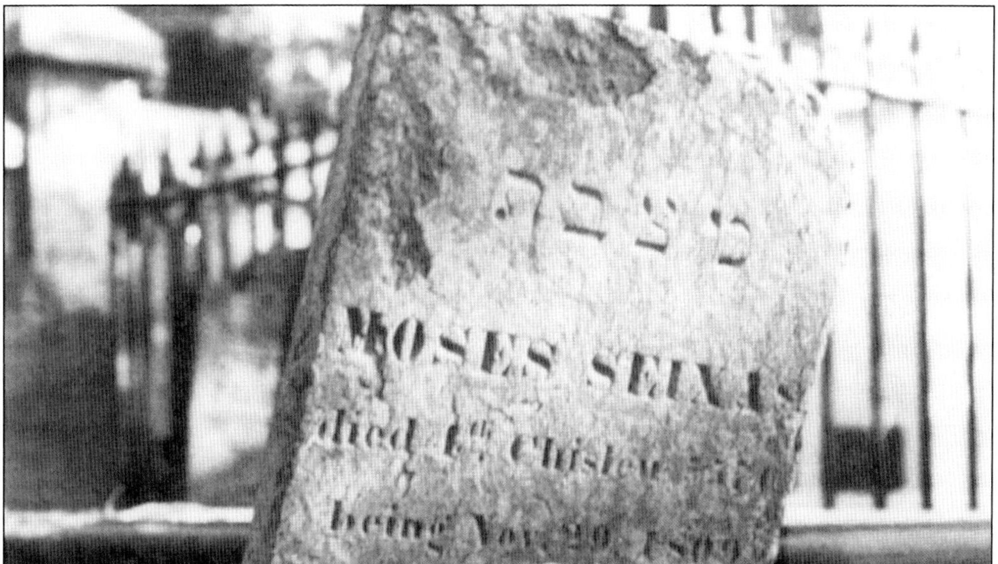

The gravestone of Moses Seixas, merchant and warden of Congregation Yeshuat Israel. Moses Seixas also took on the duties of "mohel" (Heb. ritual circumciser) for the community after learning the delicate procedure through correspondence with a New York "mohel." Seixas became first Grand Master of the King David Masonic Lodge, and in 1795 he helped establish the Bank of Rhode Island. He served as cashier until his death in 1809. (Photograph by Edwin Connelly.)

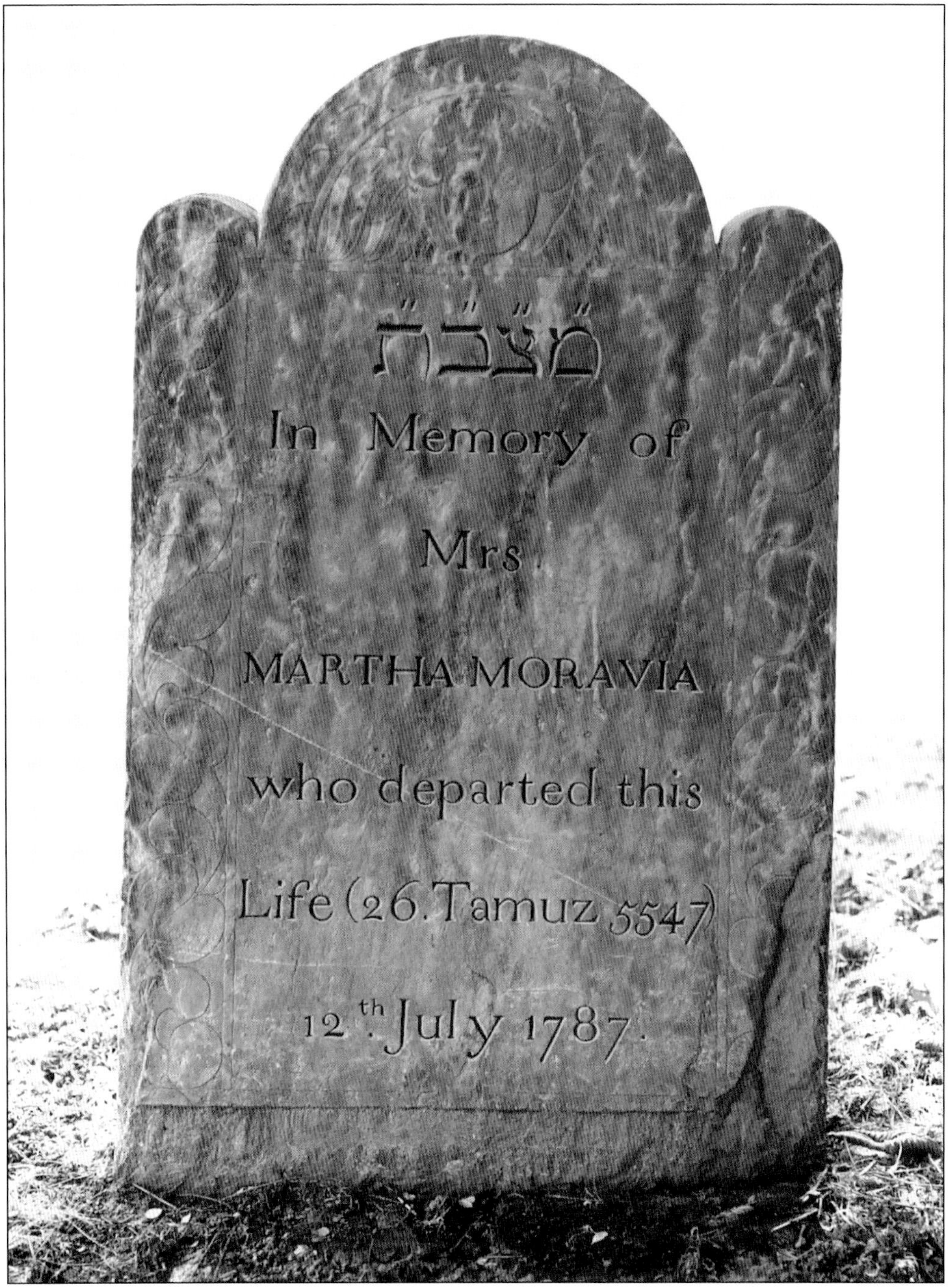


The gravestone of Martha Moravia. (Photograph by Edwin Connelly.)

Aaron Lopez, an eminent businessman with considerable interests in shipping, imports, and exports. The secret of Lopez's great success lay in the variety of his commercial enterprise, as witnessed by the copy of one of his contracts pictured below. Lopez was also frequently cited for his sense of honor and his philanthropy. A patriot, he and his family fled to Leicester, Massachusetts, when the British occupied Newport. He perished in an accident while returning to Newport after the Revolutionary War. (Courtesy of American Jewish Historical Society.)

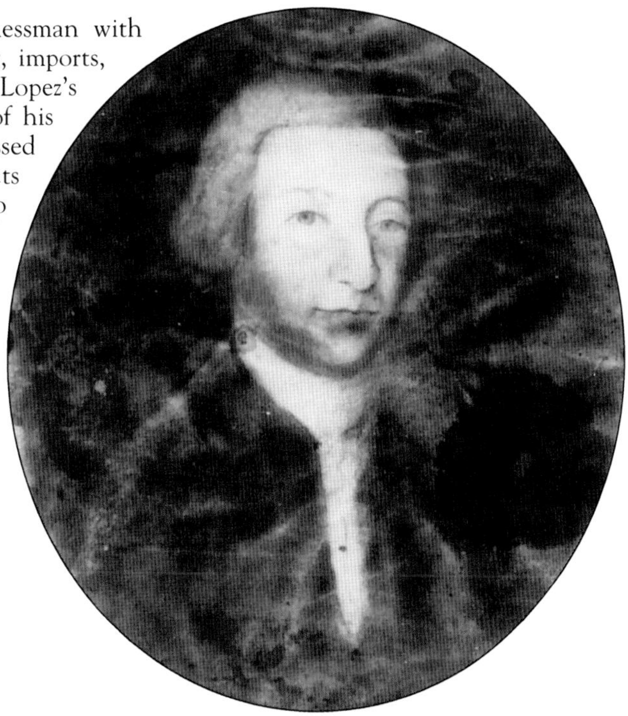

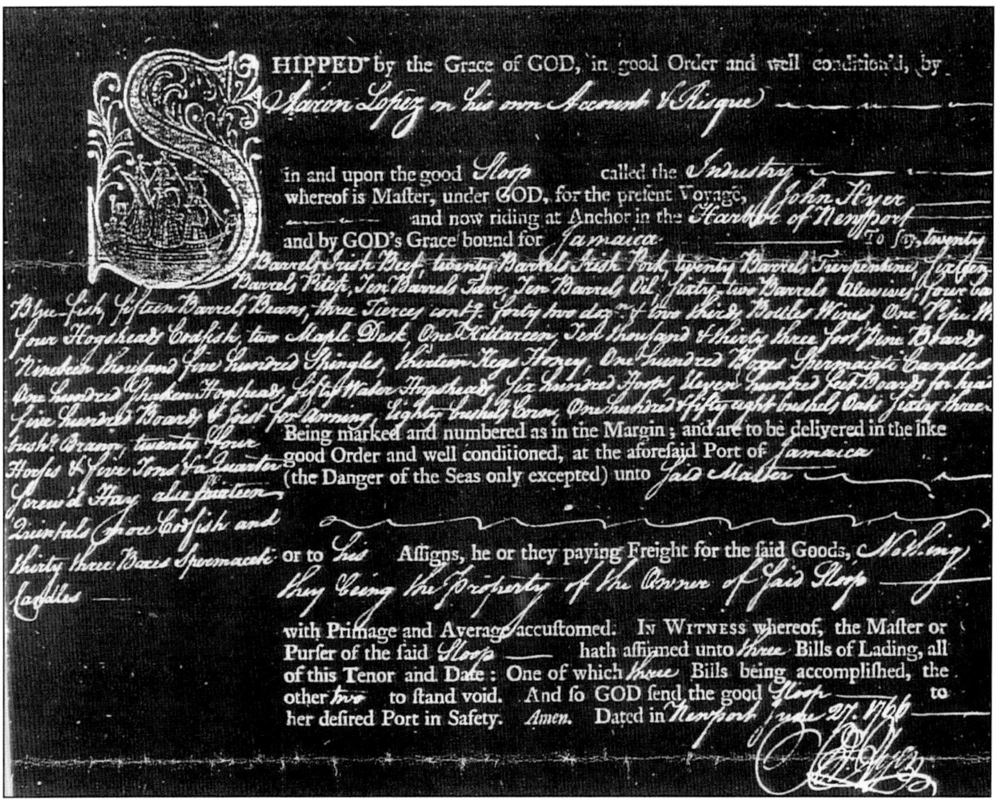

SHIPPED by the Grace of GOD, in good Order and well condition'd, by Aaron Lopez on his own Account & Risque

in and upon the good Sloop called the Industry whereof is Master, under GOD, for the present Voyage, John Ayer and now riding at Anchor in the Harbor of Newport and by GOD's Grace bound for Jamaica To say, twenty Barrels Irish Beef, twenty Barrels Irish Pork, twenty Barrels Turpentine, Sixteen Barrels Pitch, Ten Barrels Tar, Ten Barrels Oil, sixty two Barrels Alewives, four ba[illegible] Blue-fish, fifteen Barrels Beans, three Tierces cont. forty two doz. of two thirds Bottles Wines, One Pipe W[illegible] four Hogsheads Codfish, two Maple Desk, One Kittareen, Ten thousand & thirty three foot Pine Boards Nineteen thousand five hundred Shingles, Thirteen Kegs Honey, One hundred Boxes Spermaceti Candles One hundred Shaken Hogsheads, Fifty Water Hogsheads, Six hundred Hoops, Eleven hundred feet Boards for hea[illegible] five hundred Boards & Joist for Awning, Eighty bushels Corn, One hundred & fifty eight bushels Oats, Sixty three bush. Bran, twenty four Horses & five Tons & a Quarter Screw'd Hay, also fourteen Quintals of Codfish and thirty three Boxes Spermaceti Candles

Being marked and numbered as in the Margin; and are to be delivered in the like good Order and well conditioned, at the aforesaid Port of Jamaica (the Danger of the Seas only excepted) unto said Master or to his Assigns, he or they paying Freight for the said Goods, Nothing they being the property of the Owner of said Sloop with Primage and Average accustomed. IN WITNESS whereof, the Master or Purser of the said Sloop hath affirmed unto three Bills of Lading, all of this Tenor and Date: One of which three Bills being accomplished, the other two to stand void. And so GOD send the good Sloop to her desired Port in Safety. *Amen.* Dated in Newport June 27. 1766

One of Aaron Lopez's bills of lading. (Courtesy of American Jewish Historical Society.)

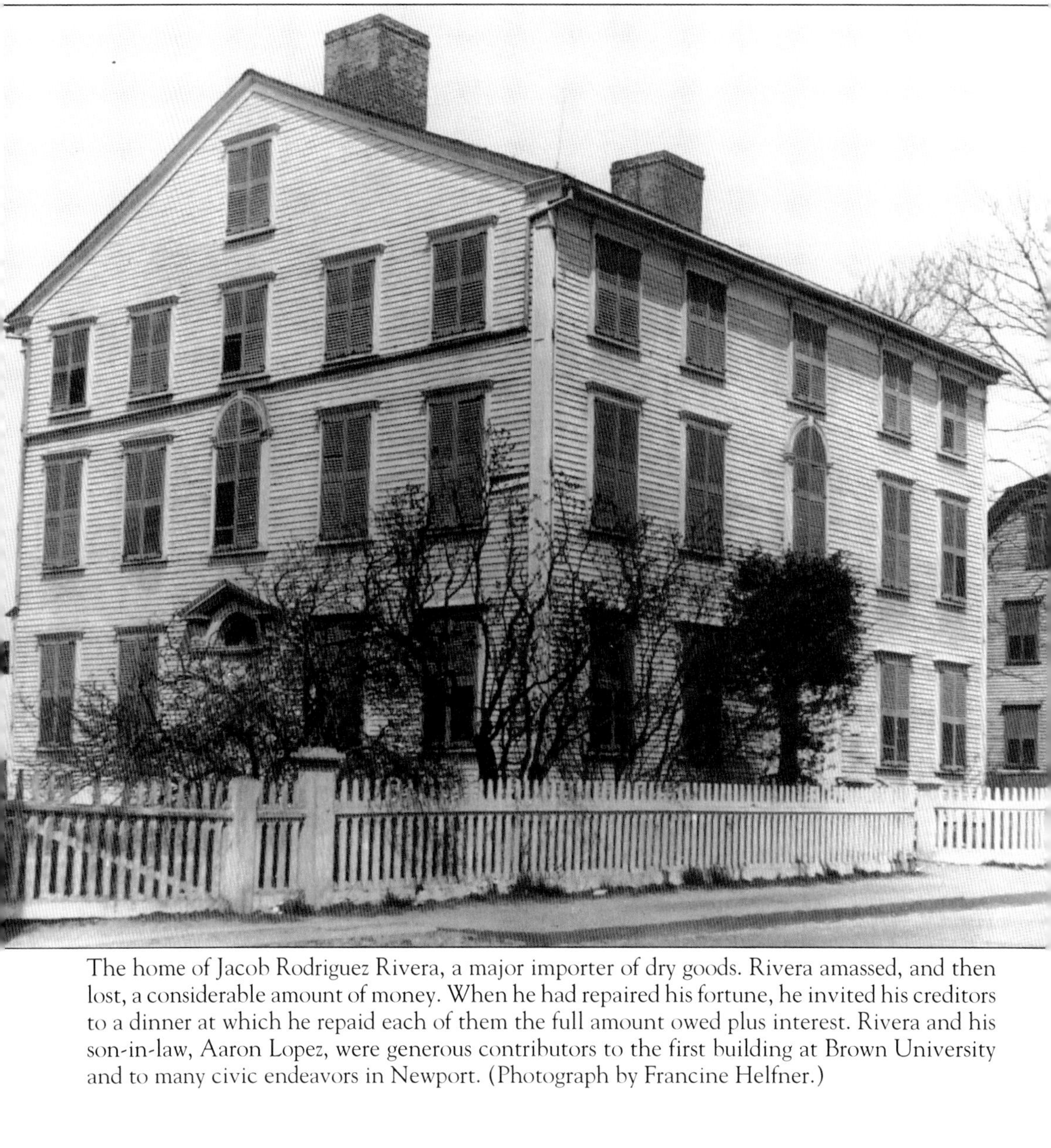

The home of Jacob Rodriguez Rivera, a major importer of dry goods. Rivera amassed, and then lost, a considerable amount of money. When he had repaired his fortune, he invited his creditors to a dinner at which he repaid each of them the full amount owed plus interest. Rivera and his son-in-law, Aaron Lopez, were generous contributors to the first building at Brown University and to many civic endeavors in Newport. (Photograph by Francine Helfner.)

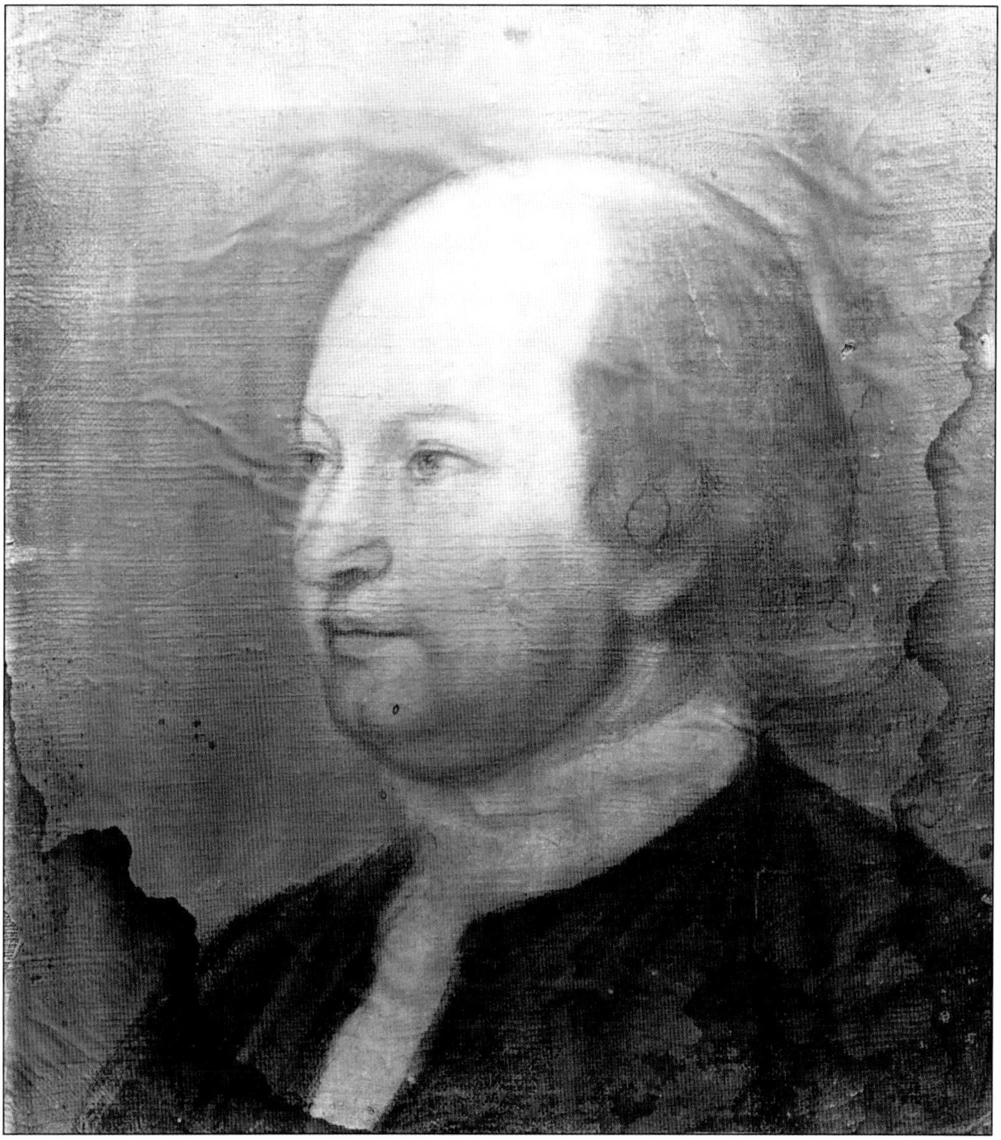

Reverend Isaac Touro in a pastel by Gilbert Stuart. Reverend Touro was one of the founders of the Touro Synagogue. He came to Newport in 1758 and served as the congregation's first religious leader. He married Reyna Hays in 1773; three children were born of this union. During the American Revolution, he took his family to New York City, and later to Kingston, Jamaica, where he died at the age of 46. Left penniless, his wife and children were brought to Boston by her brother, Moses Michael Hays. (Courtesy of Phillips Library, Peabody Essex Museum, Salem, Massachusetts.)

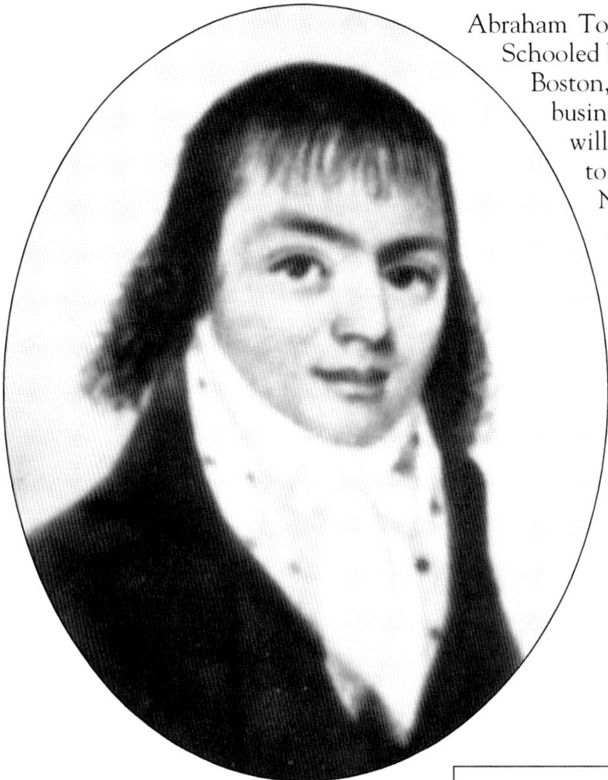

Abraham Touro, one of Isaac Touro's two sons. Schooled by his uncle, Moses Michael Hays, in Boston, Abraham became a very successful businessman. During his lifetime and in his will, he gave considerable sums of money to preserve the old Jewish cemetery of Newport as well as the synagogue. At his request, he was buried in the cemetery he saved from disrepair and neglect. (Courtesy of Newport Historical Society.)

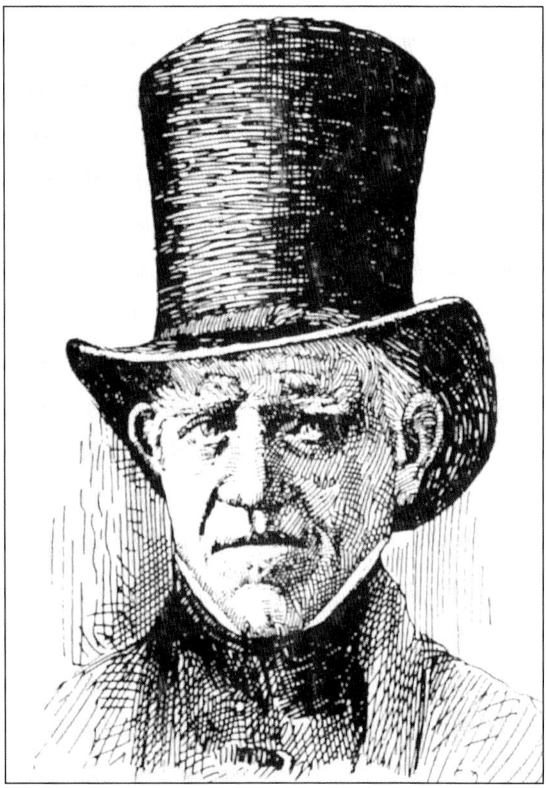

Judah Touro, son of Isaac Touro. Judah Touro, the self-effacing philanthropist, gained his business acumen from his uncle, Moses Michael Hays. He left Boston for New Orleans, where, through commerce and prudent investment in real estate, he became very successful. In his will he left an endowment entrusted to the Newport Town Council to pay for the services of "a reader or minister" to officiate at the synagogue. (Courtesy of American Jewish Historical Society.)

"TO THE HEBREW CONGREGATION IN NEWPORT
RHODE ISLAND

Gentlemen.

While I receive, with much satisfaction, your address replete with expressions of affection and esteem, I rejoice in the opportunity of assuring you, that I shall always retain a grateful remembrance of the cordial welcome I experienced in my visit to Newport, from all classes of Citizens.

The reflection on the days of difficulty and danger which are past is rendered the more sweet, from a consciousness that they are succeeded by days of uncommon prosperity and security. If we have wisdom to make the best use of the advantages with which we are now favored, we cannot fail, under the just administration of a good government, to become a great and a happy people.

The Citizens of the United States of America have a right to applaud themselves for having given to mankind examples of an enlarged and liberal policy: a policy worthy of imitation. All possess alike liberty of conscience and immunities of citizenship. It is now no more that toleration is spoken of, as if it was by the indulgence of one class of people, that another enjoyed the exercise of their inherent natural rights. For happily the Government of the United States, which gives to bigotry no sanction, to persecution no assistance requires only that they who live under its protection should demean themselves as good citizens, in giving it on all occasions their effectual support.

It would be inconsistent with the frankness of my character not to avow that I am pleased with your favorable opinion of my administration, and fervent wishes for my felicity. May the Children of the Stock of Abraham, who dwell in this land, continue to merit and enjoy the good will of the other Inhabitants; while every one shall sit in safety under his own vine and figtree, and there shall be none to make him afraid. May the father of all mercies scatter light and not darkness in our paths, and make us all in our several vocations useful here, and in his own due time and way everlastingly happy.

G. WASHINGTON"

*The famous letter by President George Washington to the Hebrew Congregation in Newport, August 21, 1790. It is interesting to note that Washington uses the same words that were addressed to him by Moses Seixas, President of the Newport Congregation, "to bigotry no sanction, to persecution no assistance" . . .*

George Washington's letter to the Jewish Congregation of Newport. This letter was written in response to an inquiry by Moses Seixas concerning the disposition of the government regarding liberty. Washington's memorable reply is an affirmation of civil and religious freedoms. The letter is the centerpiece of an annual commemoration at the Touro Synagogue.

## THE JEWISH CEMETERY AT NEWPORT

by Henry Wadsworth Longfellow

How strange it seems! These Hebrews in their graves,
Close by the street of this fair seaport town,
Silent beside the never-silent waves,
At rest in all this moving up and down!

And these sepulchral stones, so old and brown,
That pave with level flags their burial-place,
Seem like the tablets of the Law, thrown down
And broken by Moses at the Mountain's base.

Closed are the portals of their Synagogue,
No Psalms of David now the silence break,
No Rabbi reads the ancient Decalogue
In the grand dialect the Prophets spake.

How came they here? What burst of Christian hate,
What persecution, merciless and blind,
Drove o'er the sea—that desert desolate—
These Ishmaels and Hagers of mankind?

Pride and humiliation hand in hand
Walked with them through the world where'er they went;
Trampled and beaten were they as the sand,
And yet unshaken as the continent.

"The Jewish Cemetery at Newport" (1852), a poem by H.W. Longfellow, abridged. Although moving, Longfellow's words were not quite accurate. The five years of British occupation during the Revolutionary War ruined Newport's economy and divided the small Jewish community. After the war, some of those who sided with the patriot's cause returned, but in 1822, Moses Levy, the last Jew in Newport, left. In the following decades a summer colony arose, and services were held on an irregular basis, until the next permanent settlement occurred in the 1870s.

# *Two*

# Waves of Immigration

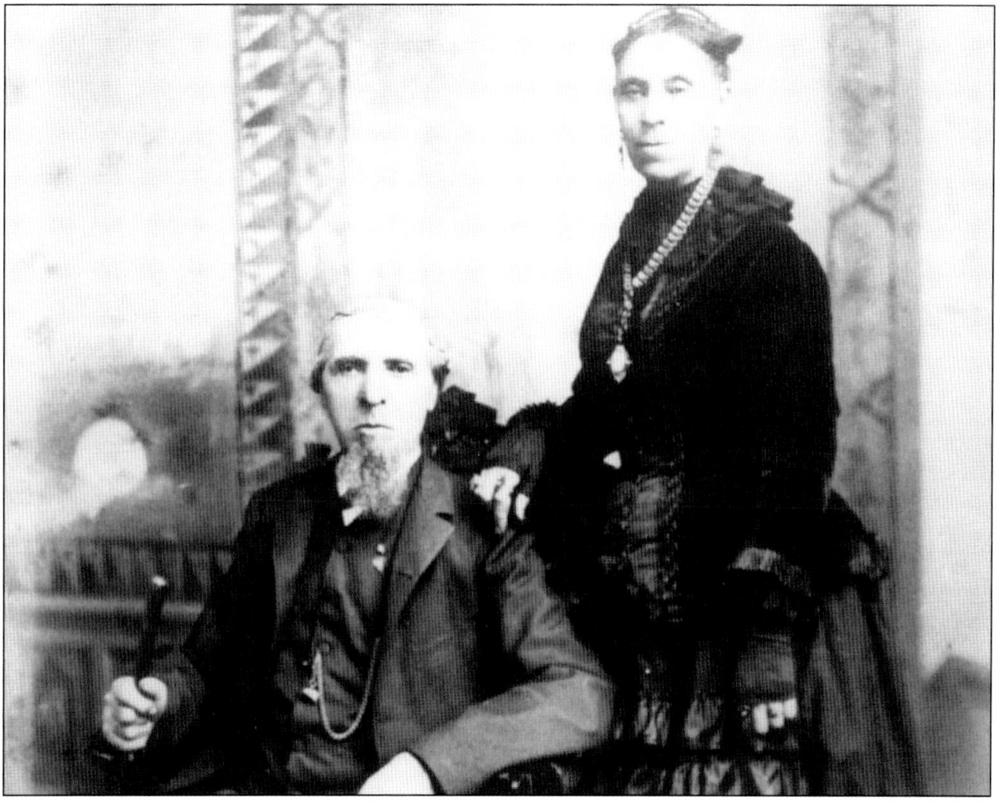

Solomon and Miriam Pareira. The first Jews to arrive on these shores were Sephardic Jews, who originated in the Iberian Peninsula. The second wave of immigrants (*c.* 1840) came mainly from Germany and Central European countries. These newcomers were, for the most part, young and well educated. Considered the first Jewish settlers in Providence and part of this second wave was the Pareira family from Holland. Pareira operated clothing stores in the Westminster Street area and lived nearby.

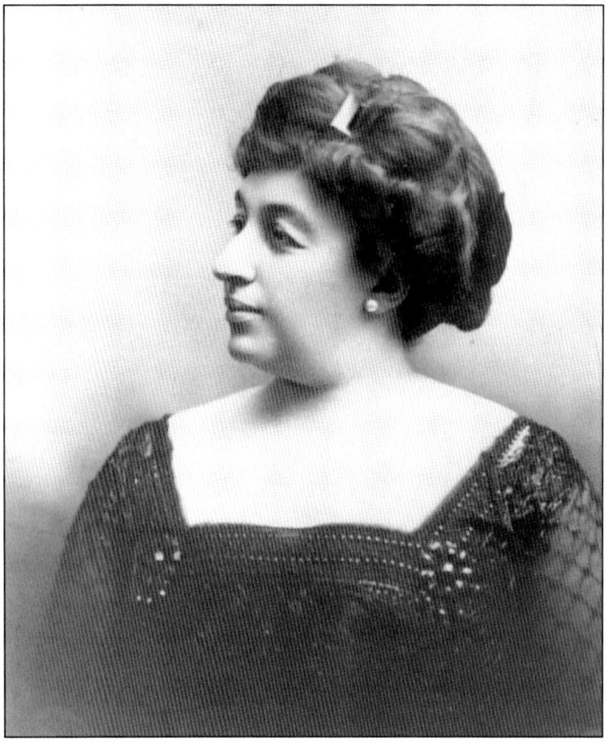

Estelle Dimond. The German Jews were organizers and joiners. The first Jewish charitable organization in Providence was a women's group, Montefiore Lodge Ladies Benevolent Association, established by young German Jews. The lodge was the focus not only of the charitable activities of the membership, but of their social activities as well. Estelle Dimond served on a number of the lodge's committees.

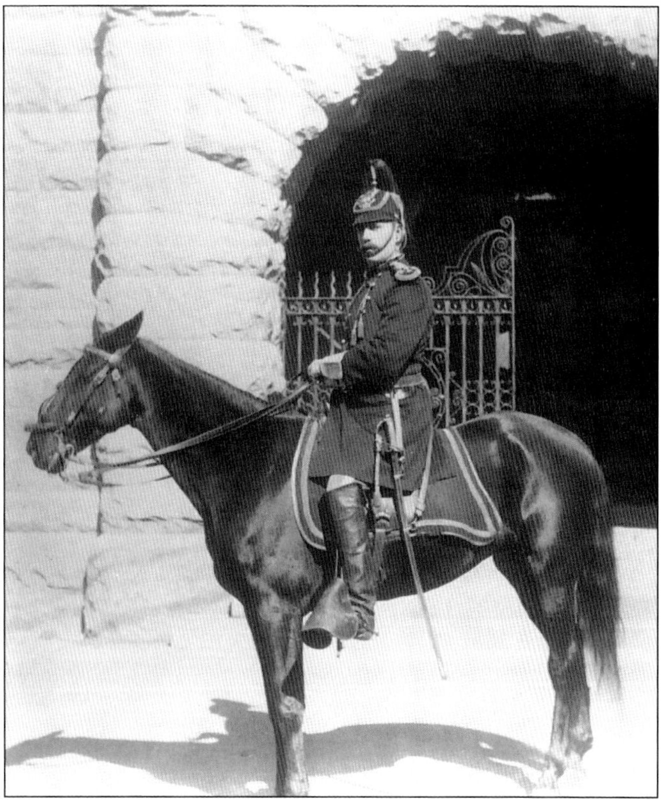

Alexander Strauss. Alexander Strauss, a president of the Congregation Sons of Israel and David (Temple Beth El), came from Germany as a young man. Active in the Rhode Island Militia, he rose from private to the rank of major in 27 years. His services were recognized at a banquet and testimonial given by his officer staff and former comrades.

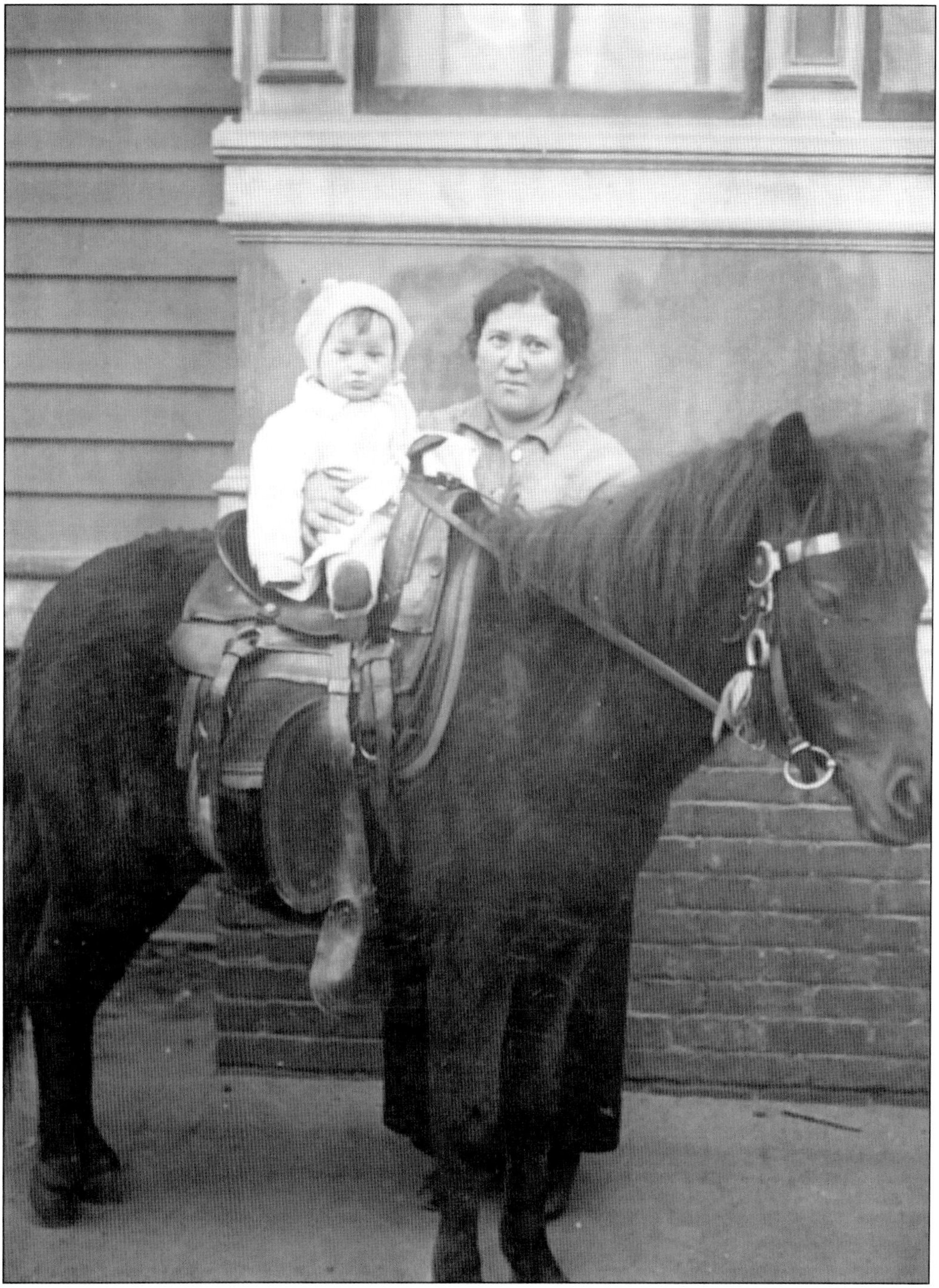

Rose Norman and her son. A third wave of immigration began about 1880. Conditions in Eastern Europe worsened for Jews due to persecutions by the government. The first of these immigrants settled in the North End, bringing with them their Yiddish language, their vibrant culture, and hopes for the future. Rose Norman, who settled in the North End, holds her son on the pony of an itinerant photographer who canvassed neighborhoods to take pictures of their frightened (of the pony) children, as keepsakes of their Americanization.

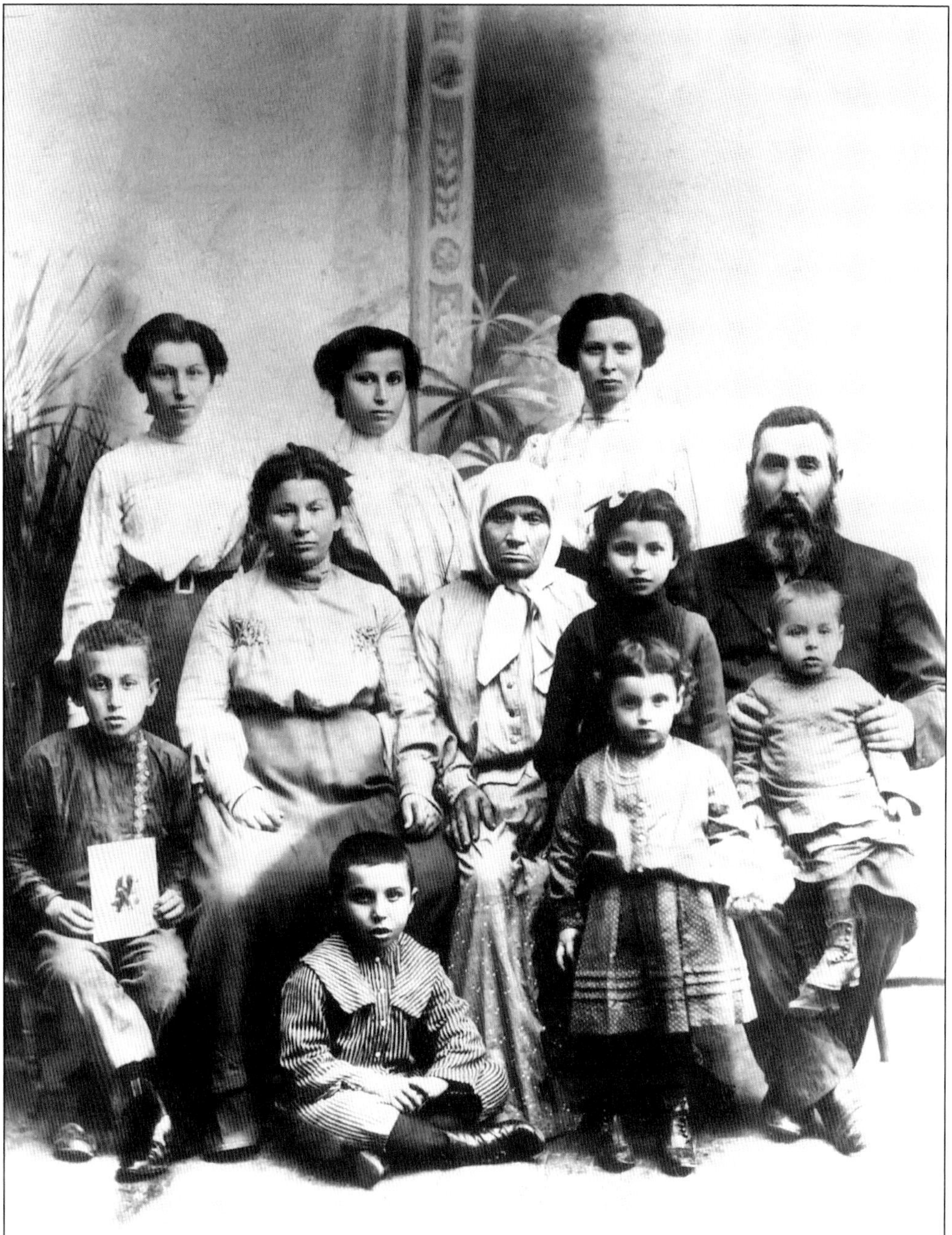

The Lasker family. Often a whole family would pose together, either before they left from Europe or after they had established themselves in their new surroundings. The Lasker family, who had migrated from Russia in 1905, is an example of such portraits. Hyman B. Lasker (holding his son Meir) became a distinguished teacher and principal of the Congregation Sons of Zion Talmud Torah (an afternoon/Sunday school where Hebrew and Judaic subjects were taught).

The Feital family: Pincus (Peney), Jacob, and Annie, c. 1900. The Feital family settled in Pawtucket. Peney Feital was first listed in the Pawtucket and Central Falls City Directory as being in the shoe and boot repair business. He eventually became a shoe manufacturer.

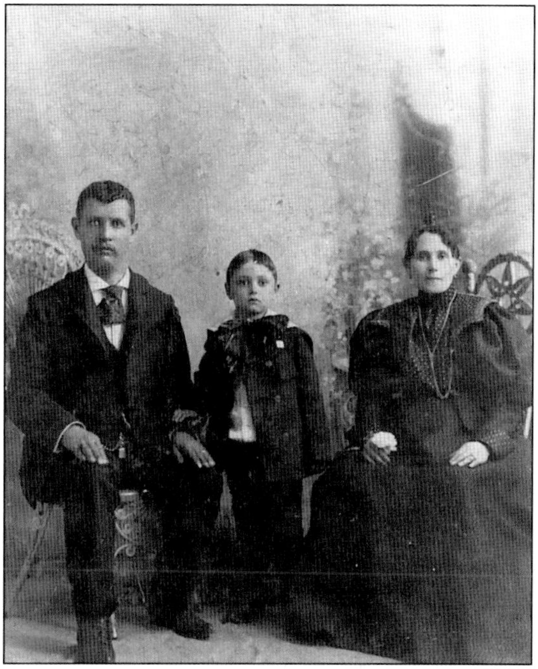

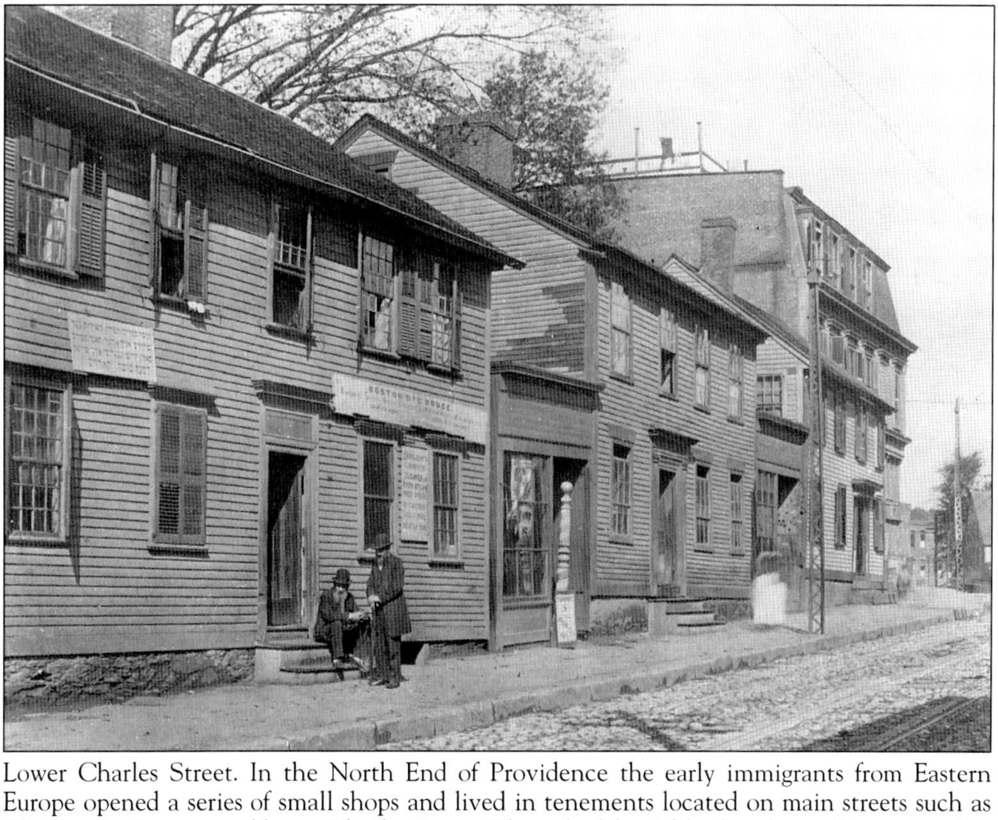

Lower Charles Street. In the North End of Providence the early immigrants from Eastern Europe opened a series of small shops and lived in tenements located on main streets such as Chalkstone Avenue and lower Charles Street. The colorful neighborhood was often referred to as "Jewtown." (Courtesy of Rhode Island Historical Society.)

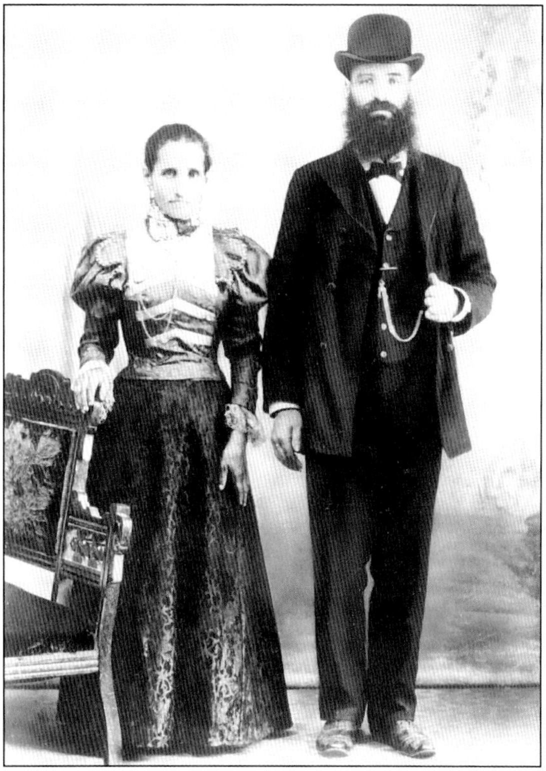

Lena and Nathan Zurier, *c.* 1900.

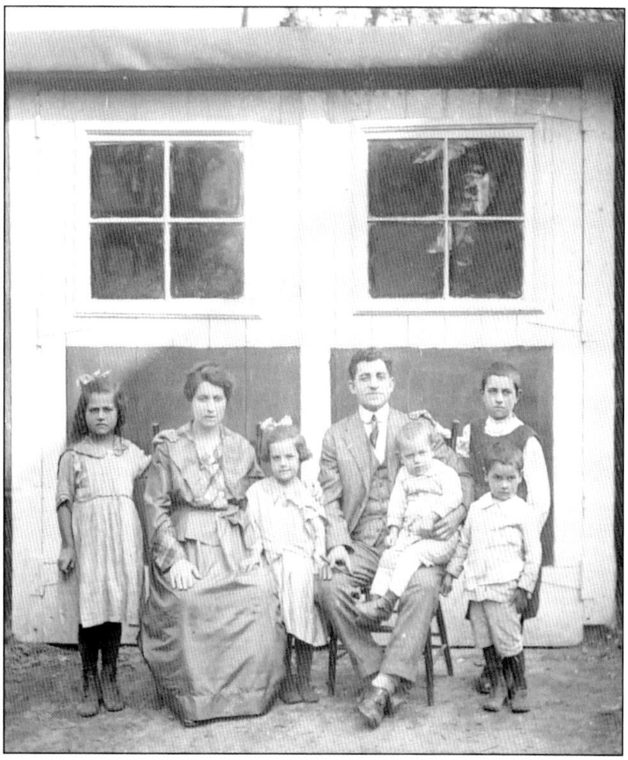

An unidentified family. By 1890, the newest immigrants began to settle in South Providence, which became a second center of Jewish life. Pictured is a typical neighborhood with three-decker houses built close together.

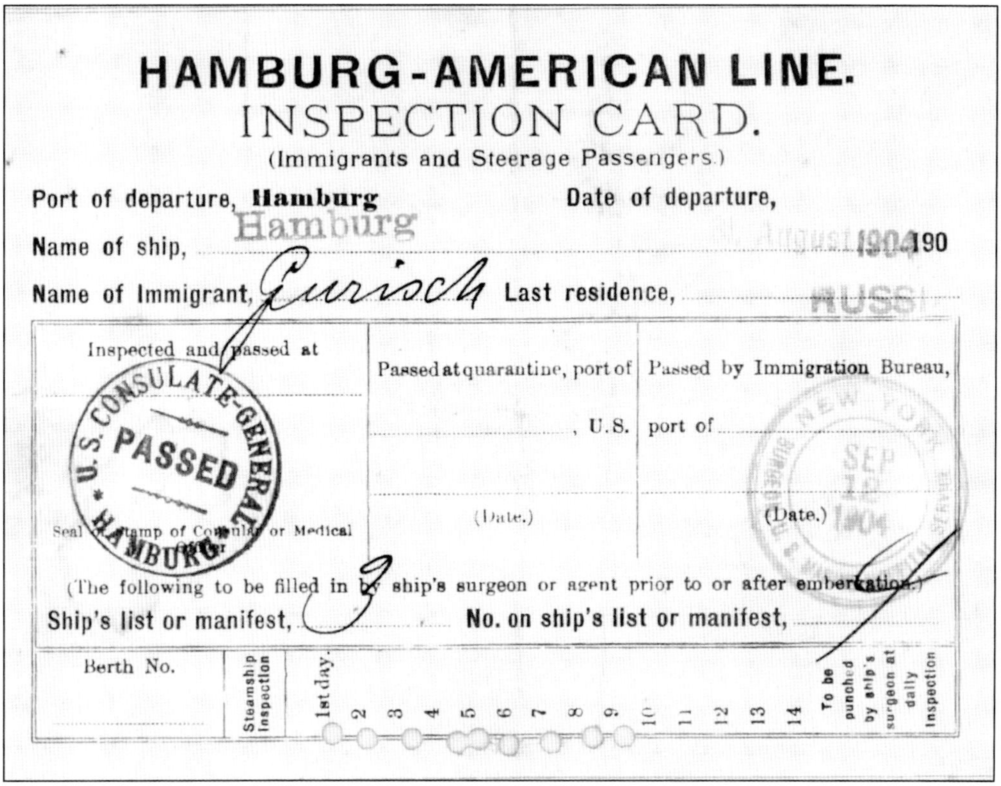
HAMBURG-AMERICAN LINE.
INSPECTION CARD.
(Immigrants and Steerage Passengers.)

Port of departure, **Hamburg** Hamburg
Date of departure, August 1904 190
Name of ship,
Name of Immigrant, Gurisch
Last residence, RUSS

| Inspected and passed at | Passed at quarantine, port of | Passed by Immigration Bureau, |
|---|---|---|
| U.S. CONSULATE-GENERAL PASSED HAMBURG | , U.S. | port of |
| Seal or stamp of Consular or Medical Officer | (Date.) | (Date.) SEP 12 1904 |

(The following to be filled in by ship's surgeon or agent prior to or after embarkation.)
Ship's list or manifest, 3 No. on ship's list or manifest, 4

| Berth No. | Steamship Inspection | 1st day. | 2 | 3 | 4 | 5 | 6 | 7 | 8 | 9 | 10 | 11 | 12 | 13 | 14 | To be punched by ship's surgeon at daily inspection |
|---|---|---|---|---|---|---|---|---|---|---|---|---|---|---|---|---|

The inspection card of Jacob Horvitz, 1904. Jacob Horvitz kept among his prize possessions his inspection card (his name is spelled in Russian fashion) from the Hamburg-American Line.

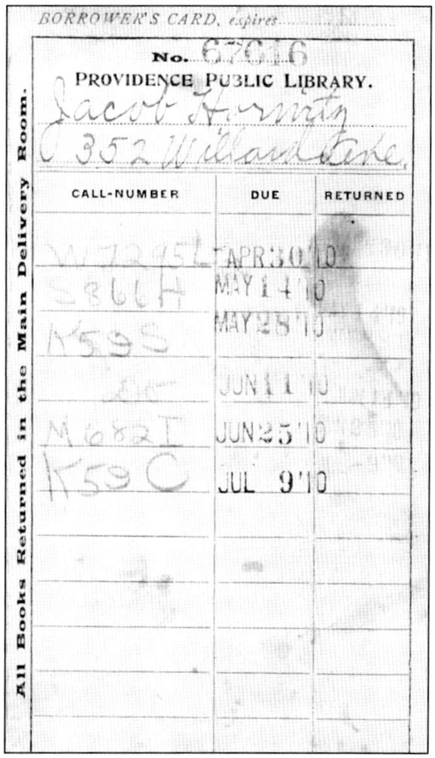
BORROWER'S CARD, expires
No. 67616
PROVIDENCE PUBLIC LIBRARY.
Jacob Horvitz
352 Willard Ave.
All Books Returned in the Main Delivery Room.

| CALL-NUMBER | DUE | RETURNED |
|---|---|---|
| W7295L | APR 30'10 | |
| S86H | MAY 14'10 | |
| K59S | MAY 28'10 | |
| | JUN 11'10 | |
| M682T | JUN 25'10 | |
| K59C | JUL 9'10 | |

The library card of Jacob Horvitz, 1910. Like many immigrants, Mr. Horvitz so valued his first library card that he also kept it among his most prized possessions. It was issued by the Providence Public Library.

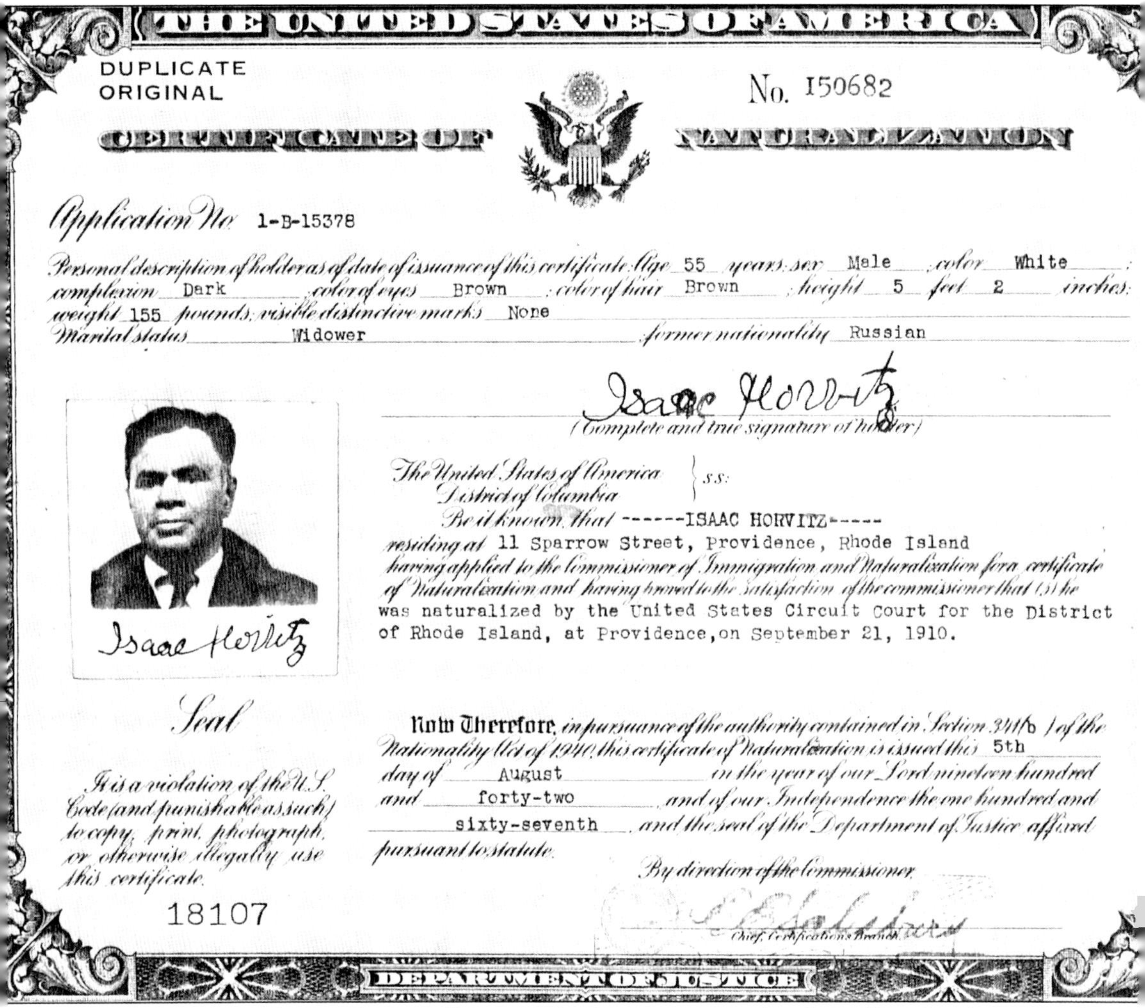

THE UNITED STATES OF AMERICA

DUPLICATE
ORIGINAL

No. 150682

CERTIFICATE OF NATURALIZATION

Application No. 1-B-15378

Personal description of holder as of date of issuance of this certificate: Age 55 years; sex Male; color White; complexion Dark; color of eyes Brown; color of hair Brown; height 5 feet 2 inches; weight 155 pounds; visible distinctive marks None

Marital status Widower; former nationality Russian

Isaac Horvitz
(Complete and true signature of holder)

Isaac Horvitz

The United States of America
District of Columbia } ss:

Be it known, that ------ISAAC HORVITZ-----
residing at 11 Sparrow Street, Providence, Rhode Island
having applied to the Commissioner of Immigration and Naturalization for a certificate of Naturalization and having proved to the satisfaction of the commissioner that (s)he was naturalized by the United States Circuit Court for the District of Rhode Island, at Providence, on September 21, 1910.

Seal

It is a violation of the U.S. Code (and punishable as such) to copy, print, photograph, or otherwise illegally use this certificate.

18107

Now Therefore, in pursuance of the authority contained in Section 341(b) of the Nationality Act of 1940, this certificate of Naturalization is issued this 5th day of August in the year of our Lord nineteen hundred and forty-two and of our Independence the one hundred and sixty-seventh, and the seal of the Department of Justice affixed pursuant to statute.

By direction of the Commissioner,

Chief, Certifications Branch

DEPARTMENT OF JUSTICE

The certificate of naturalization (later copy) of Isaac Horvitz, brother of Jacob. The original certificate was issued on September 21, 1910.

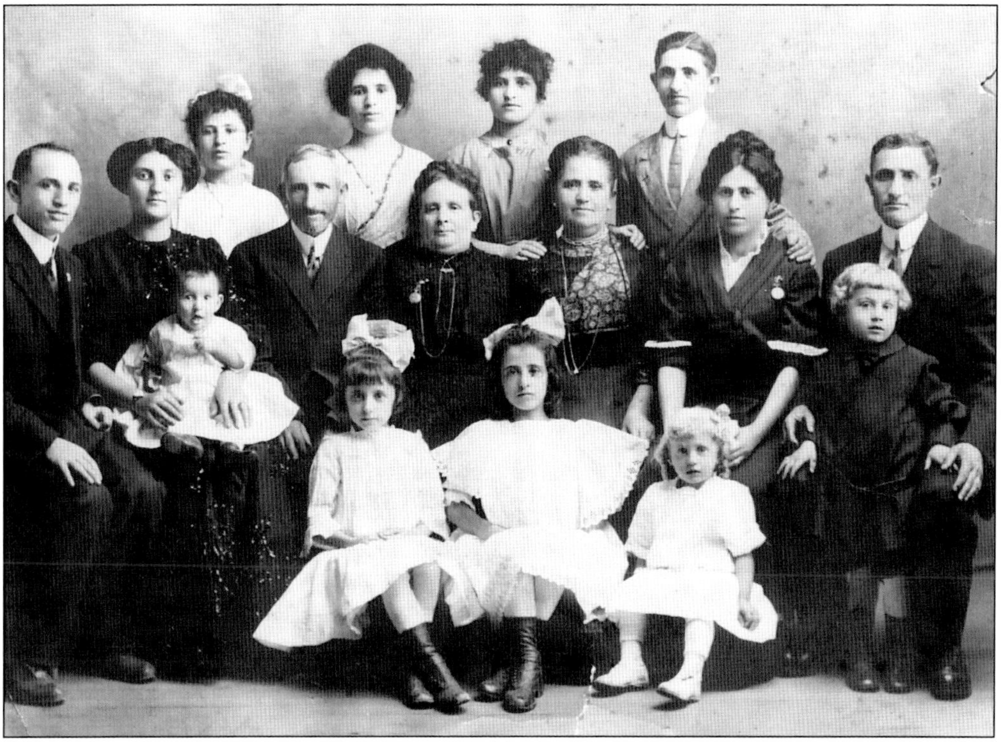

The Goldman family. To have free access to a library with limitless books to borrow, to be able to take advantage of Americanization classes and school, and to live in a democracy were opportunities cherished by families like the Goldmans. They lived on Whitmarsh Street.

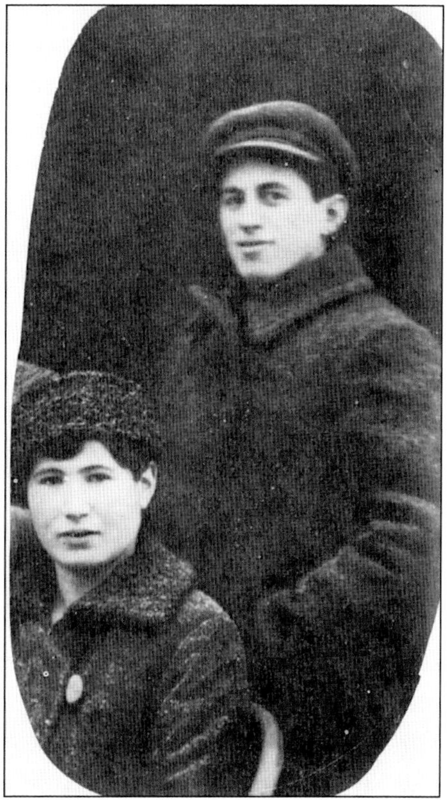

Beryl and Chaya Segal. Mr. and Mrs. Segal, photographed in 1920 just before leaving their home in Orinen, Ukraine, were among the fortunate able to enter the United States before restrictive quotas went into effect. They surreptitiously crossed the border into Romania, then made their way to Holland to board the SS *Ryndam* for Ellis Island and freedom. Beginning in 1921, the numbers of immigrants from Central and Eastern Europe were drastically cut by Congress.

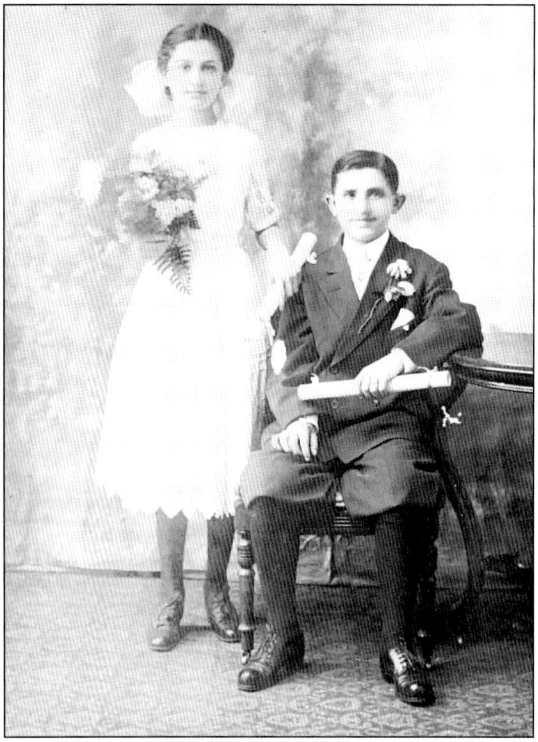

Irving Goldman and a friend. Education was considered essential by the Jewish immigrants. The importance of a graduation was underscored by having the graduate pose for a professional photographer. Irving Goldman displays his diploma, while his friend holds her graduation bouquet.

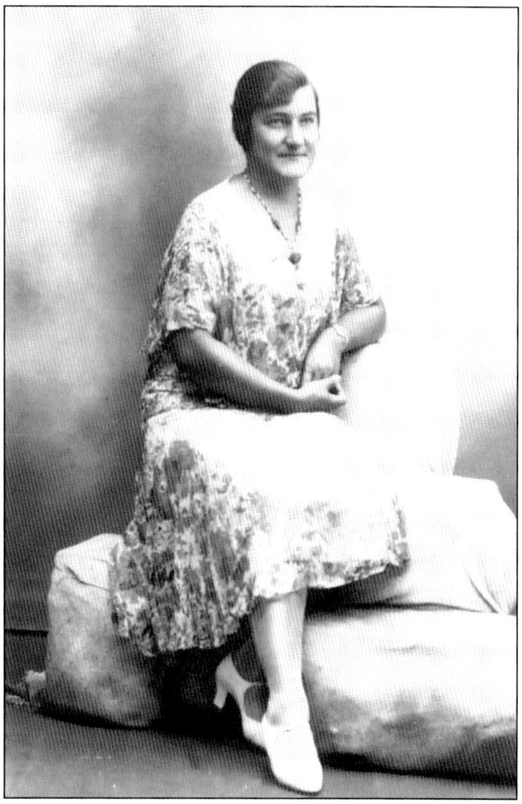

Elizabeth Guny. Providence was also a port of entry for immigrants. The French Fabre Line established direct links between Mediterranean ports and Providence. Elizabeth Guny met every Fabre Line ship carrying Jewish immigrants from 1917 until 1930. The immigrants were given clothing if needed, as well as other services to put them in touch with relatives. The Hebrew Aid Society, headed by Archibald Silverman, loaned money for newcomers to travel to their planned destination.

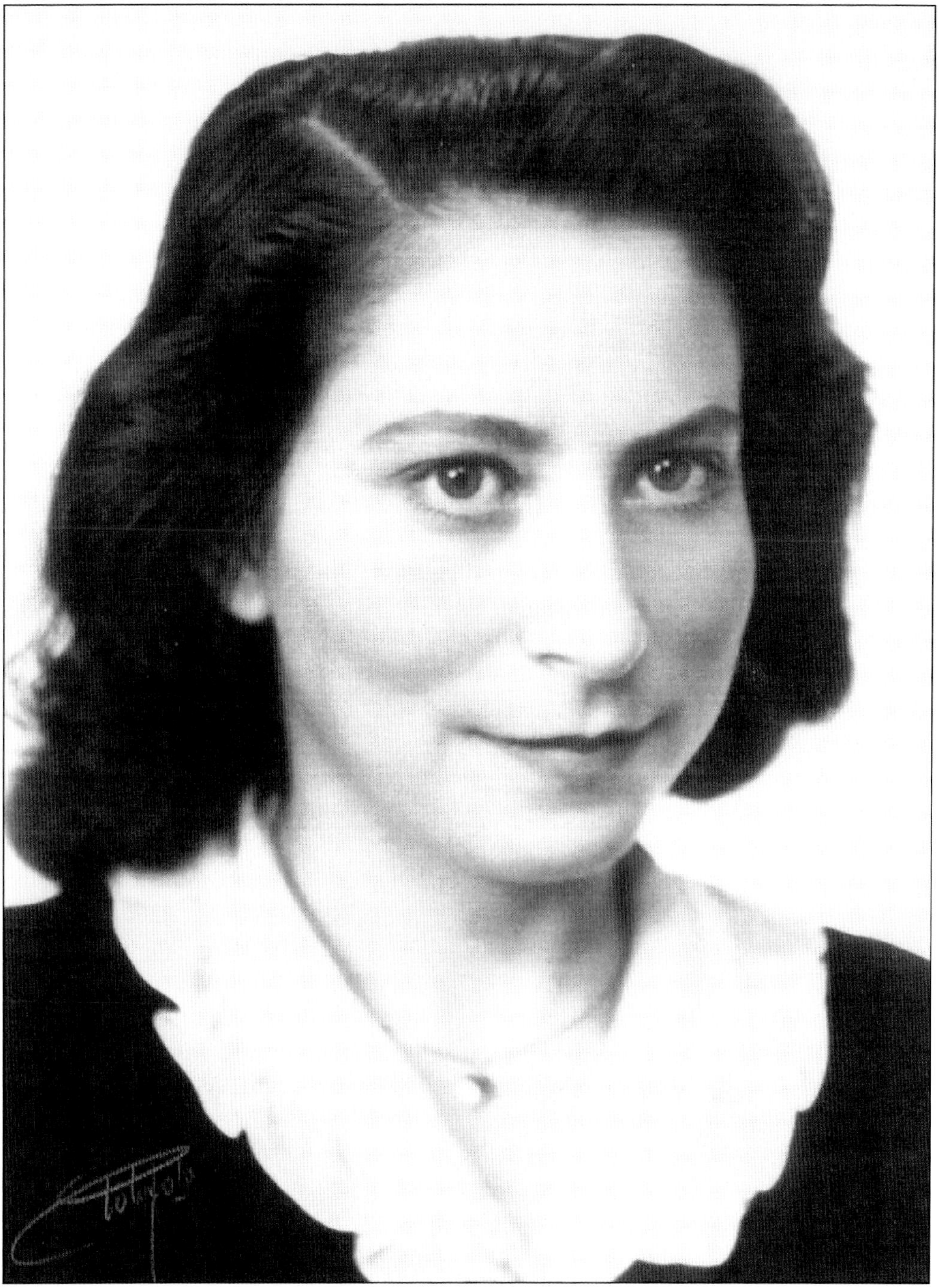

Lenka Kopolowitz (Rose), Sweden, 1946. Lenka Kopolowitz was born in Czechoslovakia, one of six children. She and two of her brothers survived the Holocaust. In 1945, she was carried from Bergen Belsen on a stretcher and brought to Sweden for medical treatment and recuperation. She remained there for two and a half years and then left for the United States, where she had relatives.

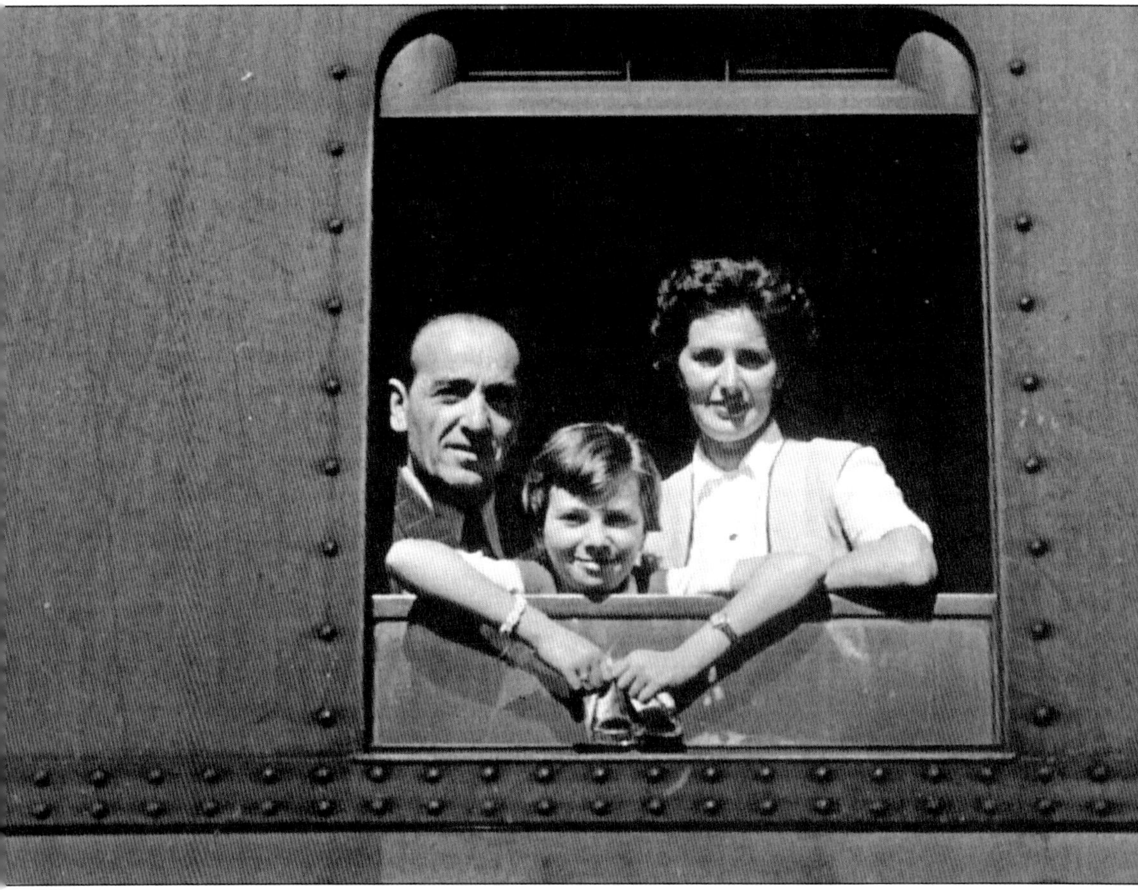

Solomon, Asya, and Lea Eliash (from left to right), Bremen, 1951. Gazing out from the train, the reunited Eliash family were on their way to the United States, to Providence. Having survived the Holocaust, they looked forward to their new life of freedom. Lea Eliash received an Honorary Doctorate of Public Service from Rhode Island College at commencement, May 22, 1997, for her volunteer work in educating children and adults about the dark years of the Holocaust. (Courtesy of Lea Eliash.)

Raymond and Alice Handel Eichenbaum, 1957. Raymond Eichenbaum was 16 when he was liberated, having spent his teen years in the Lodz Ghetto, Mathausen, and Auschwitz camps. He alone of his family survived. He came to Rhode Island in 1947 where he was placed with a caring family and allowed to continue his education (he eventually graduated from URI). Alice Handel spent the war years in Bulgaria, her family having left Vienna in 1937. Until forced to change, the Bulgarians protected their Jewish population. The Eichenbaums met in Europe, were married in Vienna, and then moved to the United States. (Courtesy of Alice Eichenbaum.)

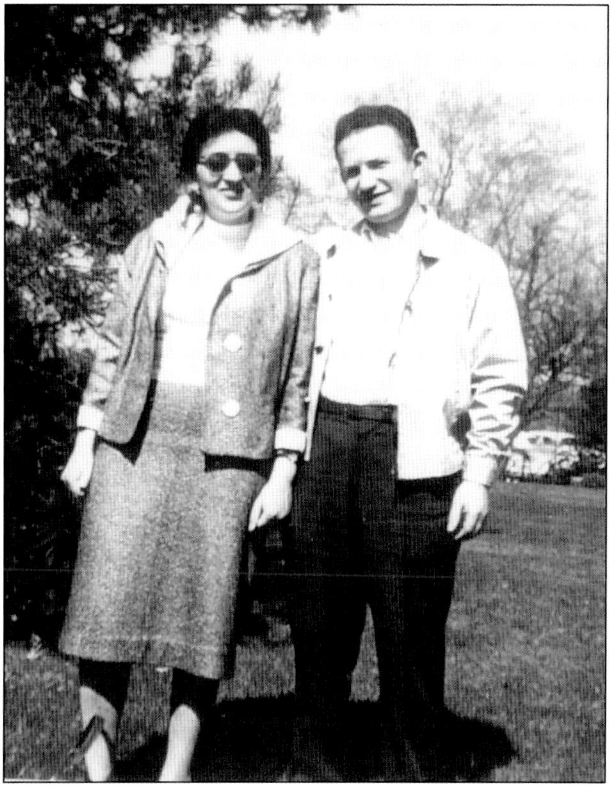

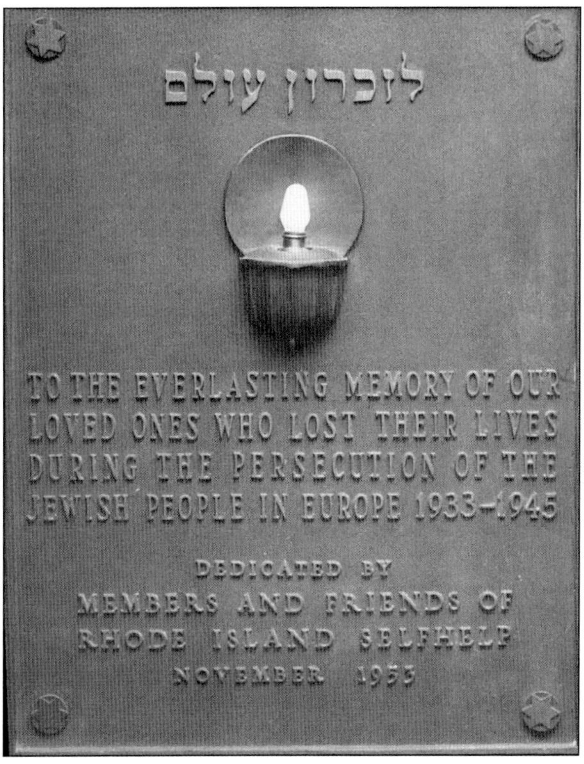


A plaque affixed in the Rhode Island Holocaust Museum, 1953. Rhode Island Self Help was composed of people who had come to the United States from Germany and Austria in the 1930s to escape the Hitler terror. Although small in number, they organized to assist other refugees from Europe with their social and economic adjustment to this country. Officially chartered in 1944, the organization disbanded 40 years later, as their work had been completed. However, an annual memorial service to commemorate the victims of the Holocaust continues.

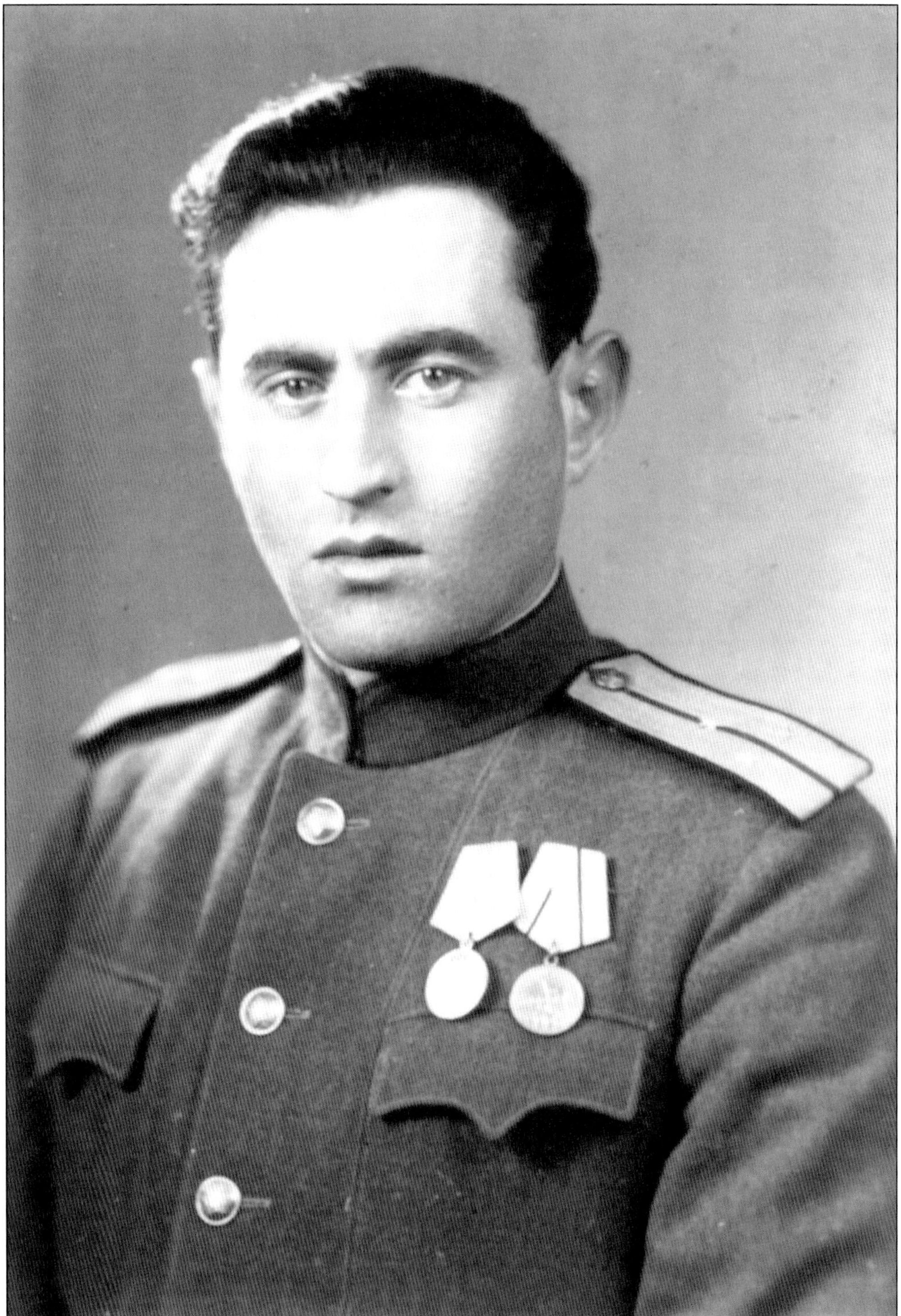

Boris Efes. A decorated veteran of the Russian Army in World War II, Boris Efes came to Providence during the most recent immigration from the former USSR. (Courtesy of Boris Efes.)

# *Three*

# Ceremonies and Milestones

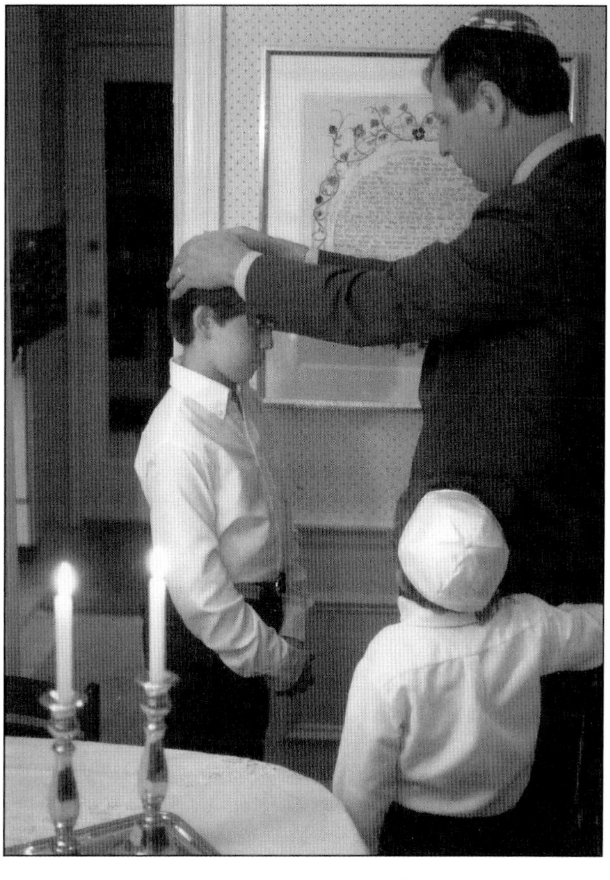

Shabbat. At sundown on Friday eve, Jews usher in Shabbat, the seventh day of the week, the scripturally ordained day of rest. Shabbat is welcomed with blessings over the Sabbath candles, Kiddush (Heb. sanctification) recited over wine, a blessing over the challot (Heb. Sabbath loaves), and song. Children of the family receive a special blessing as well. Grace and Shabbat table songs follow the meal. Synagogues have religious services on Friday evenings and on Saturday mornings, when the Torah is read. (Courtesy of Rhode Island Bureau of Jewish Education.)

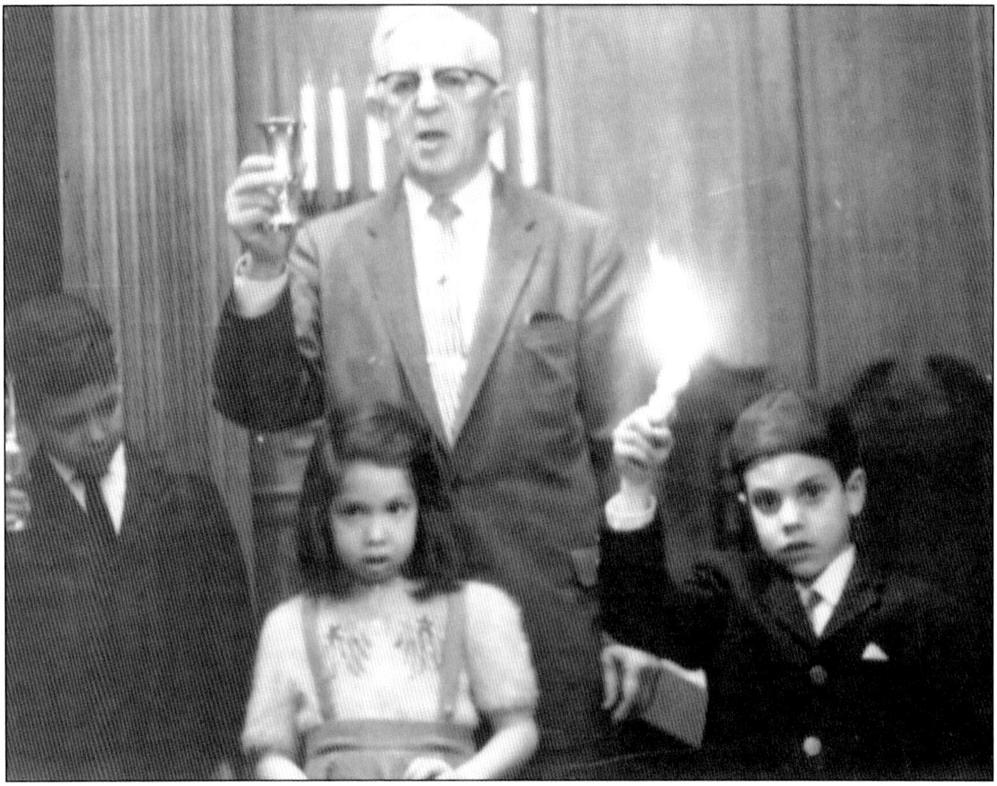

The Havdalah (Heb. distinction) ceremony observed at the close of Shabbat and festivals at home or at public worship. The prayers, recited over wine like the Kiddush, consist of four benedictions, two of which drew a distinction between the day of rest and work days, between the sacred and the ordinary. Fragrant spices in a container evoke the pleasantness of Shabbat, and a twisted candle with several wicks is extinguished in the wine to mark the resumption of the work week.

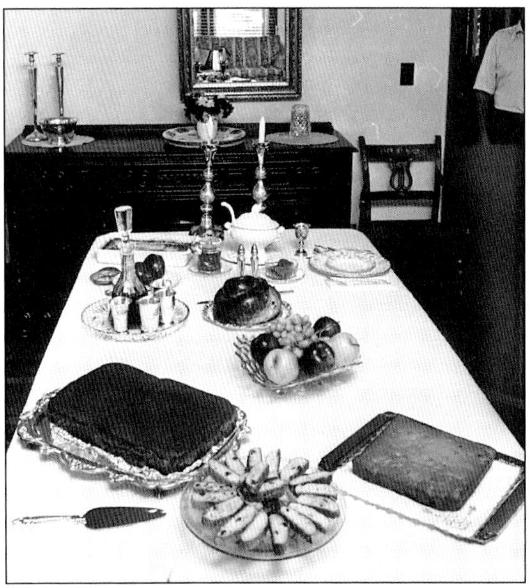

A table set with the symbols of Rosh Hashonah, the Jewish New Year. Honey cake and other sweets can be seen here, along with candles over which a blessing is said, wine for Kiddush to usher in the High Holy Day, apples dipped in honey for a sweet year, and a round challot symbolizing hope for a complete and harmonious year. Fine china and napery are used in the table setting. (Courtesy of Geraldine Foster.)

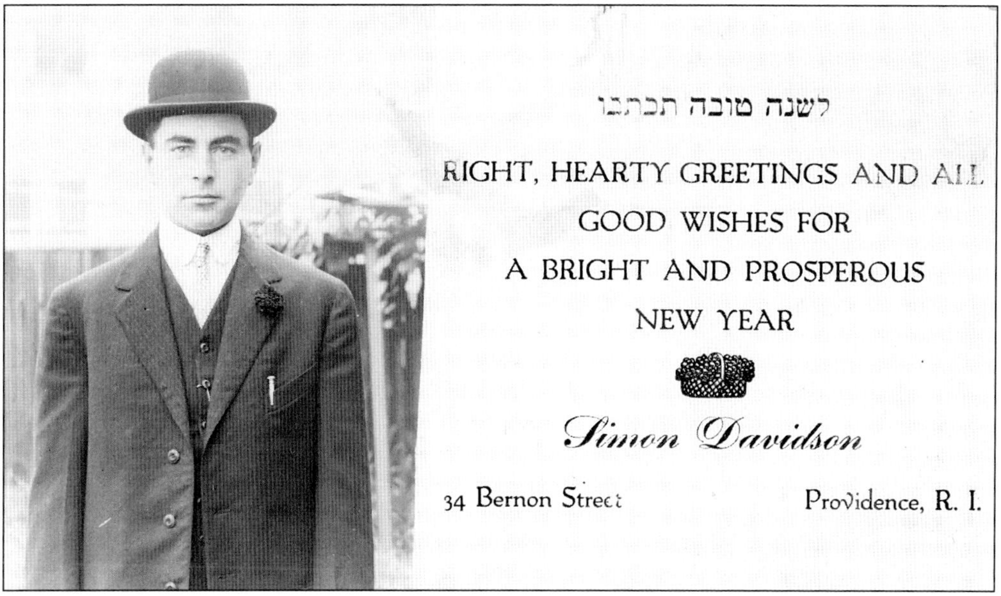


An early New Year greeting card. The Hebrew states the following: May you be inscribed for a good year.

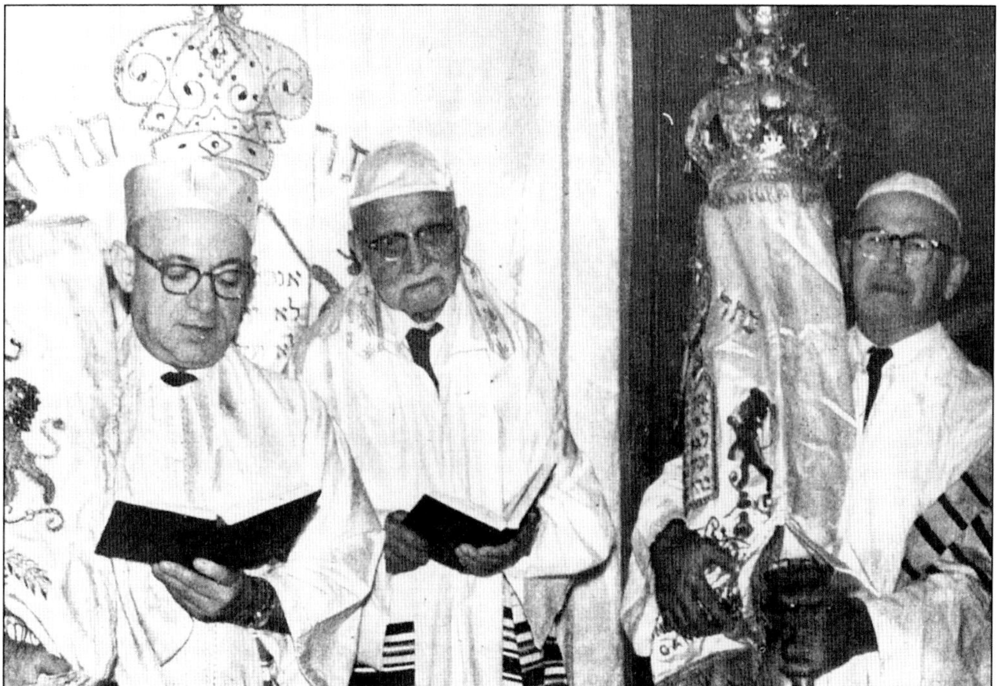

Rosh Hashonah. On Rosh Hashonah, it is written that one should not appear clothed in somber colors, but should appear in a joyous mood and festive garments, preferably white. The Torahs are also dressed in white mantles for the High Holy Days, which bespeaks of God's forgiveness.

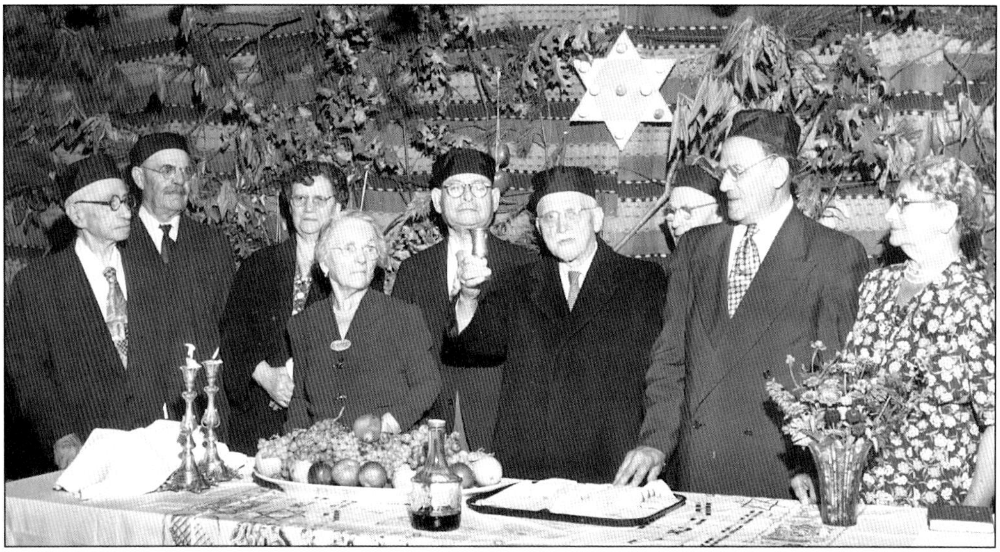

Sukkah (Heb. booth) at the Jewish Home for the Aged. The autumn festival of Sukkot commemorates the agricultural harvest and the booths in which the Israelites lived during their biblical wanderings. During Sukkot, it is traditional for men to sleep in the impermanent Sukkah and the family to take their meals there. The booths are decorated with fruits and greens. The major symbol of the holy day is an agricultural bouquet consisting of the palm branch, ethrog (citron), myrtle, and willow.

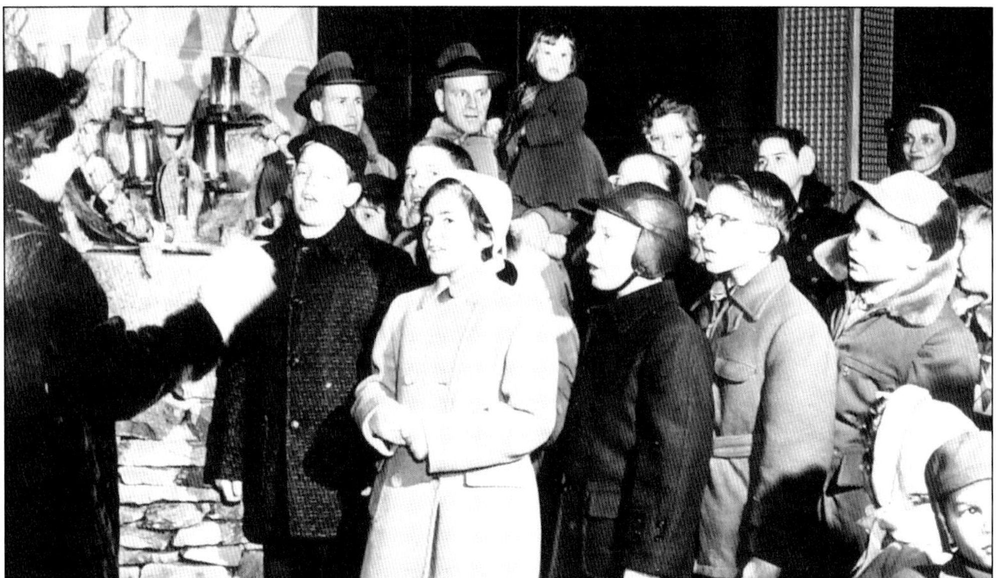

The kindling of Hanukah lights at the outdoor menorah (Heb. Candelabrum) at Temple Beth El. Hanukah, the festival of lights celebrated for eight days, commemorates the victorious struggle of the Jews against religious persecution by the Graeco-Syrians in 167 B.C.E. One candle is lit the first night, and one more is added each night using a shammash (Heb. Attendant), a ninth candle, to kindle them. Each lighting begins with the newest addition as traditional blessings are recited. Hanukah lights are kindled at home as well as in the synagogue and at public functions. (Courtesy of Temple Beth-El Archives.)

A Hanukah menorah inherited by Norma Bromberg Goodman.

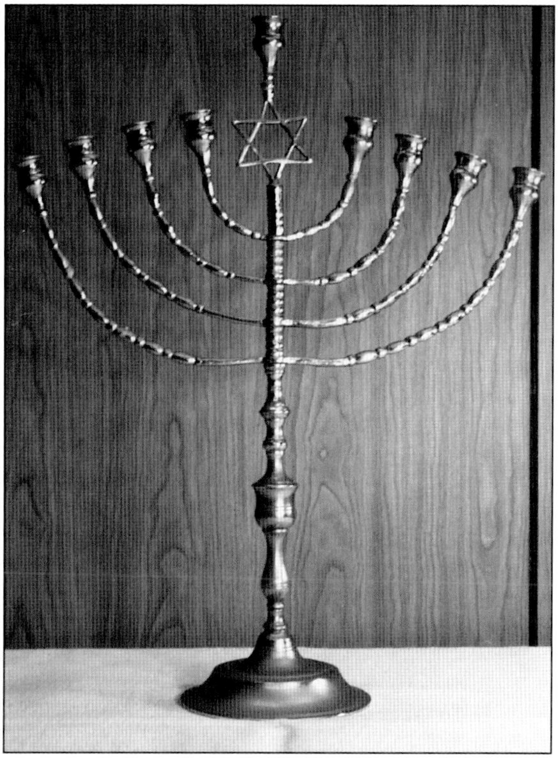

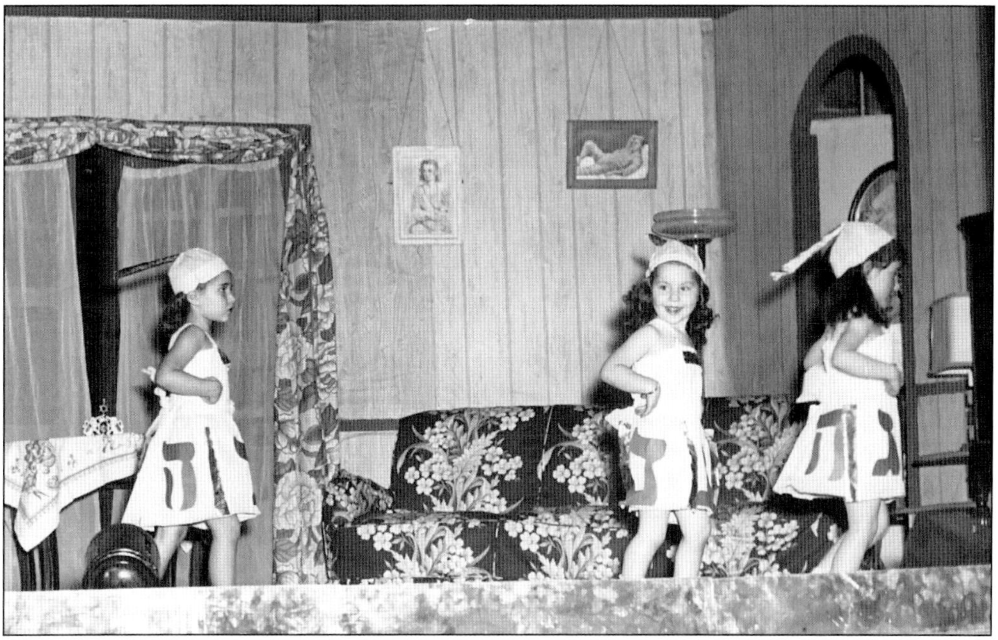

A Hanukah party at the Jewish Community Center. Games and parties have long been part of the holiday celebration. One game called dreidle (Yidd. top) uses a four-sided spinner, each side containing a Hebrew letter that represents the first letter of each word in the phrase "a great miracle happened there." Included at the parties are songs and entertainment based on the symbols of the holiday.

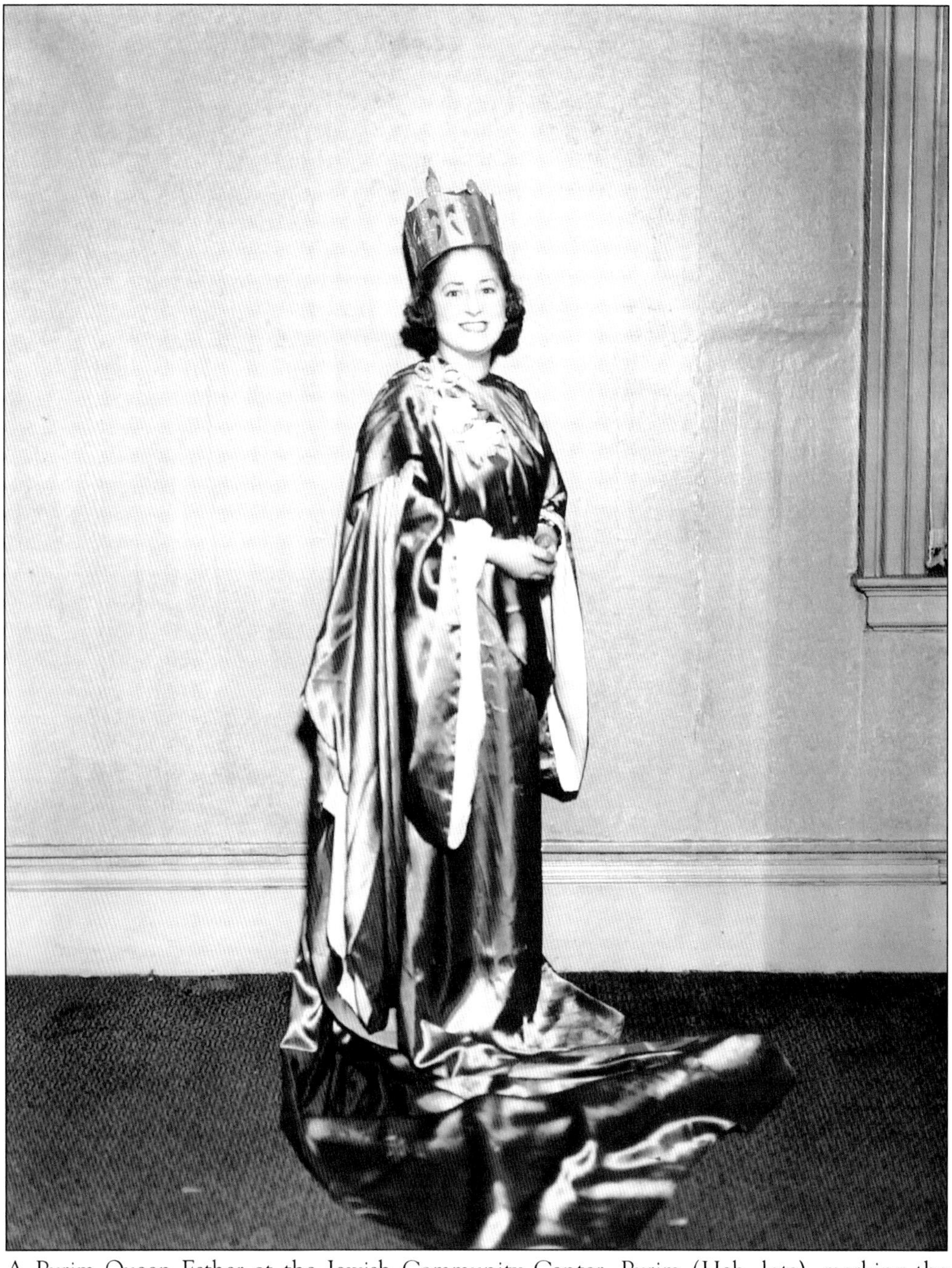

A Purim Queen Esther at the Jewish Community Center. Purim (Heb. lots), marking the deliverance of Persian Jews from an impending massacre, is celebrated in the synagogue by reading the Scroll of Esther, and by enjoying three-cornered pastries called hamantaschen. Children attending religious schools are encouraged to wear costumes to school, and there is also entertainment in the form of carnivals and Purim parties or balls, at which a Queen Esther, heroine of the Purim story, is crowned. A Purim party was a favorite way for philanthropic organizations to raise money for their projects.

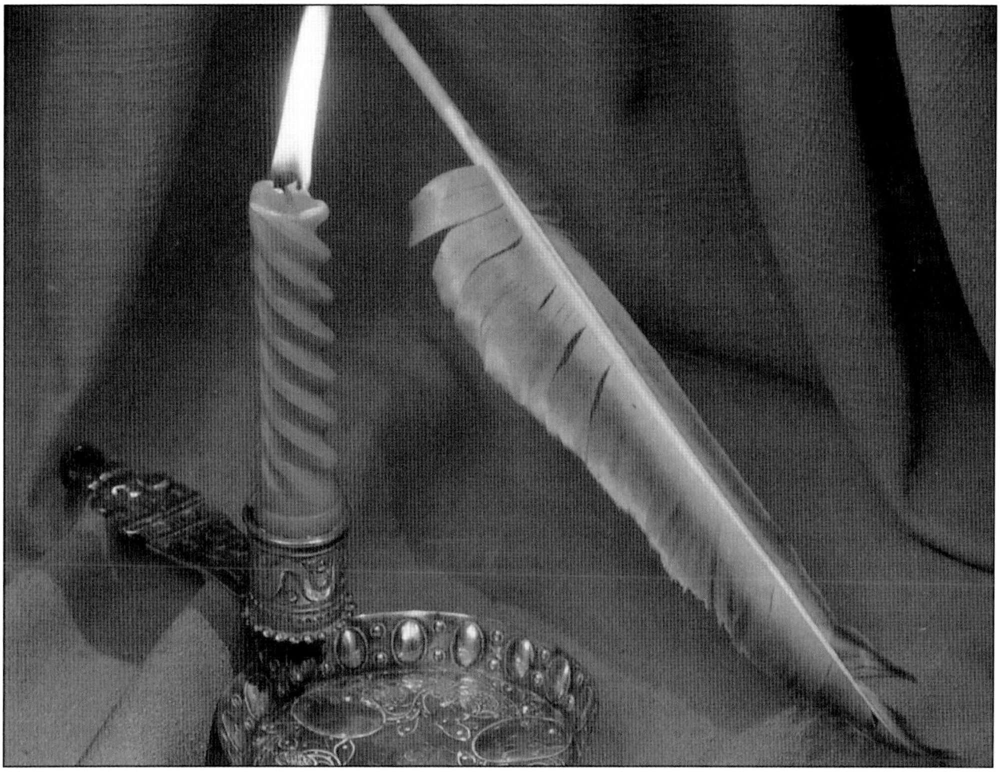

Passover, the Feast of Unleavened Bread. This holiday commemorates the exodus from Egypt. On the morning of the 14th day of Nisan, all hametz (Heb. leaven) must be cleared from the home as the celebration begins at sundown. A candle to light dark corners and a feather to root out even the tiniest crumbs are features of the symbolic search for leaven in the home. (Courtesy of Bureau of Jewish Education.)

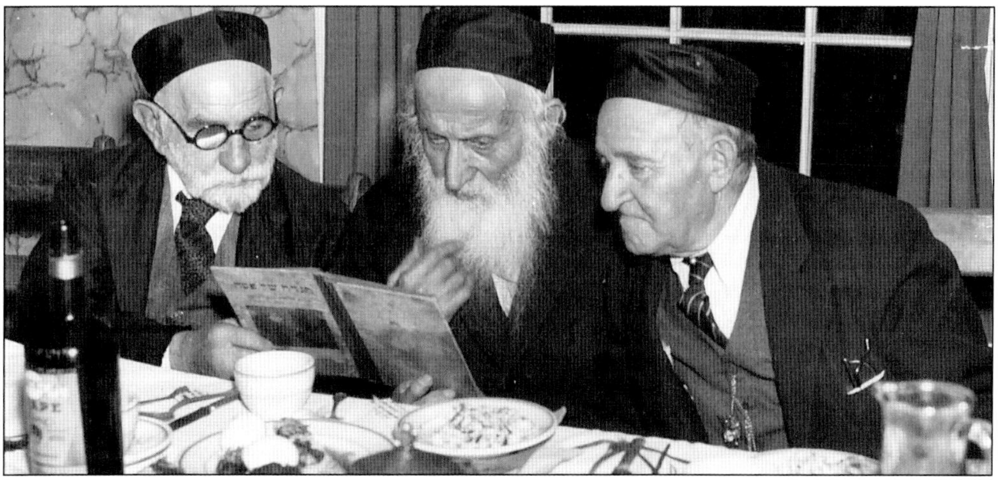

Seder at the Jewish Home for the Aged. The Haggadah (Heb. narration ) is read to accompany the seder (Heb. order, but refers to the special meal). The special liturgy tells of the Israelites' deliverance from slavery and exodus from Egypt, discussions between rabbis, the meaning of matzoh (Heb. unleavened bread) and marror (Heb. bitter herbs), and includes hymns and songs. It is customary to have discussions regarding parts of the liturgy.

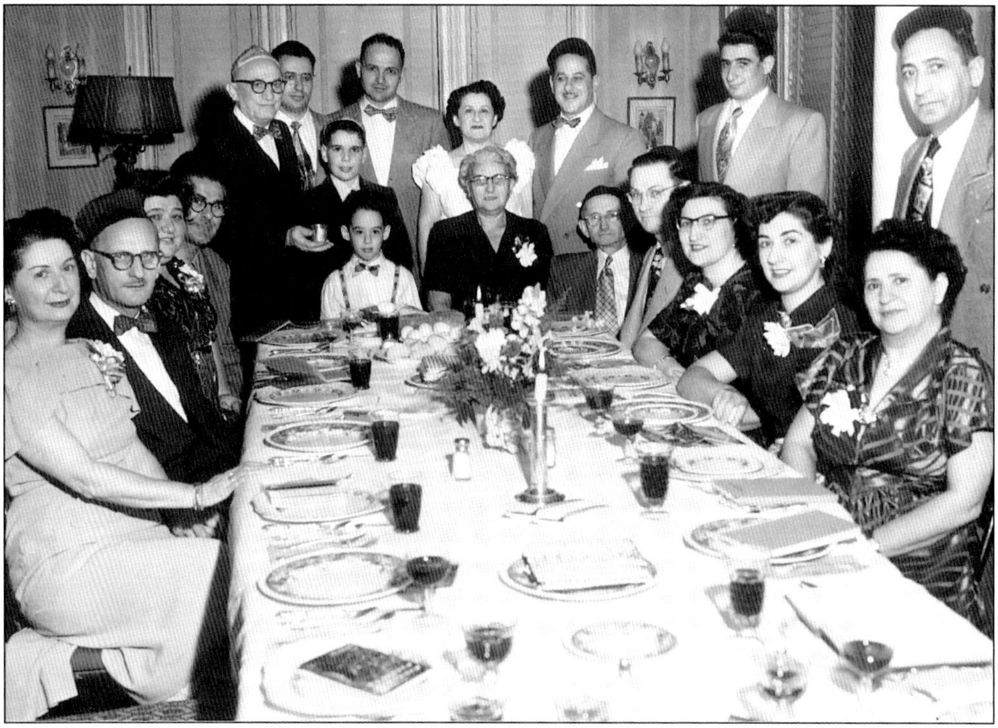

A 1951 family gathering on Passover night at the home of Dorothy and Saul Faber.

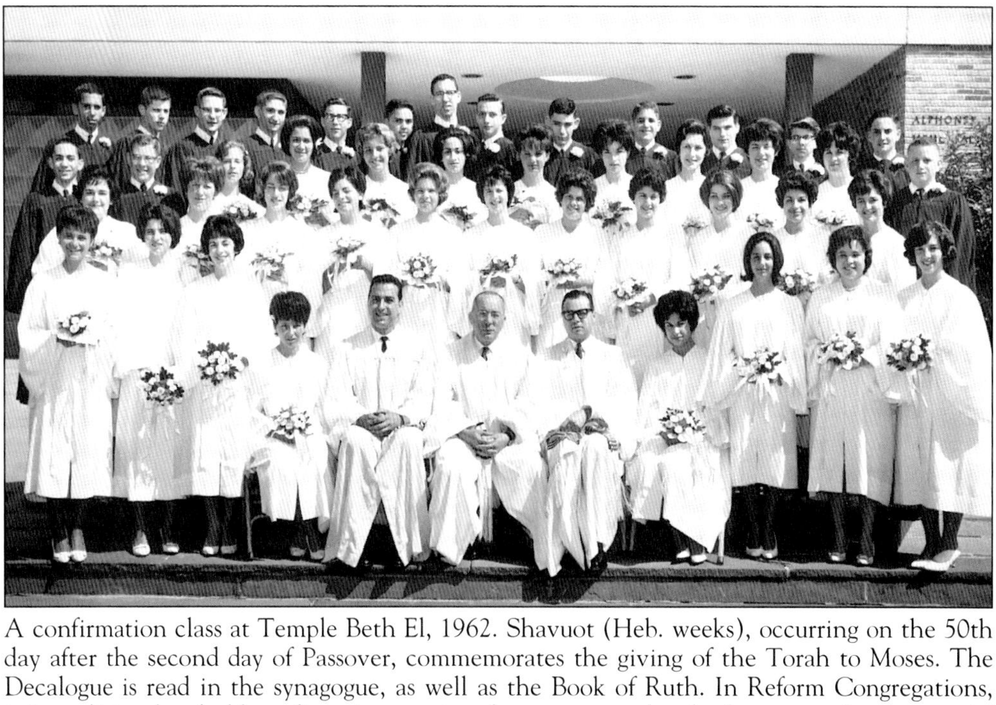

A confirmation class at Temple Beth El, 1962. Shavuot (Heb. weeks), occurring on the 50th day after the second day of Passover, commemorates the giving of the Torah to Moses. The Decalogue is read in the synagogue, as well as the Book of Ruth. In Reform Congregations, it is traditional to hold confirmation services for young people who have completed a special course of study.

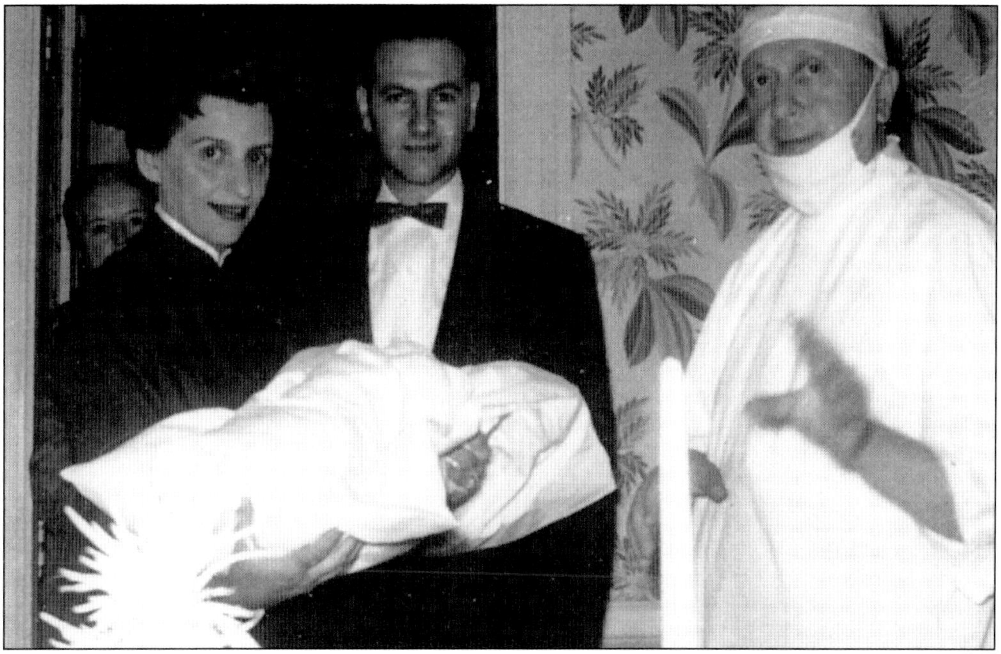

The Brit Milah (Heb. covenant of circumcision) of Stuart Cohen, son of Frances and Maurice Cohen. Rev. Meyer Smith is on the right. A major practice of Judaism, it is performed on the eighth complete day after birth. The boy receives his Hebrew name at that time. Girls are named in the synagogue.

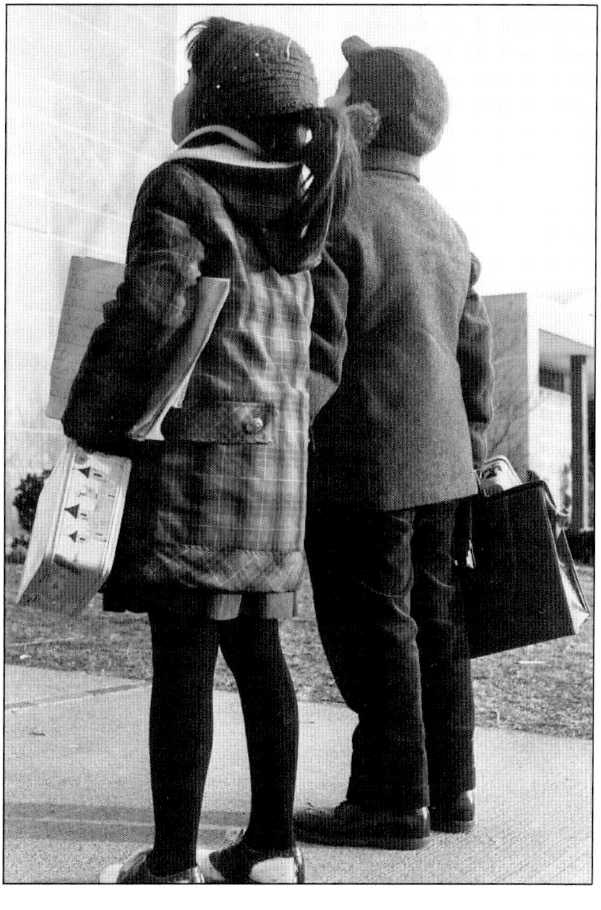

Looking to the future: students from the Providence Hebrew Day School temporarily housed at Temple Beth El. Jewish education, always a priority within the Jewish community, begins in childhood. The Providence Hebrew Day and Alperin Schechter Day Schools, congregational afternoon and Sunday schools, and a community high school provide classes for young people, while adults have their choice of classes, lectures, and discussions based on Torah. All schools are affiliated with the Bureau of Jewish Education. (Courtesy of Providence Journal Co.)

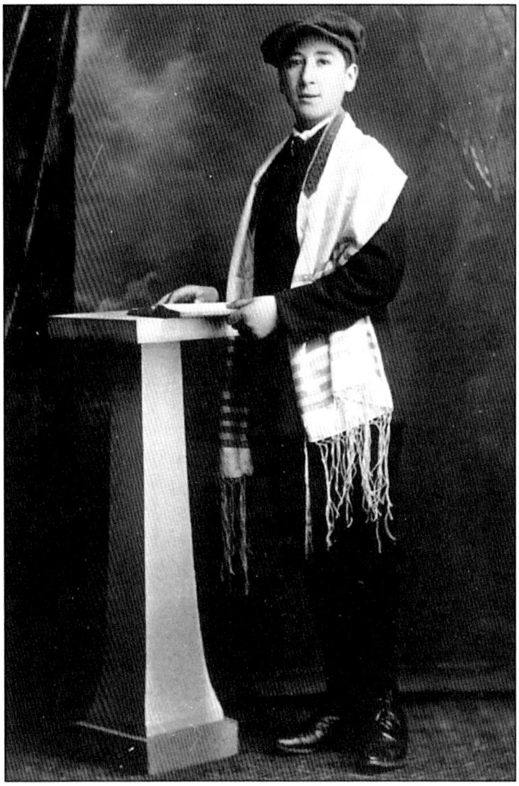

Julius Brier's bar mitzvah (Heb. literally, son of the commandment), the entry into religious manhood. At age 13, after prerequisite study, young boys are extended the privilege of being called up to the Torah during public worship. Having become bar mitzvahs, they are responsible for their religious acts, of fulfilling the mitzvot (Heb. duties) of Judaism. In recent years, girls in Reform and Conservative congregations have been accorded the same privilege, becoming bat mitzvahs, daughters of the commandment.

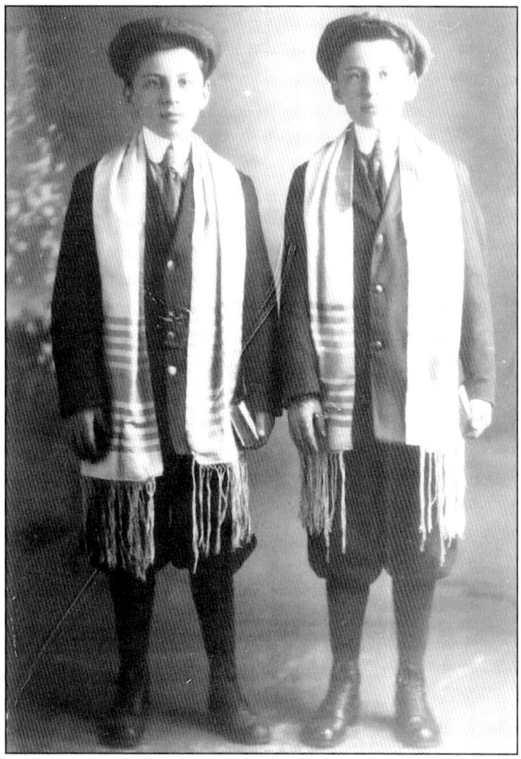

Banice and Saul Feinberg on becoming B'nai Mitzvah.

A Ketubah (Heb. marriage contract) written traditionally in Aramaic. It is a religious marriage contract, signed in front of witnesses before the marriage ceremony. Traditionally the groom pledges financial support for his bride in case of his death or of a divorce. It is also a statement of mutual love and respect. The document remains in the possession of the bride.

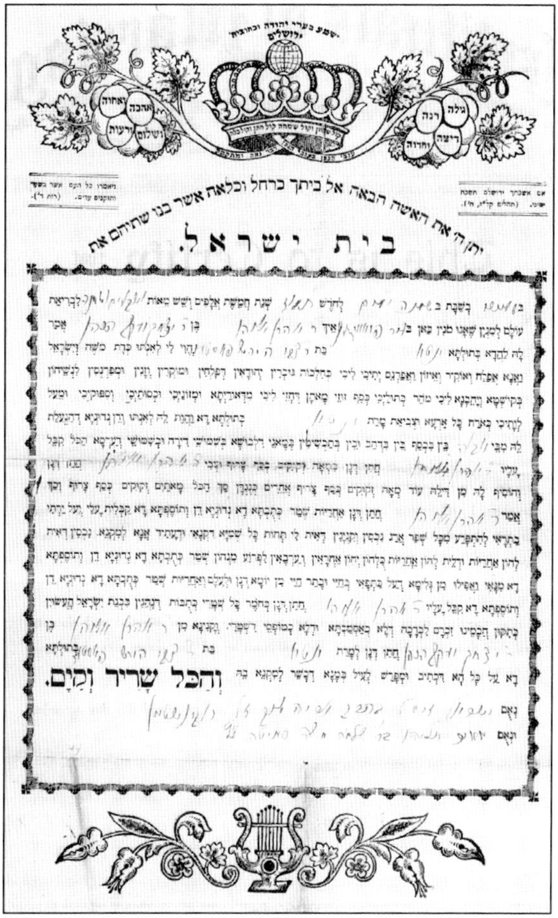


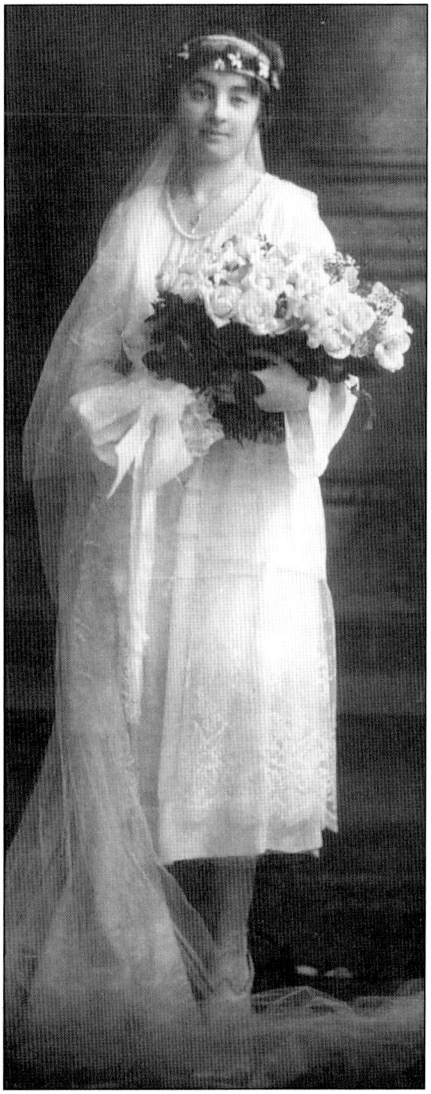

Nettie Paster as a bride before her marriage to Aaron Cohen on June 18, 1918.

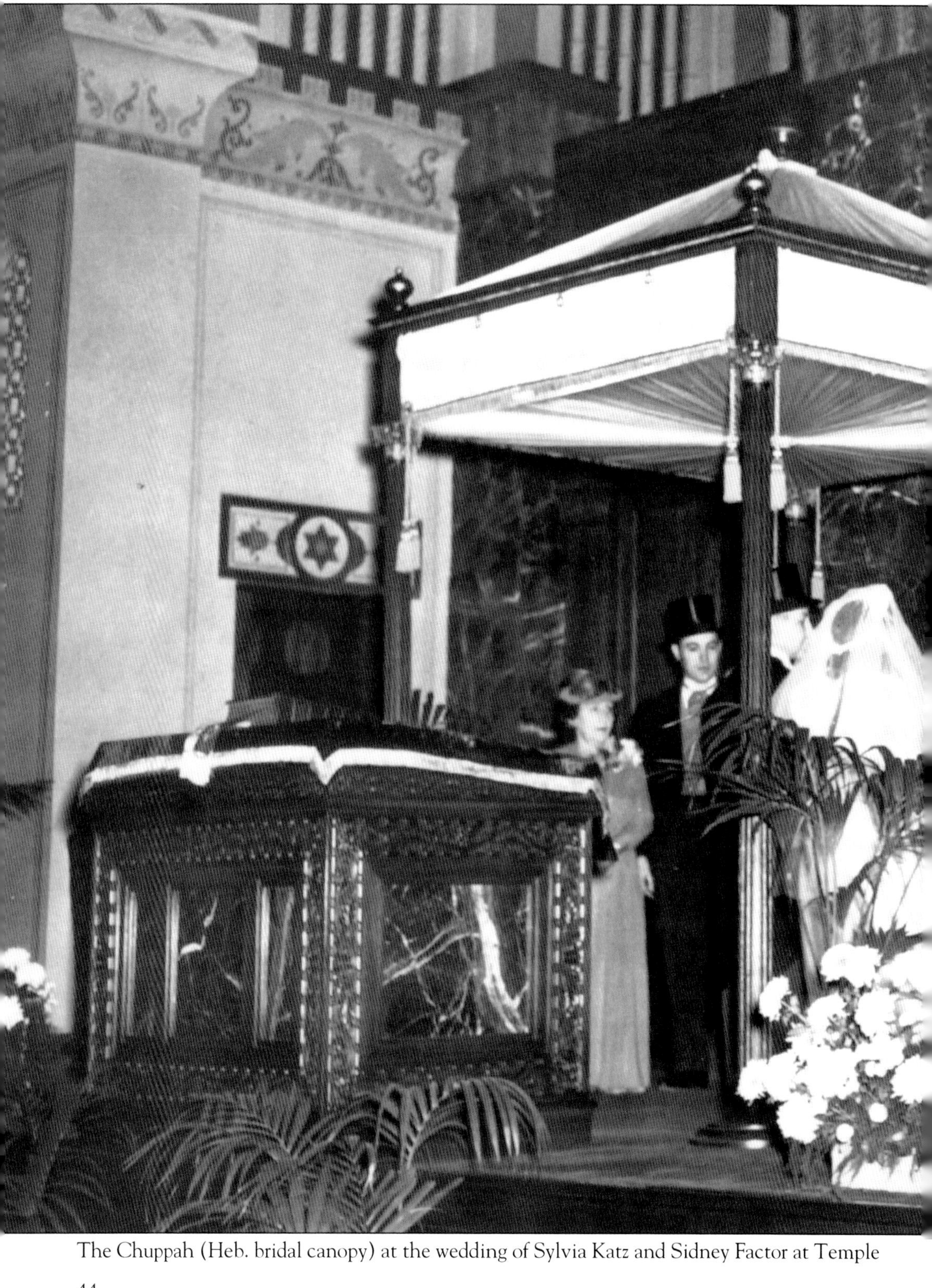

The Chuppah (Heb. bridal canopy) at the wedding of Sylvia Katz and Sidney Factor at Temple

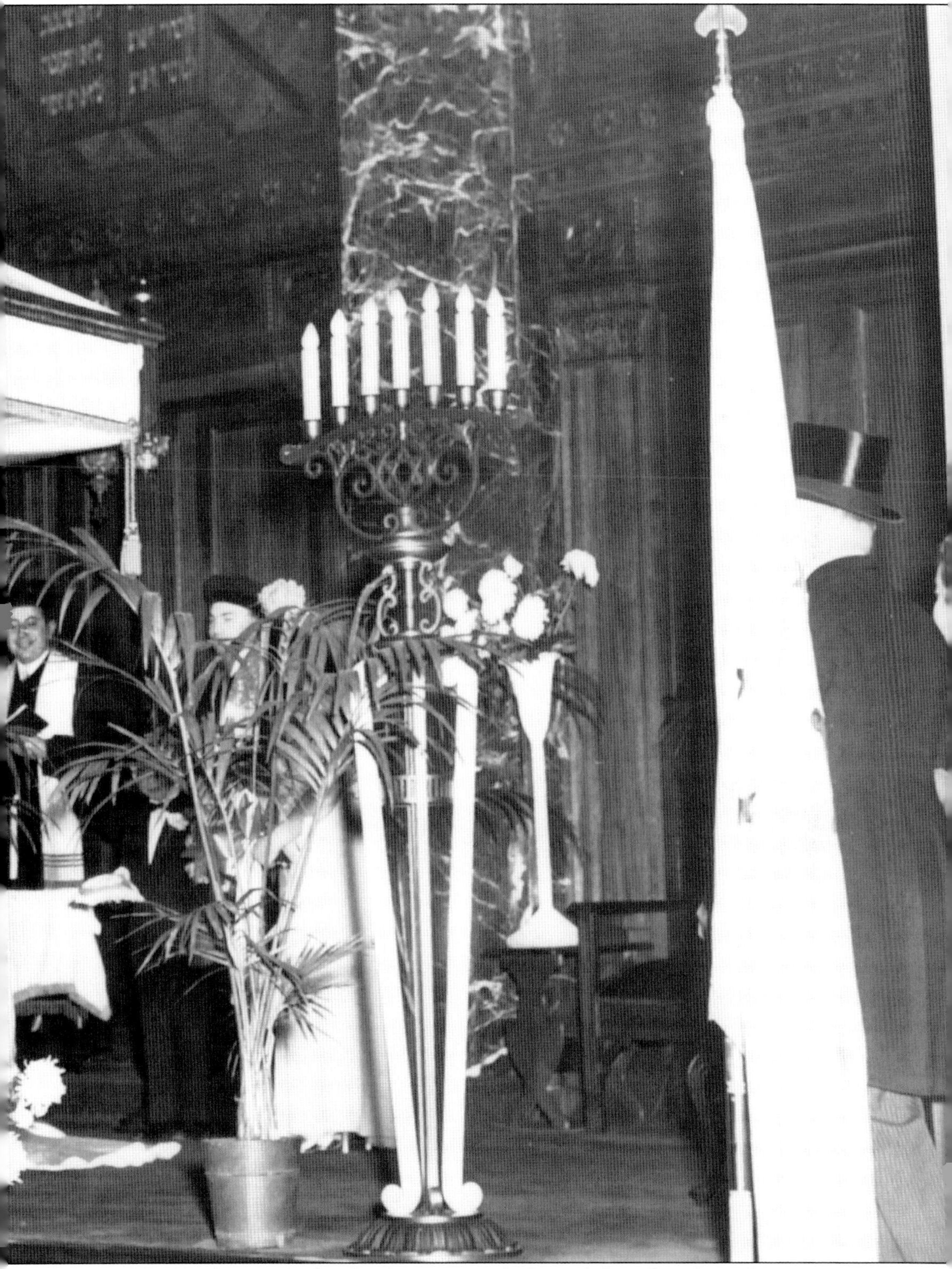

Emanu-El. A couple is married under the canopy, which symbolizes their future home.

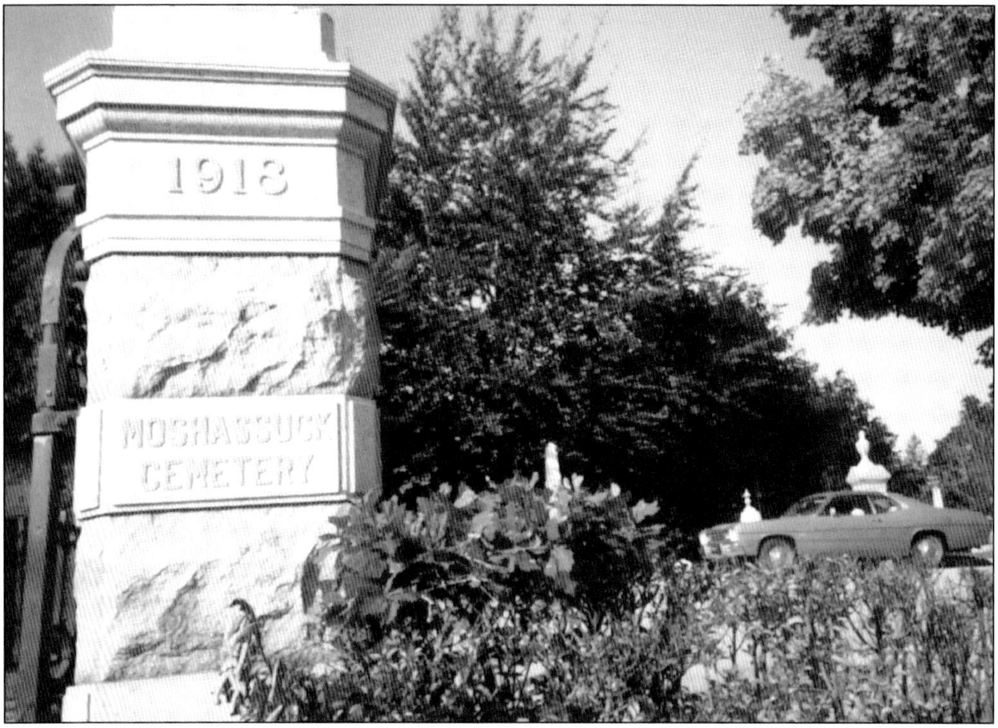

Mosshasuck Cemetery. From 1870 to 1897, as the number of Eastern European Jews increased dramatically, they organized synagogues and self-help societies. These organizations purchased contiguous plots of land in the northwest section of the Mosshasuck Cemetery for the burial of their members.

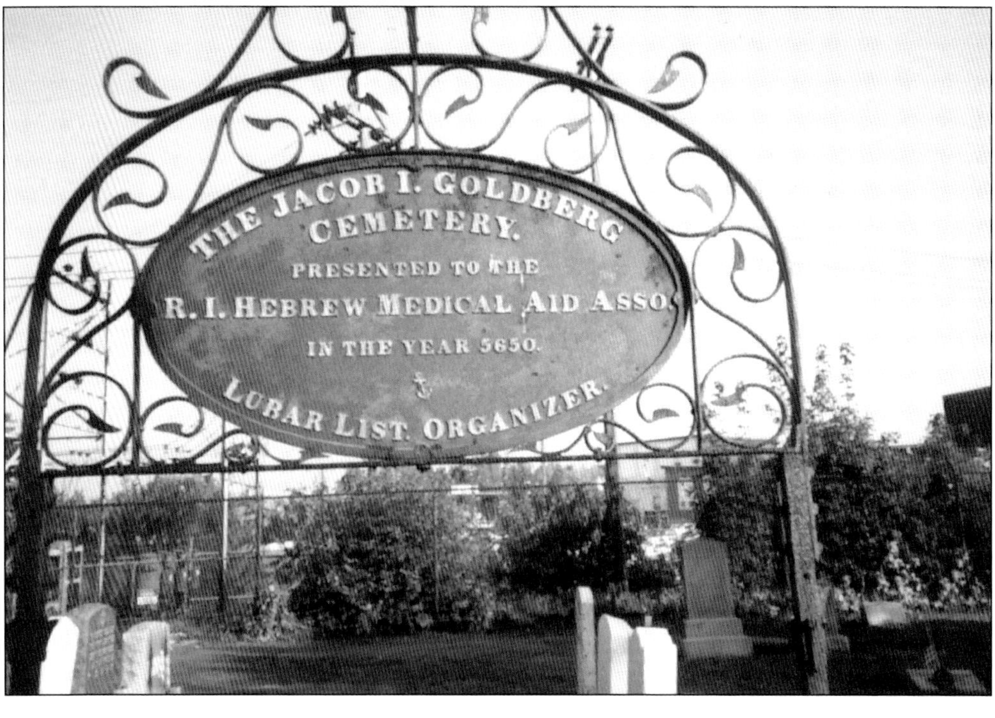

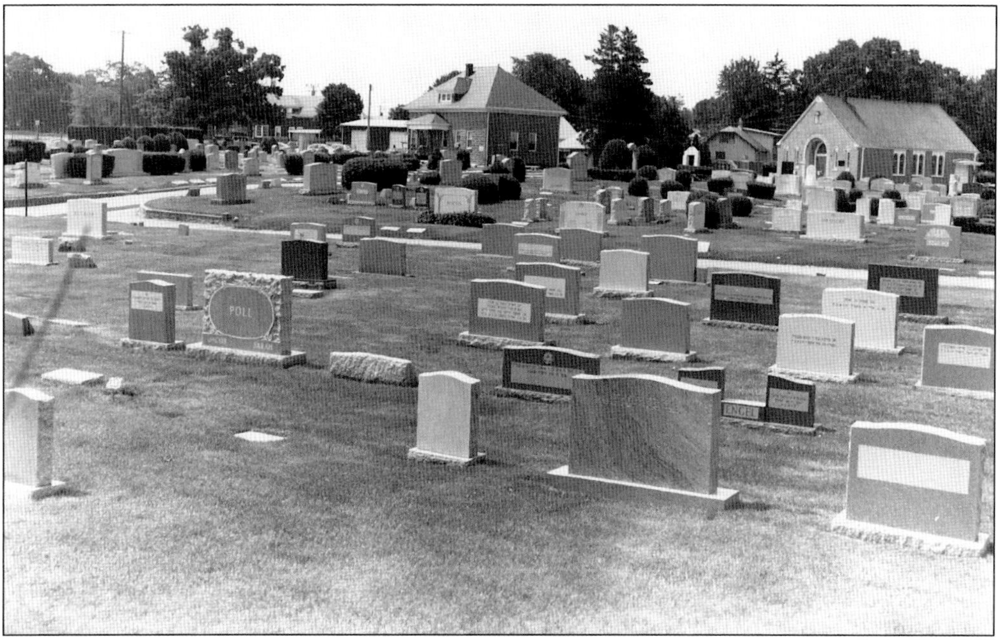

Lincoln Park Cemetery. Originally purchased by Barnet Fain under the aegis of Congregation Sons of Zion, it replaced the Mosshasuck Cemetery.

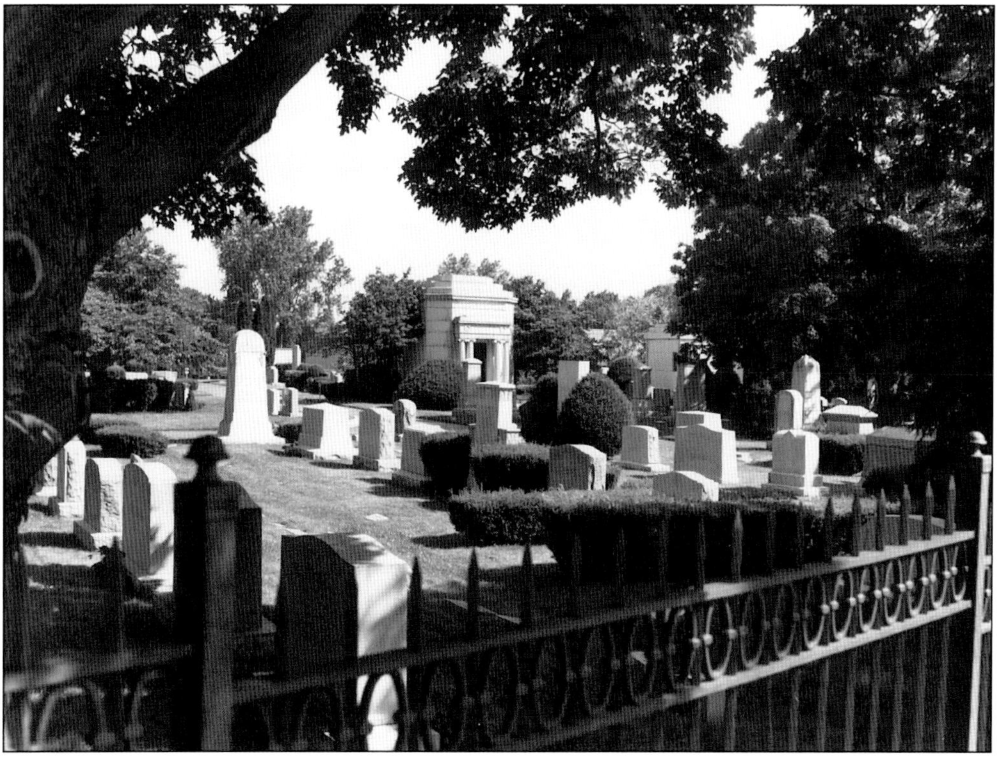

The Cemetery of the Congregation of the Sons of Israel and David, more familiarly known as Temple Beth El, on Reservoir Avenue. Originally purchased by Solomon Pareira in 1849, the land was a gift to the congregation. Burial at this cemetery is limited to members.

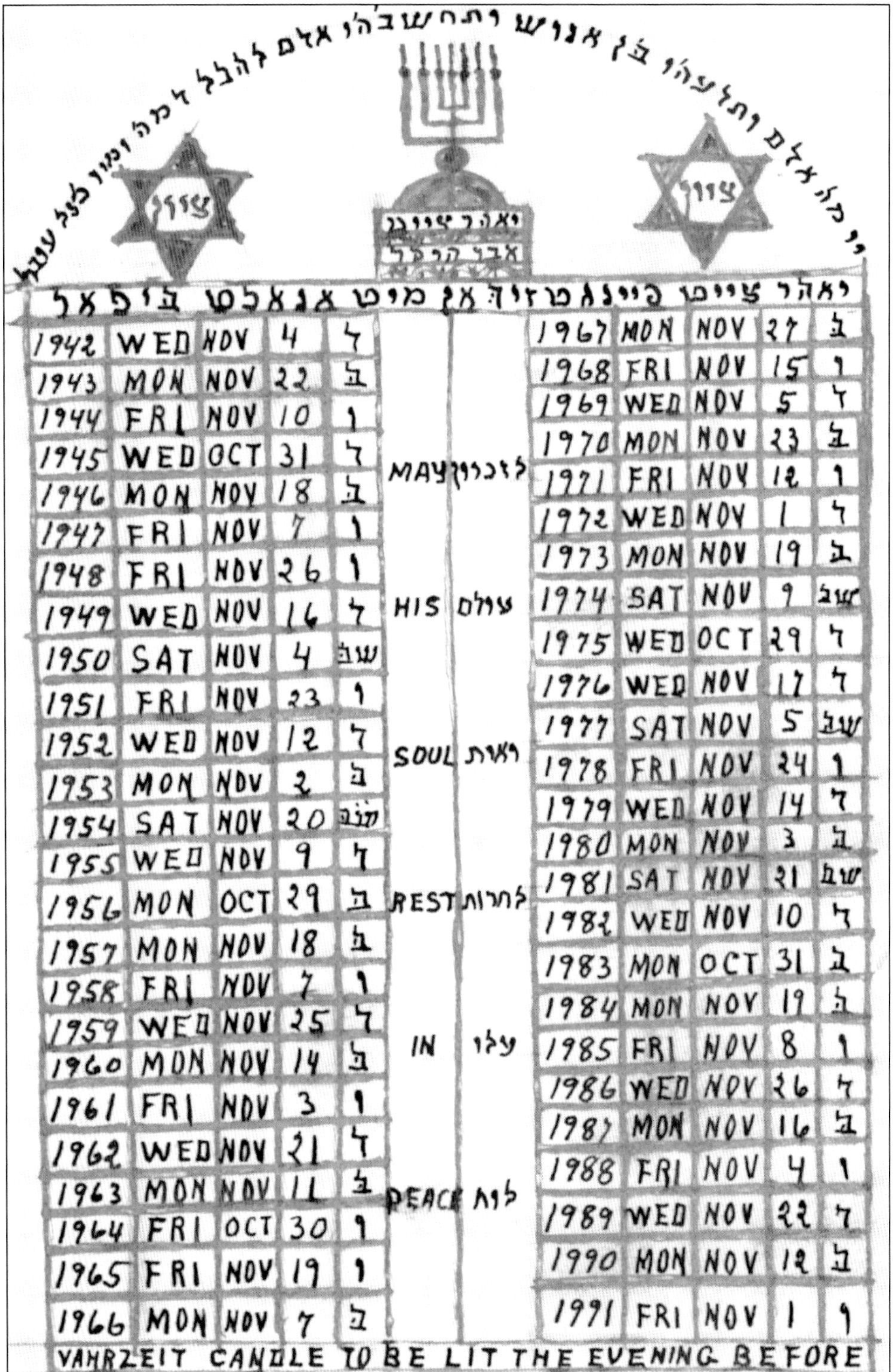


| Year | Day | Month | Date | Day (Heb.) |
|---|---|---|---|---|
| 1942 | WED | NOV | 4 | ד |
| 1943 | MON | NOV | 22 | ב |
| 1944 | FRI | NOV | 10 | ו |
| 1945 | WED | OCT | 31 | ד |
| 1946 | MON | NOV | 18 | ב |
| 1947 | FRI | NOV | 7 | ו |
| 1948 | FRI | NOV | 26 | ו |
| 1949 | WED | NOV | 16 | ד |
| 1950 | SAT | NOV | 4 | שב |
| 1951 | FRI | NOV | 23 | ו |
| 1952 | WED | NOV | 12 | ד |
| 1953 | MON | NOV | 2 | ב |
| 1954 | SAT | NOV | 20 | שב |
| 1955 | WED | NOV | 9 | ד |
| 1956 | MON | OCT | 29 | ב |
| 1957 | MON | NOV | 18 | ב |
| 1958 | FRI | NOV | 7 | ו |
| 1959 | WED | NOV | 25 | ד |
| 1960 | MON | NOV | 14 | ב |
| 1961 | FRI | NOV | 3 | ו |
| 1962 | WED | NOV | 21 | ד |
| 1963 | MON | NOV | 11 | ב |
| 1964 | FRI | OCT | 30 | ו |
| 1965 | FRI | NOV | 19 | ו |
| 1966 | MON | NOV | 7 | ב |
| 1967 | MON | NOV | 27 | ב |
| 1968 | FRI | NOV | 15 | ו |
| 1969 | WED | NOV | 5 | ד |
| 1970 | MON | NOV | 23 | ב |
| 1971 | FRI | NOV | 12 | ו |
| 1972 | WED | NOV | 1 | ד |
| 1973 | MON | NOV | 19 | ב |
| 1974 | SAT | NOV | 9 | שב |
| 1975 | WED | OCT | 29 | ד |
| 1976 | WED | NOV | 17 | ד |
| 1977 | SAT | NOV | 5 | שב |
| 1978 | FRI | NOV | 24 | ו |
| 1979 | WED | NOV | 14 | ד |
| 1980 | MON | NOV | 3 | ב |
| 1981 | SAT | NOV | 21 | שב |
| 1982 | WED | NOV | 10 | ד |
| 1983 | MON | OCT | 31 | ב |
| 1984 | MON | NOV | 19 | ב |
| 1985 | FRI | NOV | 8 | ו |
| 1986 | WED | NOV | 26 | ד |
| 1987 | MON | NOV | 16 | ב |
| 1988 | FRI | NOV | 4 | ו |
| 1989 | WED | NOV | 22 | ד |
| 1990 | MON | NOV | 12 | ב |
| 1991 | FRI | NOV | 1 | ו |

The Yahrzeit calendar, the memorial calendar showing dates corresponding to the anniversary of the death of a loved one. The anniversary is constant on the Hebrew lunar calender.

# *Four*

# Leisure Time

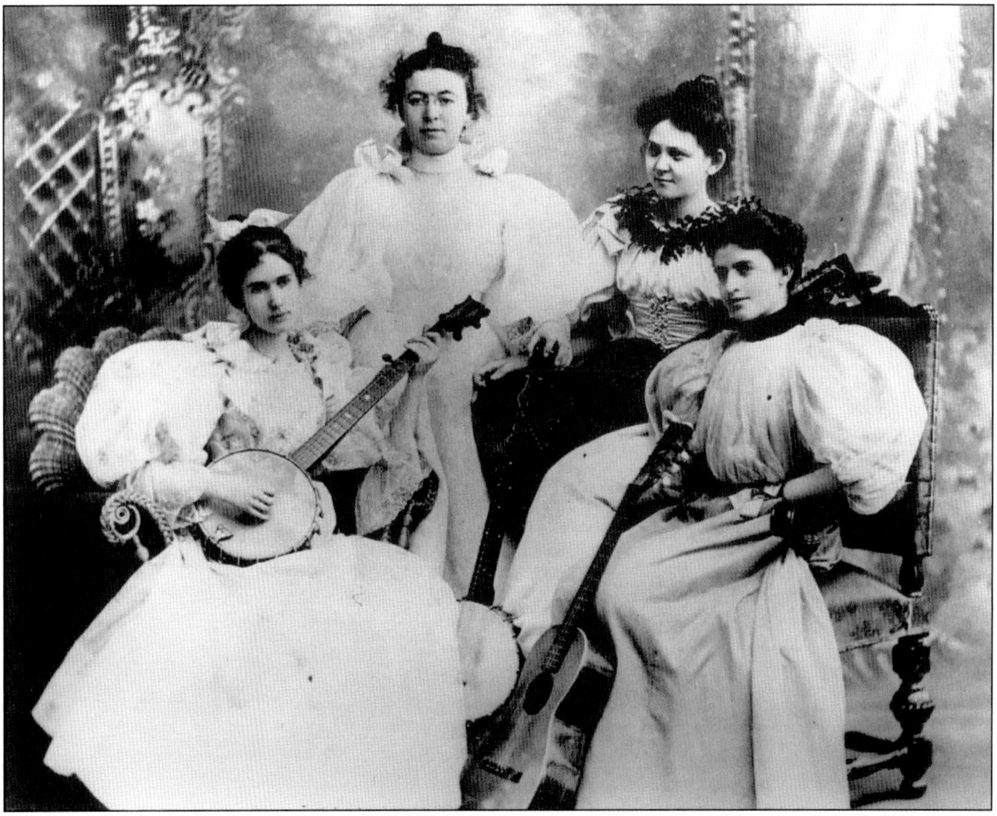

The Pembroke College Banjo and Guitar Club, 1896. Clara Gomberg is seated on the left.

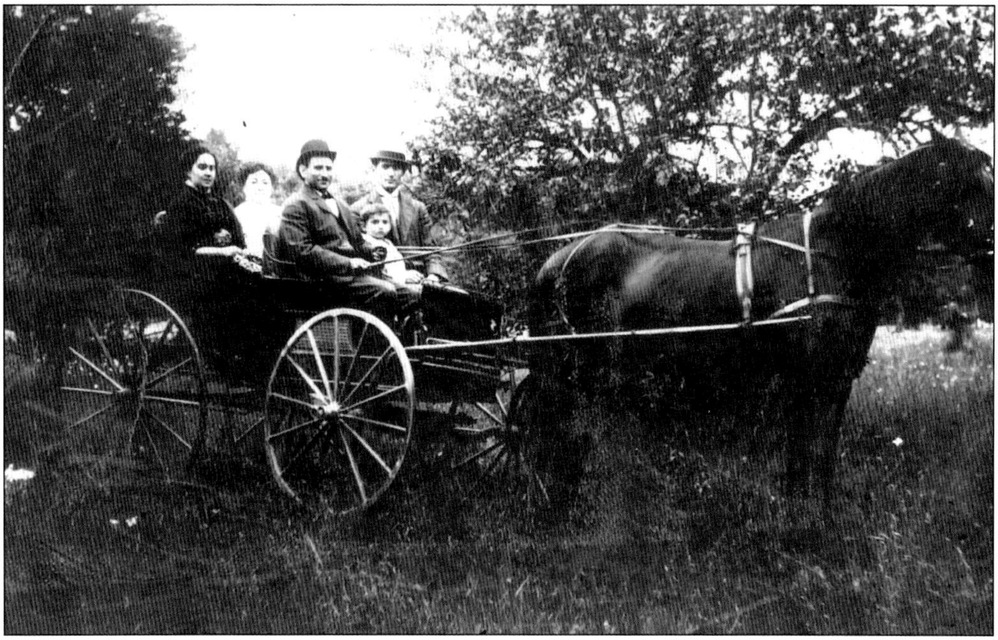

The Hornstein family. Dressed in their best clothes, the family obviously anticipates their outing. Their picnic might have taken place at Palace Gardens near Conimicut or perhaps at a farm such as the Turoff Farm in nearby Massachusetts.

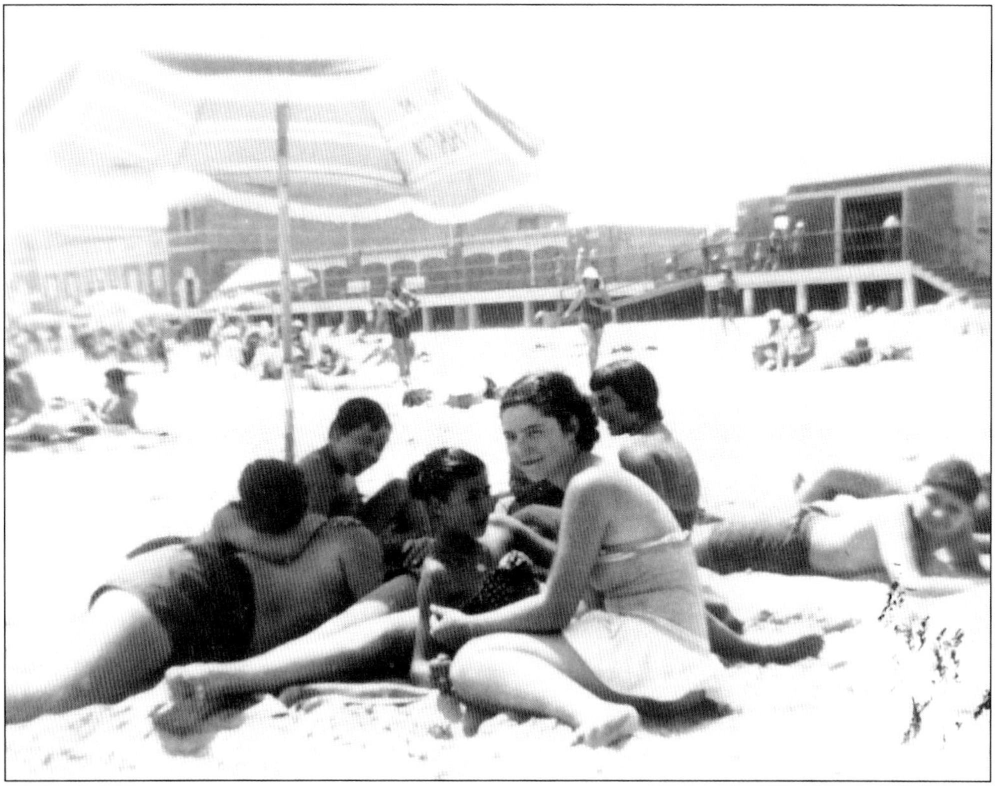

Enjoying the beach at Narragansett Pier.

A young man with a fiddle.

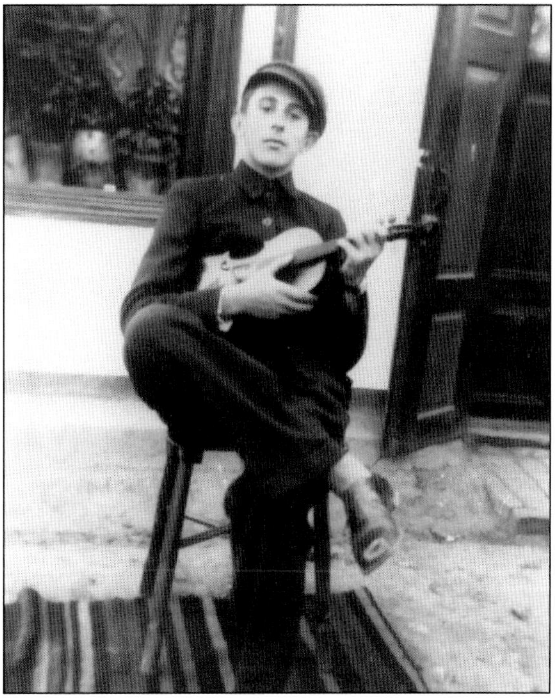

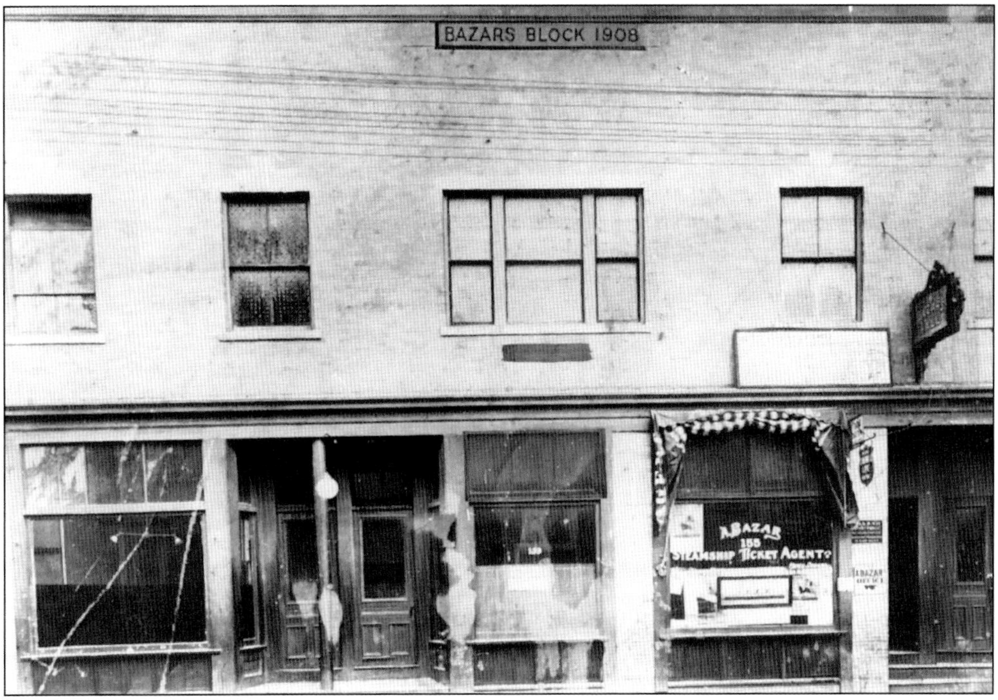


Bazar's Hall in South Providence, the location of many weddings and balls. Even though leisure time was a scarce commodity for the hard-working immigrants, there was ample mental and physical diversion such as the activities that took place in this hall. On Friday nights it was turned into the neighborhood silent movie house. The Literary and Dramatic Club also met here.

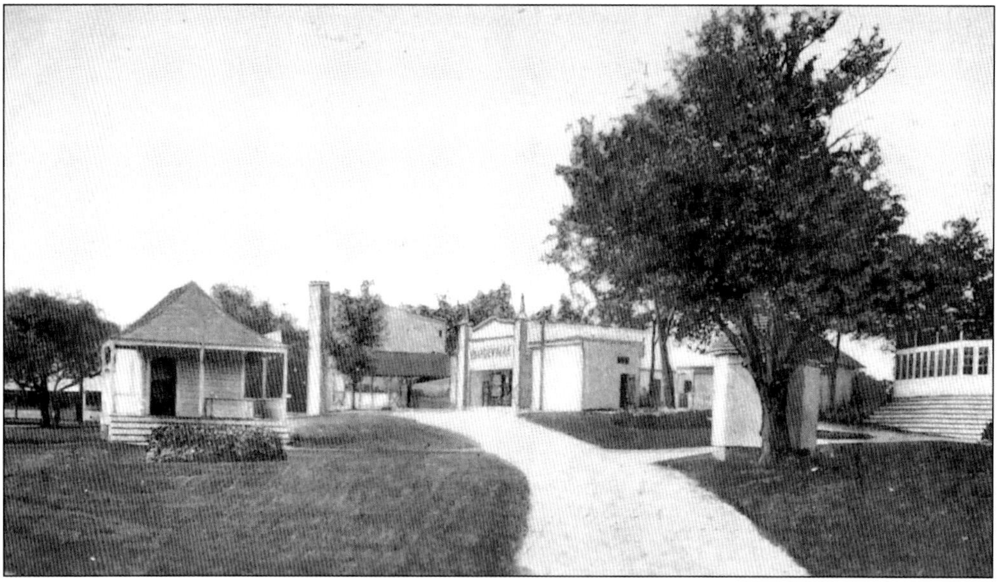

Hunt's Mills in East Providence. This was a recreational complex where the younger adults met for dancing and other social activities.

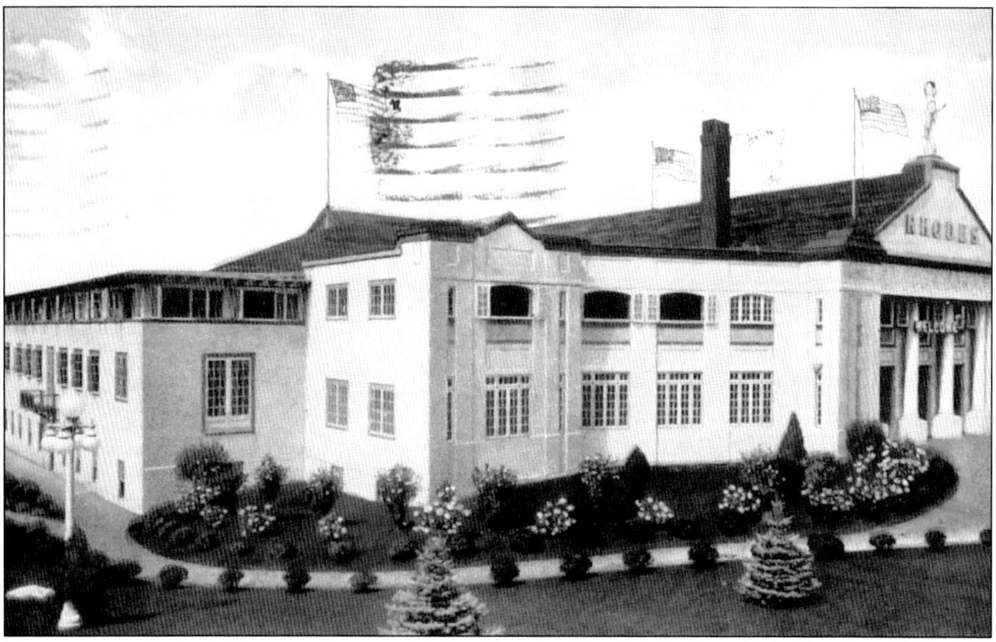

Rhode-on-the-Pawtuxet, another hall for dancing and socializing.

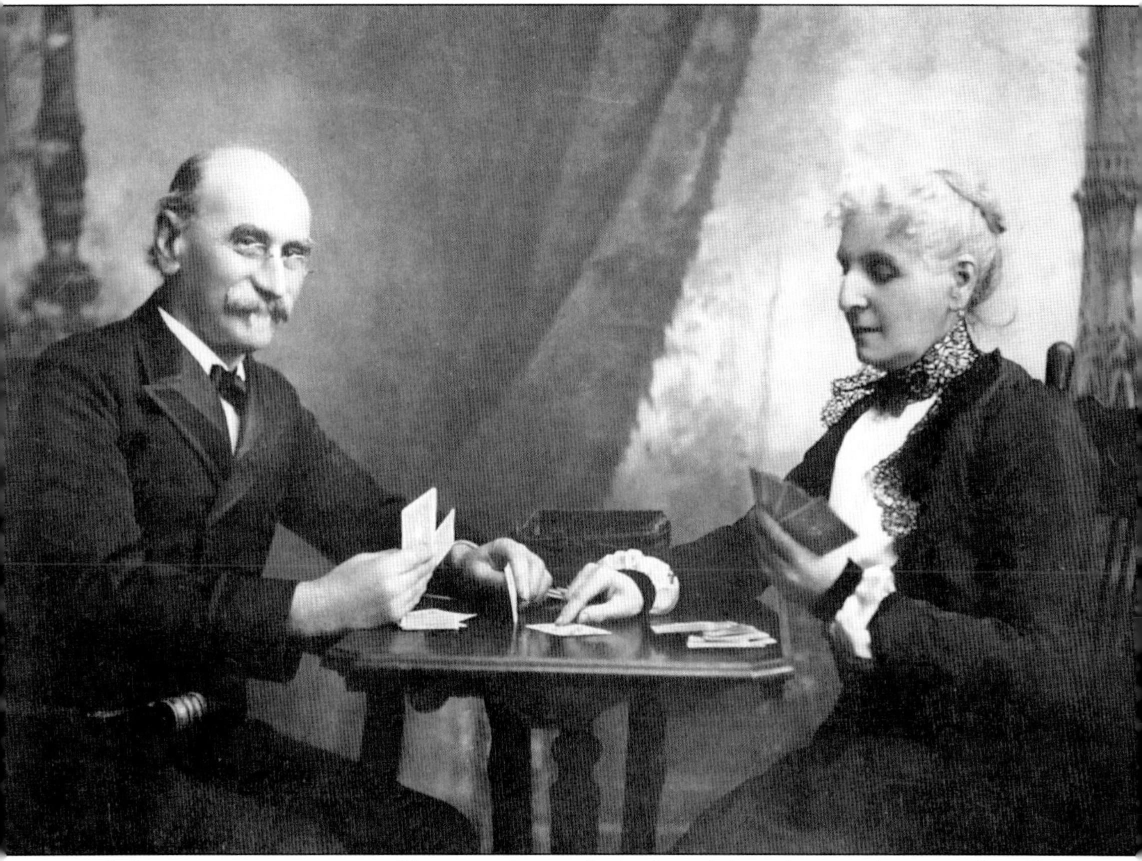

Card playing, an activity enjoyed by many. Mr. and Mrs. Joseph Hirschorn are having a friendly game of pinochle.

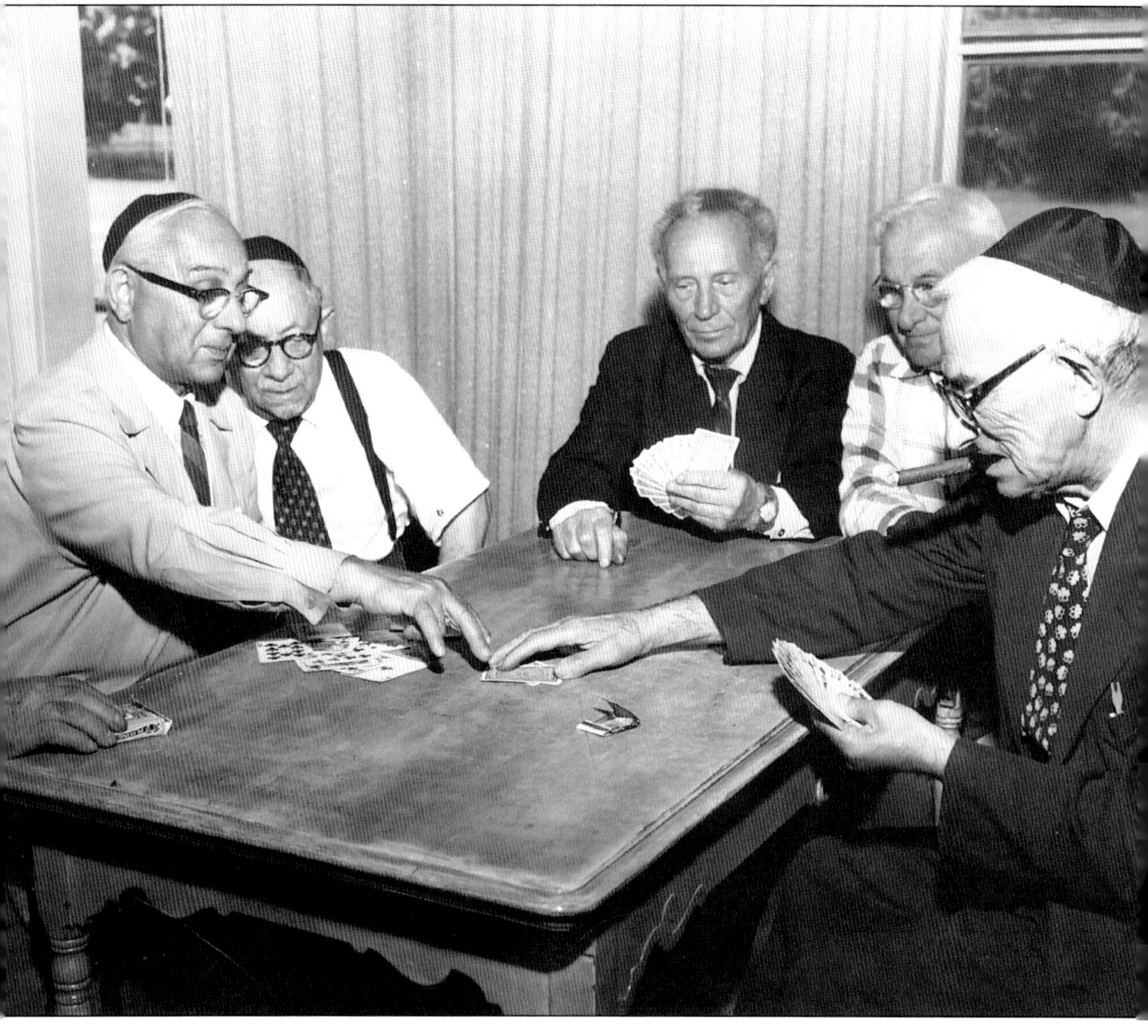

A card game at the Jewish Home for the Aged.

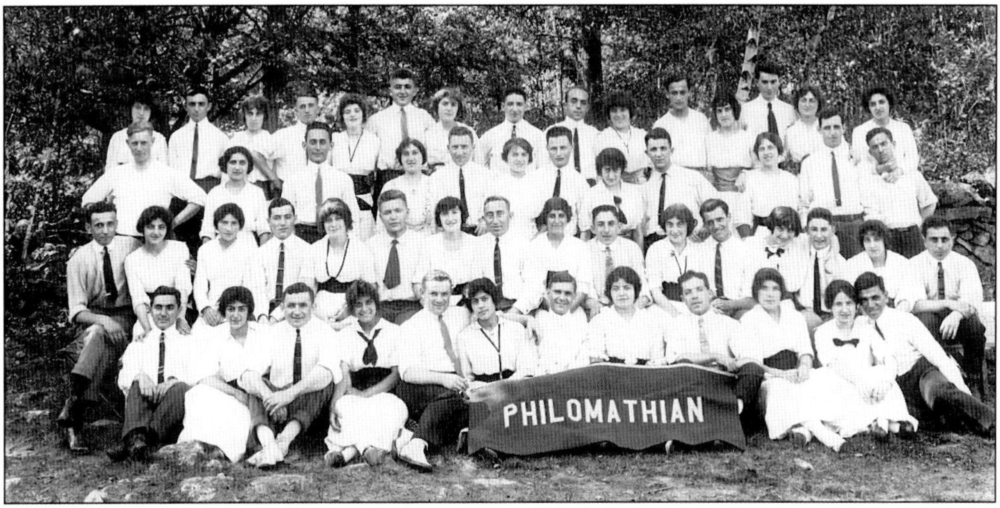


The Philomathians. The Philomathians were a group of young men who, in 1910, formed a club to promote and encourage educational, religious, charitable, and social pursuits among its members and the community at large.

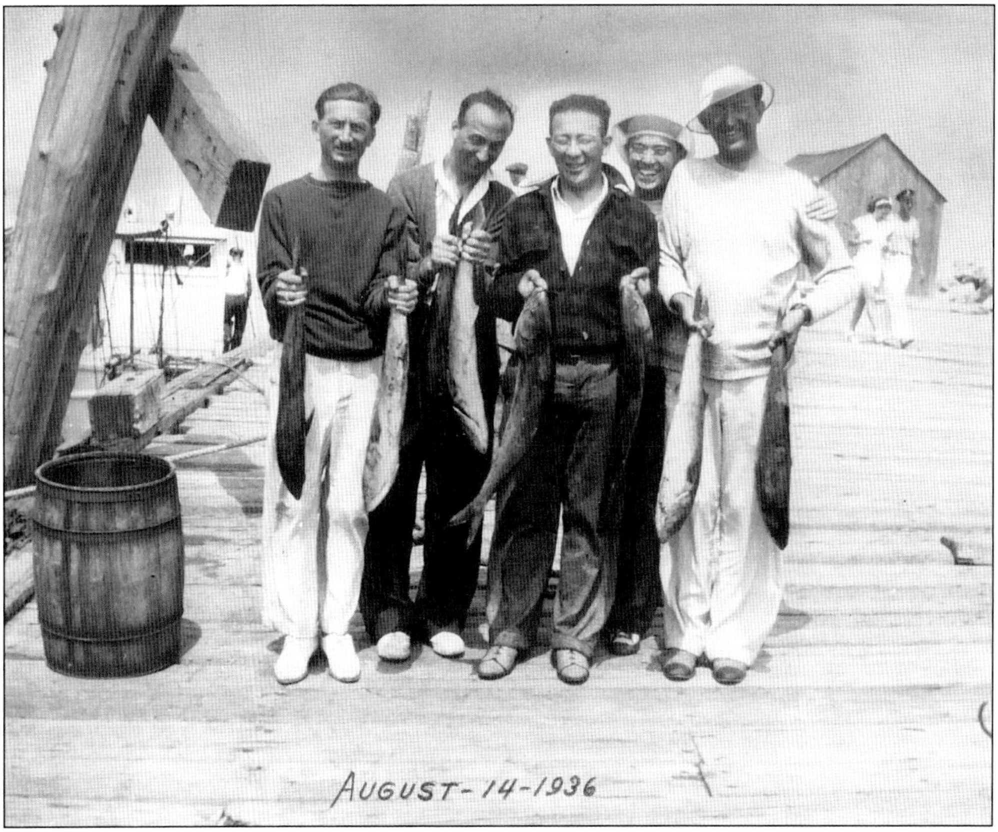


The Olneyville Hebrew Club, established in 1920 as a social club by a group of young men ages 16 to 18. They eventually changed their name to the Order of Hebraic Comradeship. In this photograph they are proudly displaying their recent catch taken during an outing.

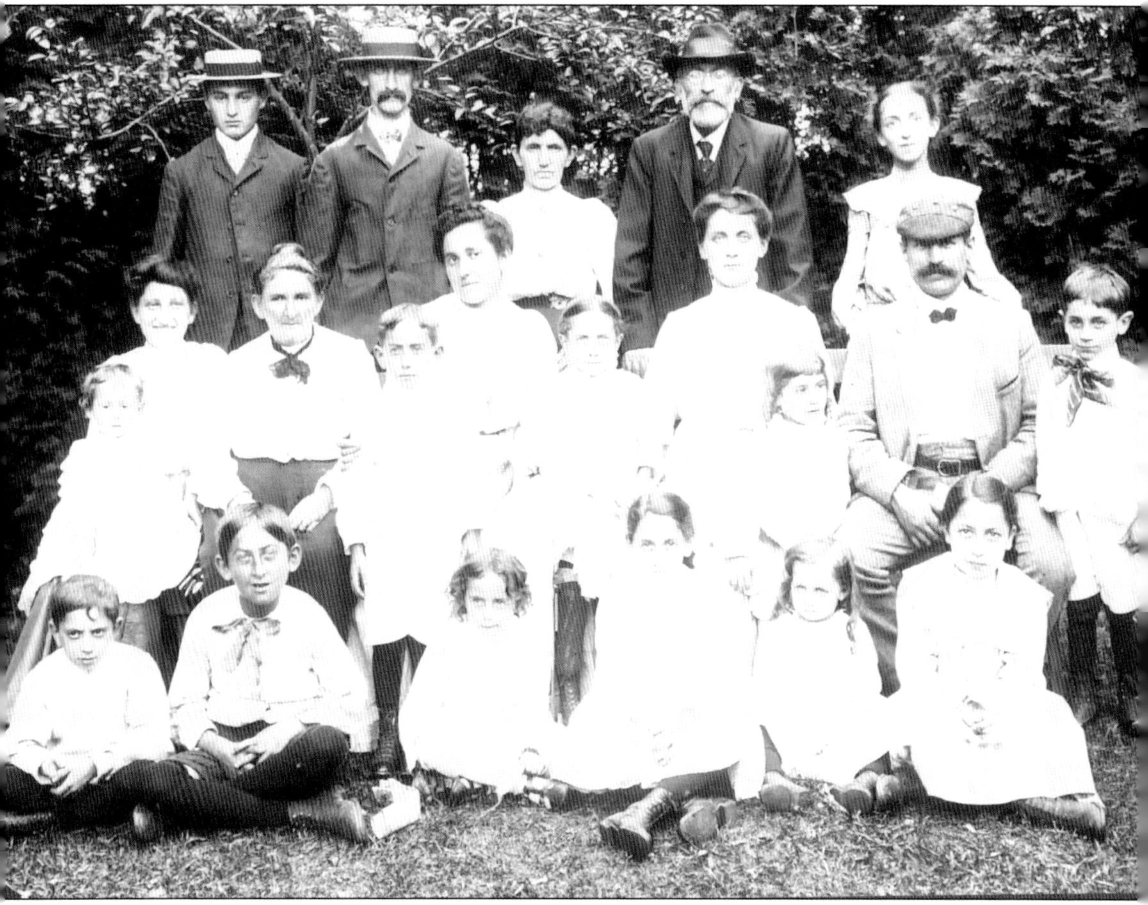

The Goldstein/Shindler family picnic at Duby's Grove, Pawtucket. Sundays were for family outings and picnics. They arrived at their destination by horse-drawn buggies or moving vans converted into buses.

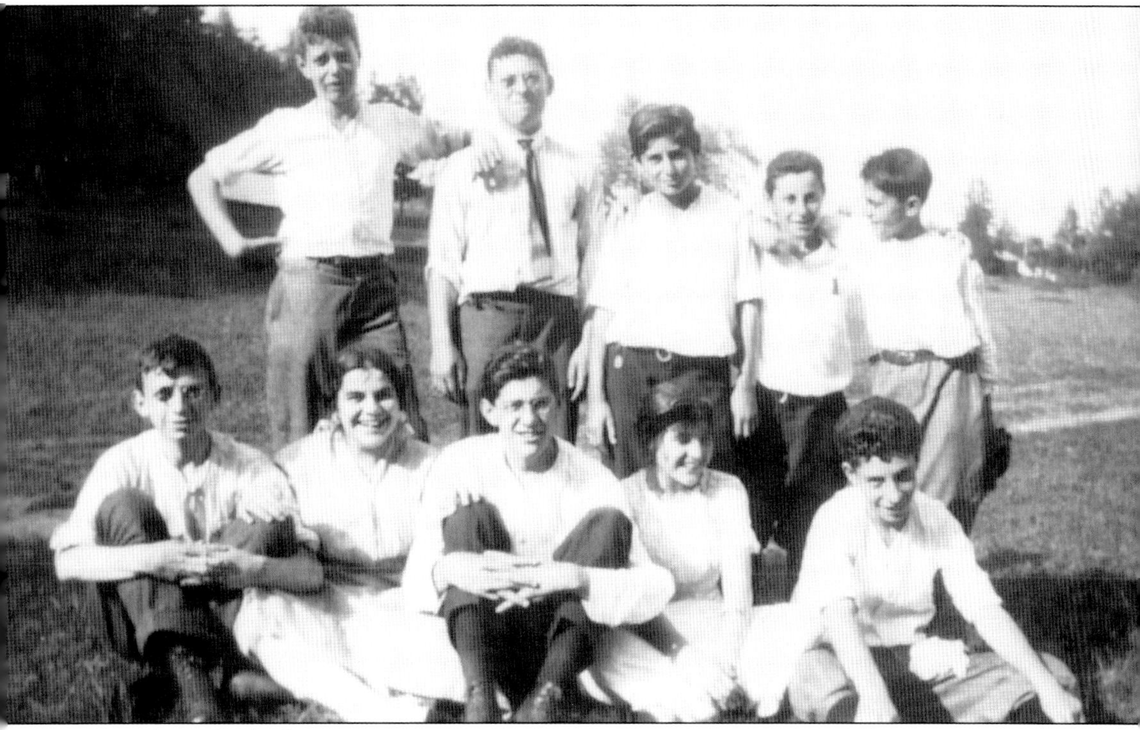

A Temple Beth El Librarians picnic, *c.* 1911.

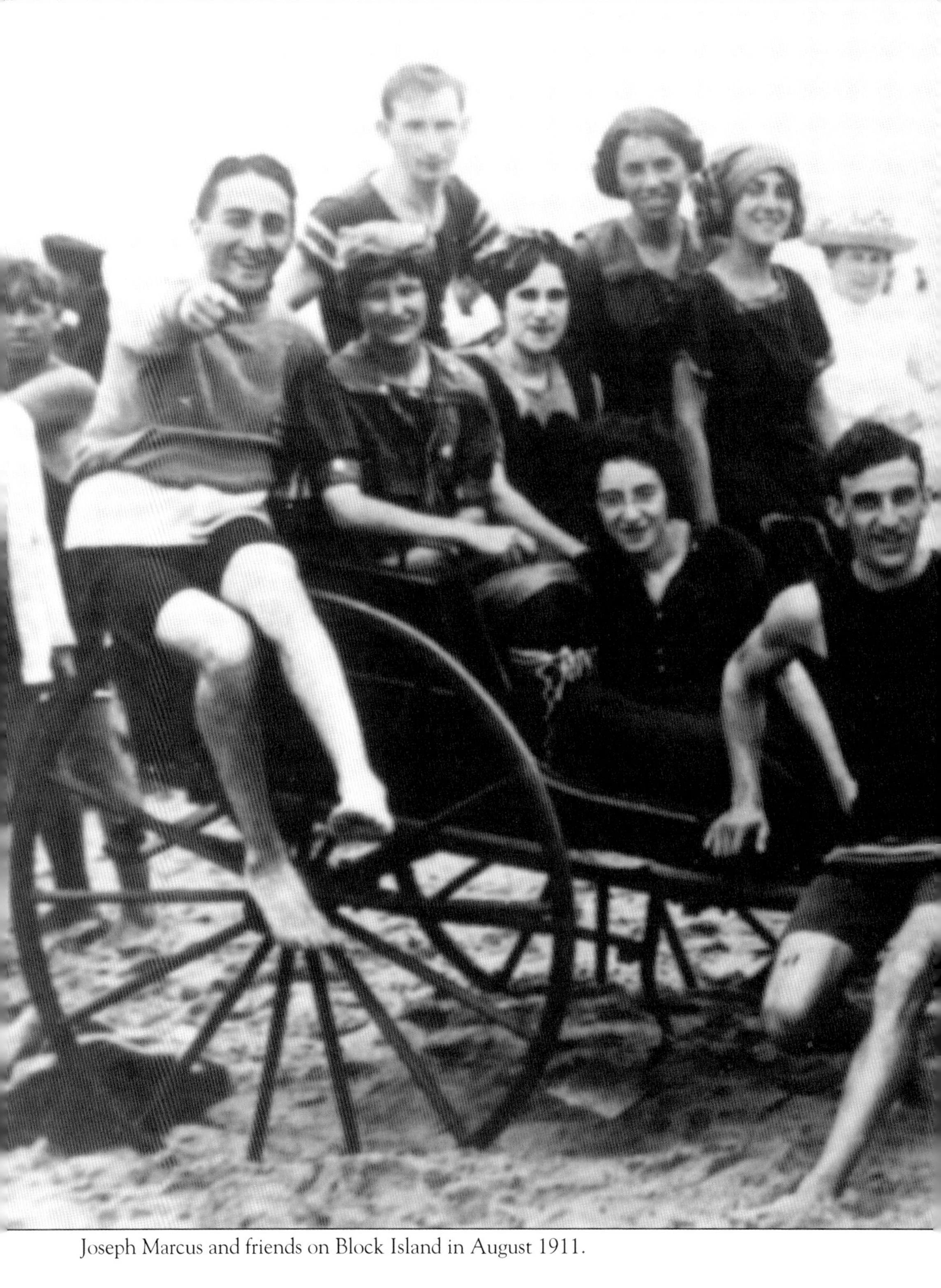

Joseph Marcus and friends on Block Island in August 1911.

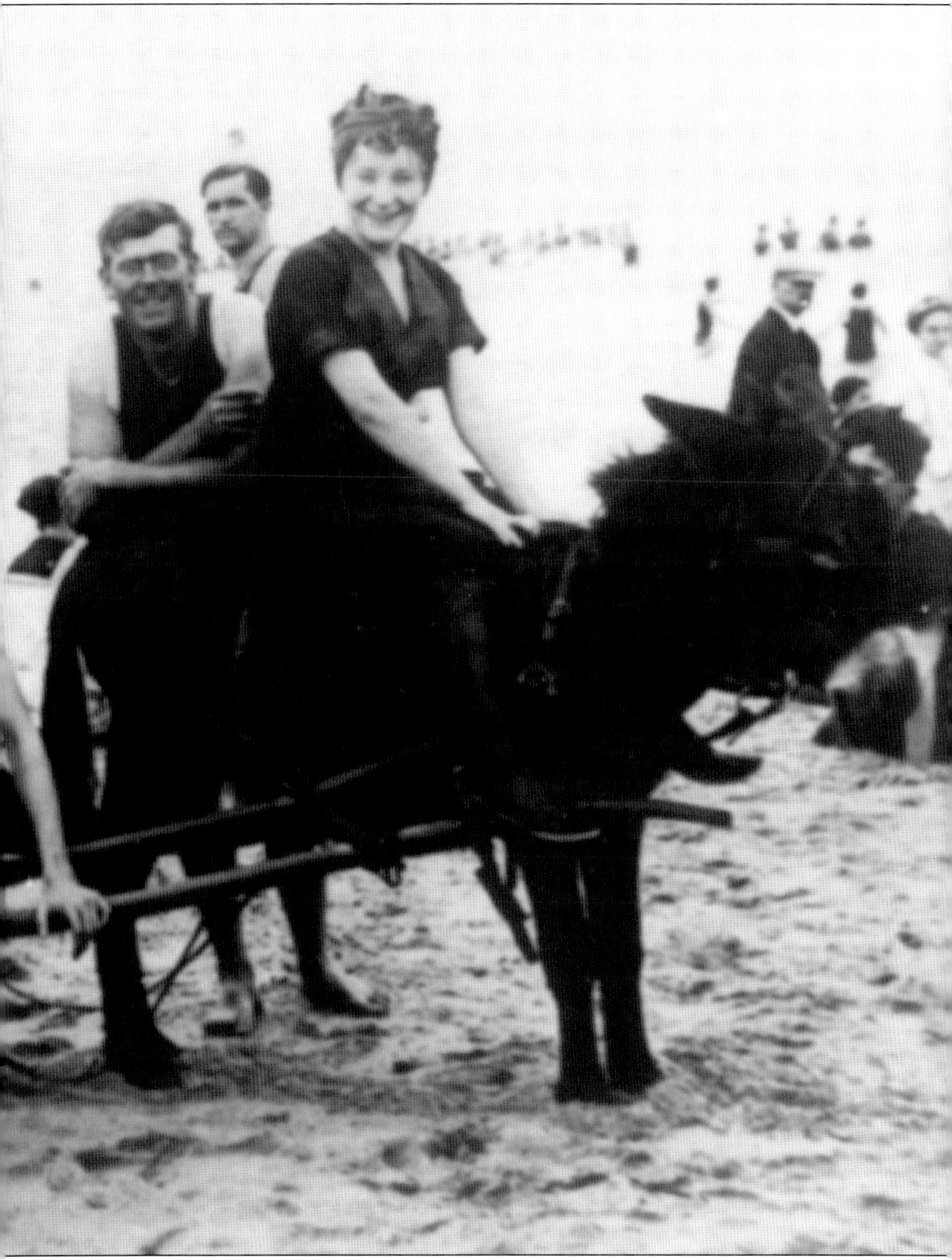

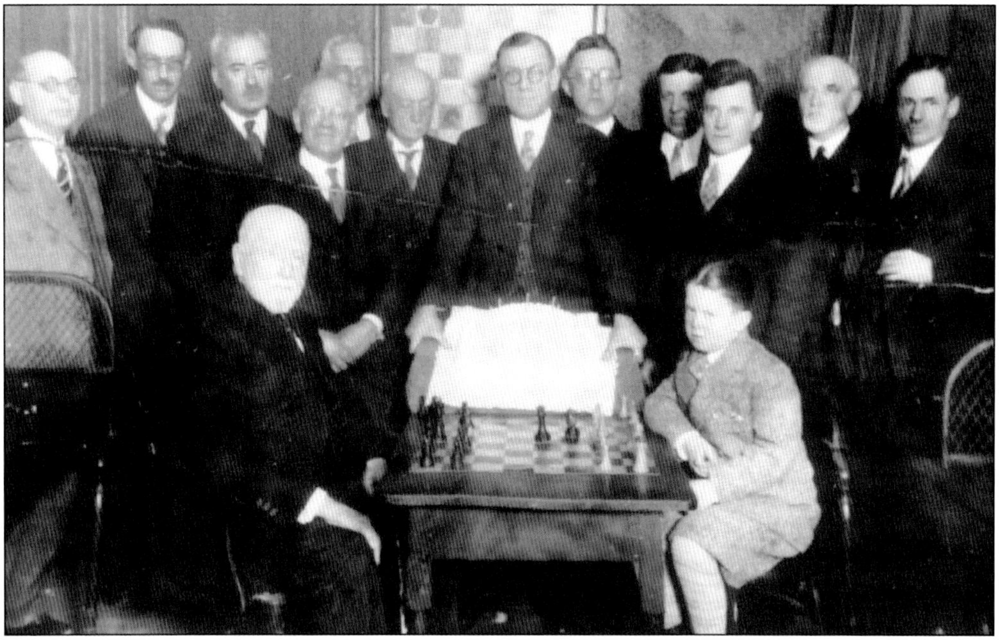

The Chess Club, 1921. Shown here playing together are the oldest member of the club at the time, Colonel Ingall, and the youngest, Frank Gomberg.

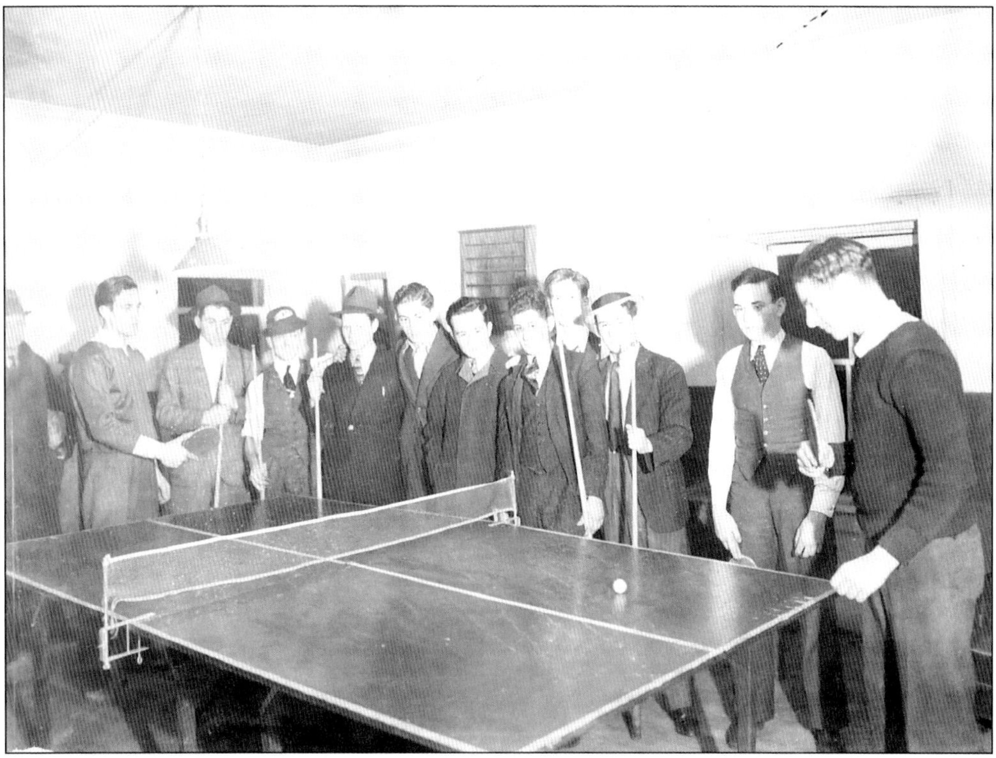

The Jewish Community Center, 65 Benefit Street, Providence. It offered facilities for all types of games and activities. This group of young men are enjoying their choice of a game of ping pong or pool, c. 1920.

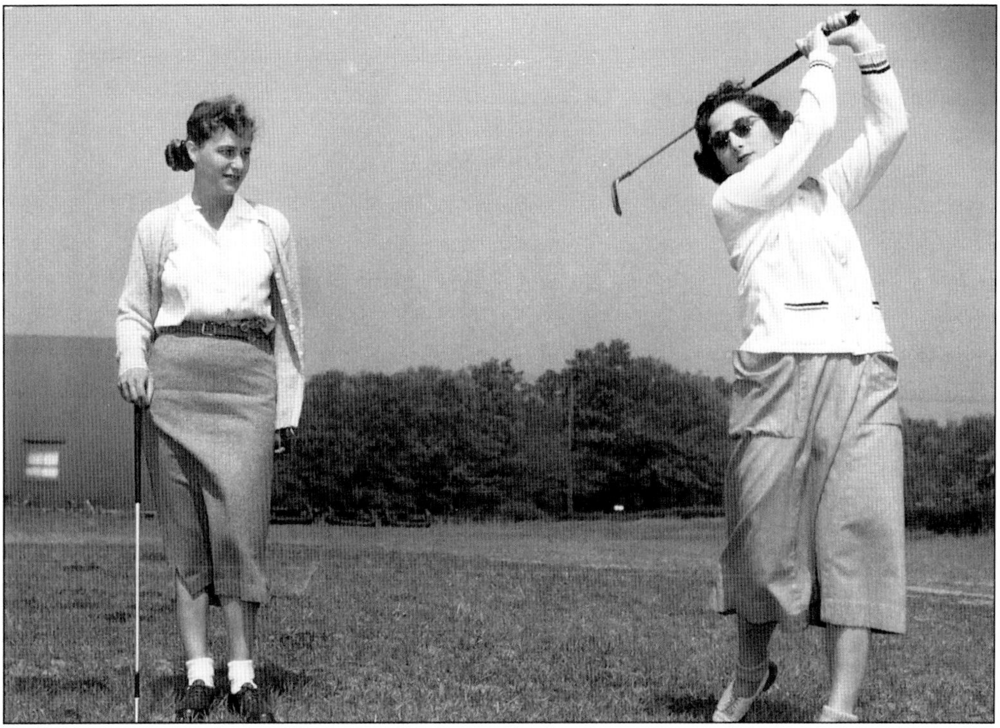

Two women enjoying a round of golf, a perennial favorite.

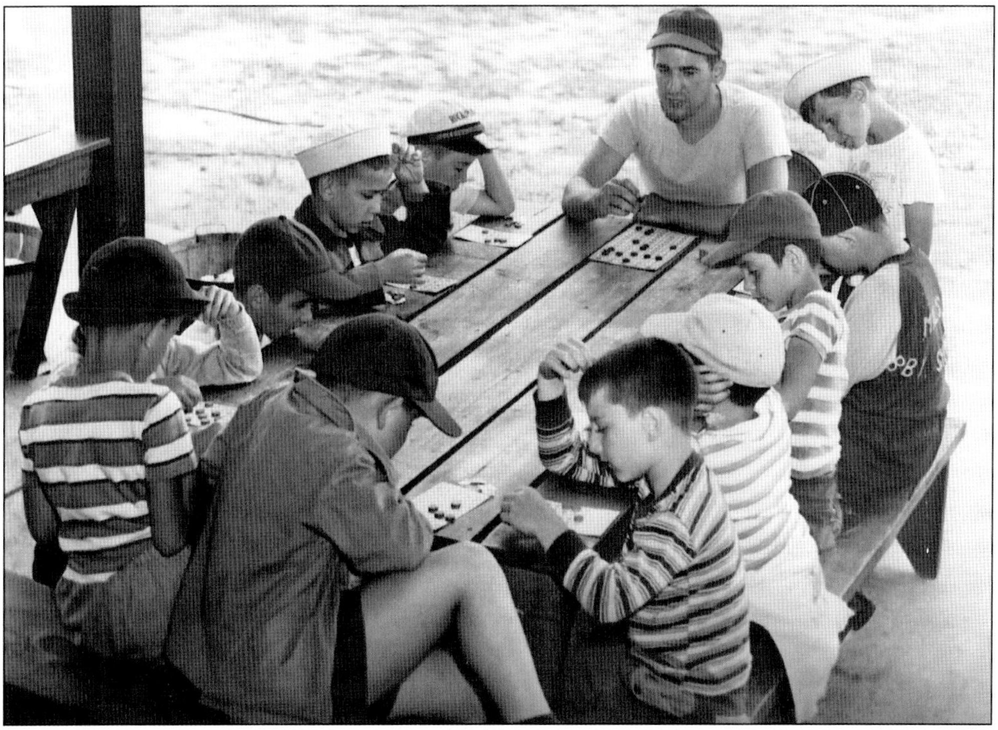

Campers at Camp Centerland. These children are playing bingo under the direction of their counselor.

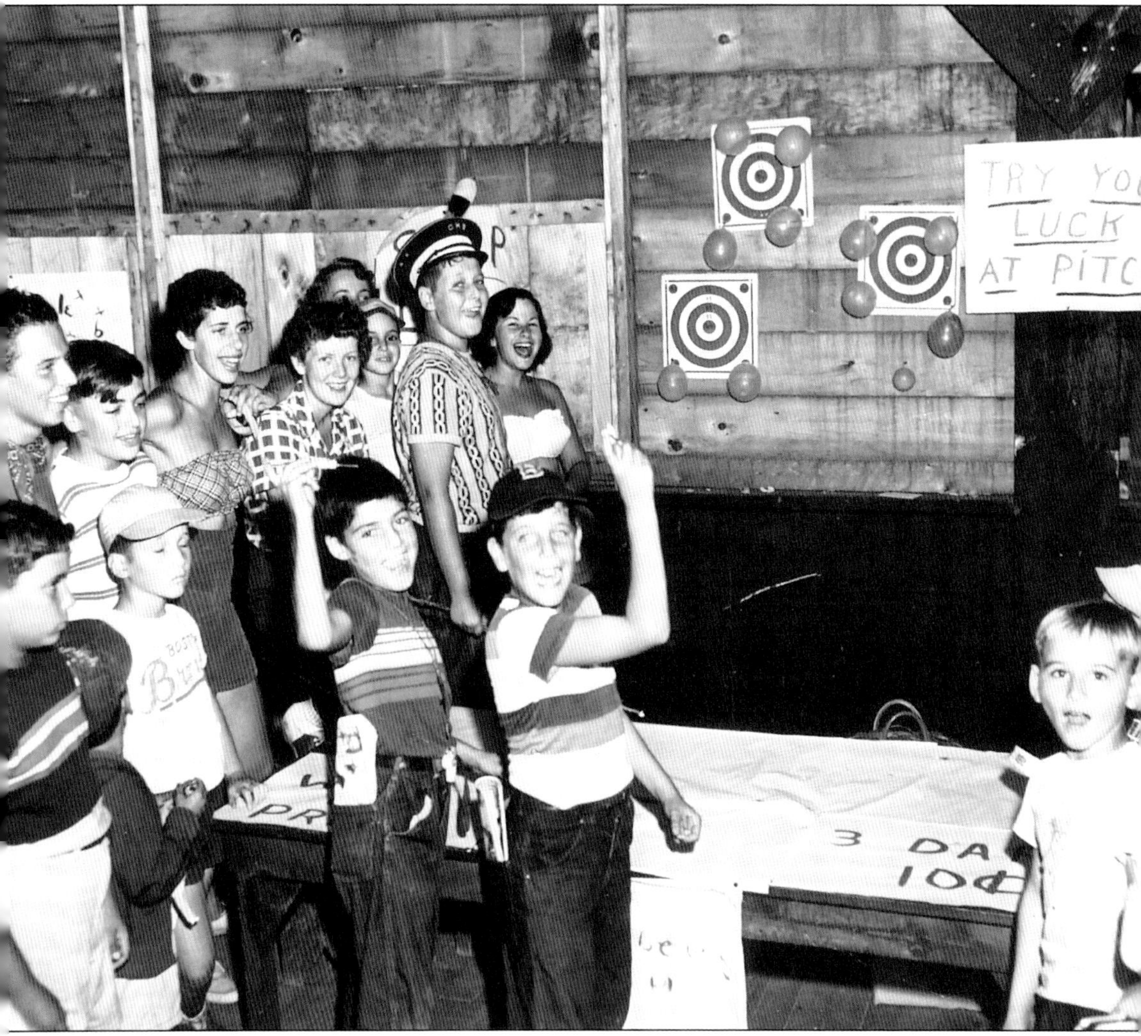


Enjoying a game of pitching at the Jewish Community Center Carnival. Although they had schooling, both secular and religious, these children had time to play organized games or attend camps. The children of an earlier generation often had jobs after school; they found their recreation in ball playing in the neighborhood, and, in the winter, sliding on the more hilly streets.

# *Five*
# Serving Their Country

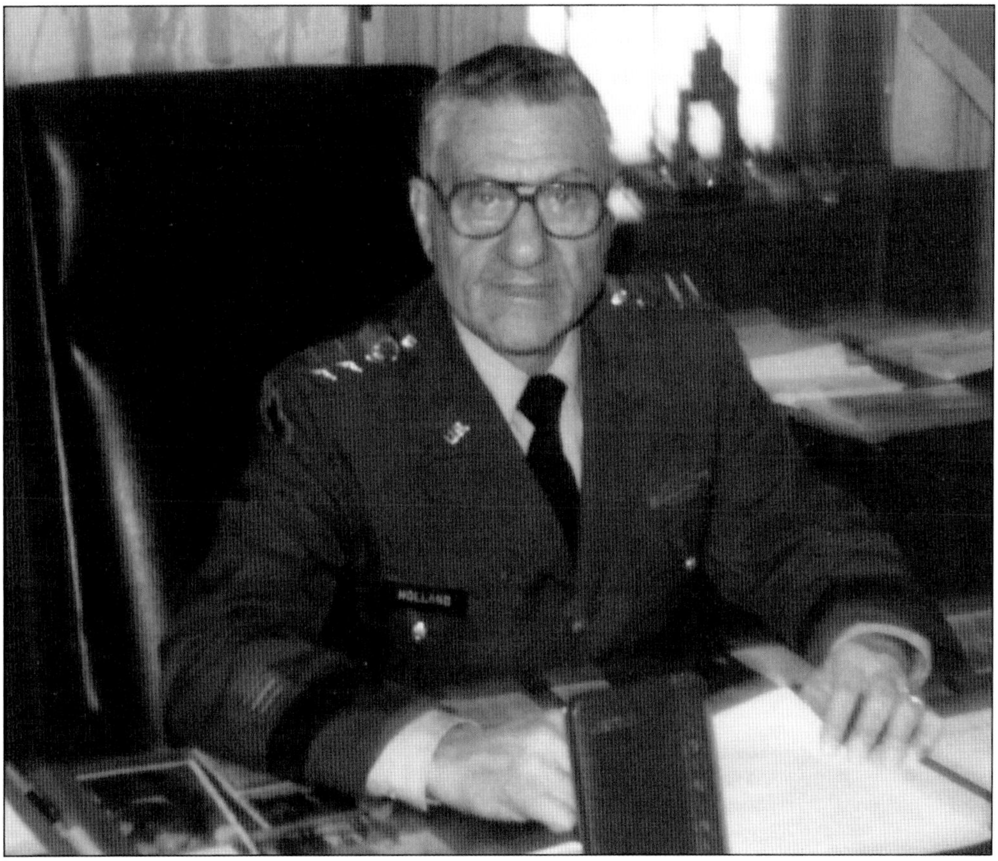

Major General Leonard Holland. Major General Holland retired on August 6, 1983, after serving as state adjutant general and commander of the Rhode Island National Guard. He saw action in every position in the army from platoon leader to regimental commander, and served in the Solomon and New Guinea Islands of the Pacific Theatre.

THE WHITE HOUSE
WASHINGTON

August 13, 1938.

Gentlemen:

The American people need no reminder of the service which those of Jewish faith have rendered our nation. It has been a service with honor and distinction. History reveals that your people have played a great and commendable part in the defense of Americanism during the World War and prior wars, and have contributed much in time of peace toward the development and preservation of the glory and romance of our country and our democratic form of government.

Franklin D Roosevelt

Jewish War Veterans of the United States,
276 Fifth Avenue,
New York, N. Y.

A letter from President Franklin Delano Roosevelt to the Jewish War Veterans.

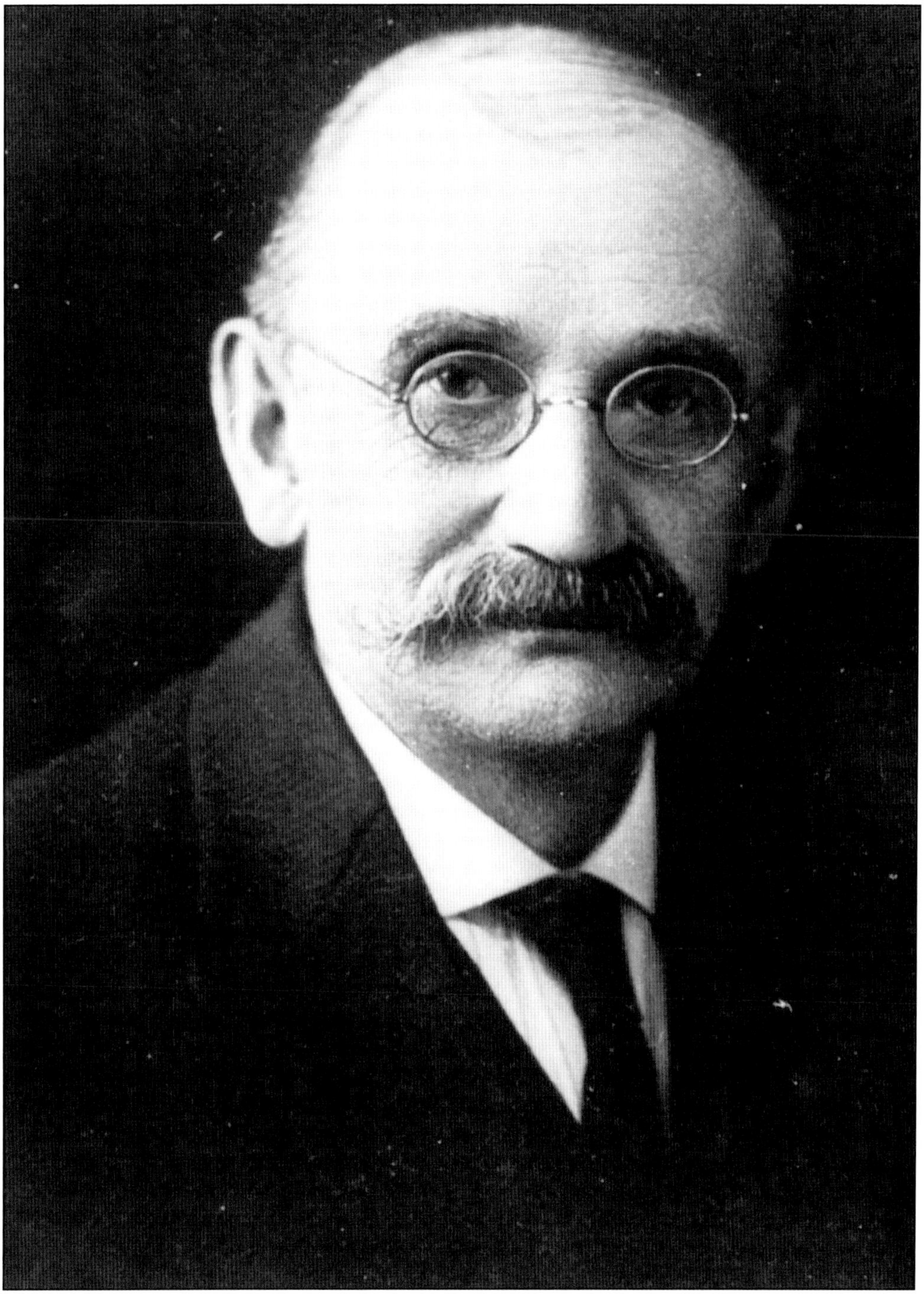

Newman Pincus. Newman Pincus came to America with his family at an early age. At the outbreak of the Civil War, he was 15 years old, but enlisted in the army (illegally), inspired by patriotism. A year after being discharged (when his true age was discovered), he re-enlisted and served in several important engagements, including the siege of Petersburg, Virginia, and the attendant battles.

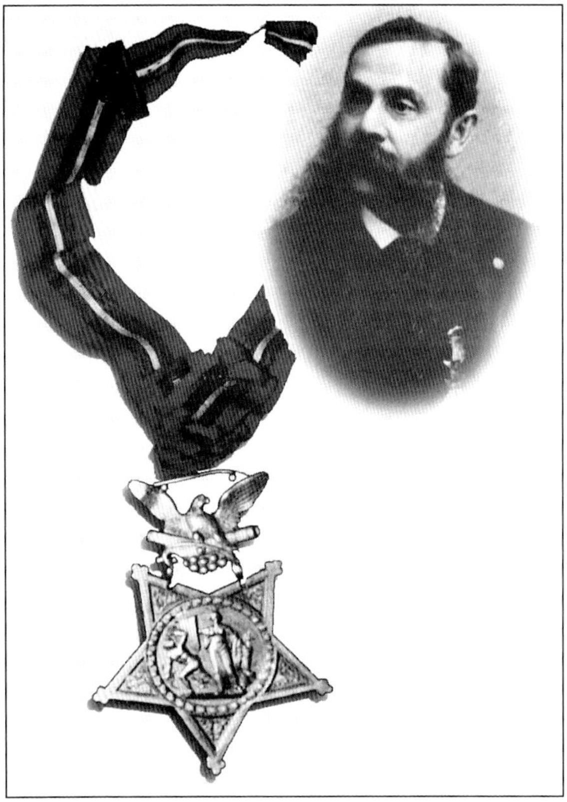

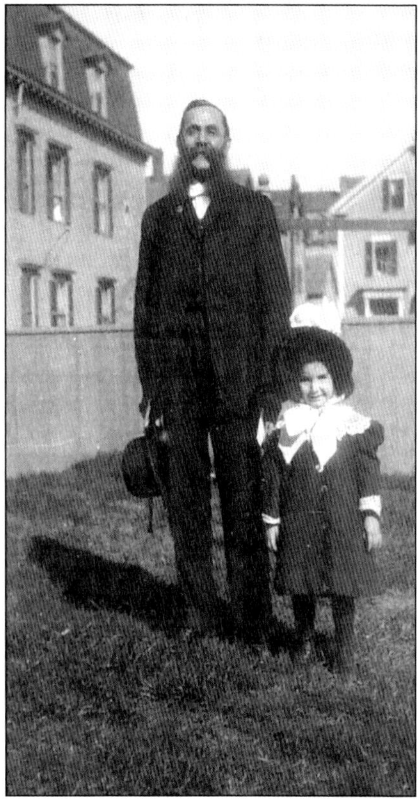

Color Sergeant Leopold Karpeles. Color Sergeant Karpeles won the Congressional Medal of Honor for bravery during the Civil War. Born in Prague, he lived in Texas and Massachusetts and, after the war, in Washington, D.C. Three of his children became Rhode Island residents. Tasy, shown to the right, later owned Chopard's, a jewelry repair shop in the Fletcher Building in Providence. Lotta Karpeles was the state psychologist of Rhode Island from 1930 to 1938, and Maurice Karpeles was a manufacturer of cultured pearls and, later, of ecclesiastical jewelry.

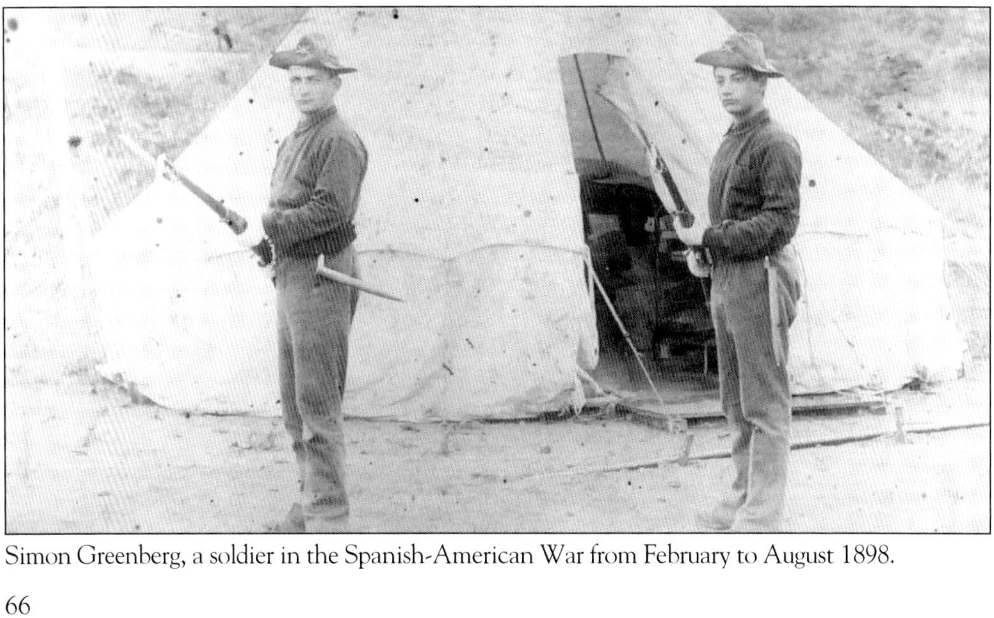

Simon Greenberg, a soldier in the Spanish-American War from February to August 1898.

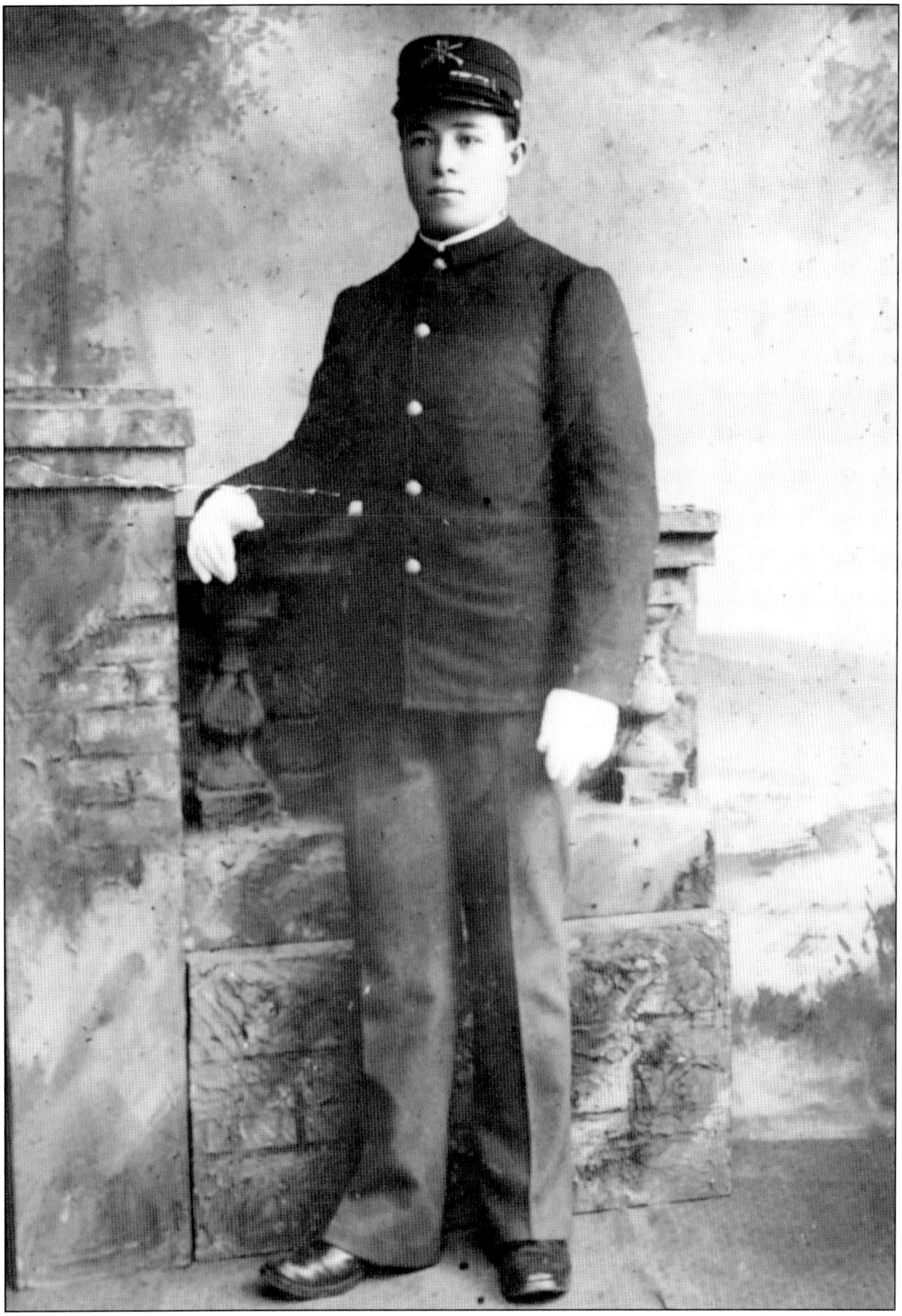

Frank A. Silberman in army dress uniform. Inspired by the Spanish-American War, he enlisted the following year in the U.S. Army, where he served in active combat during the Philippine Insurrection Campaign (1899–1902).

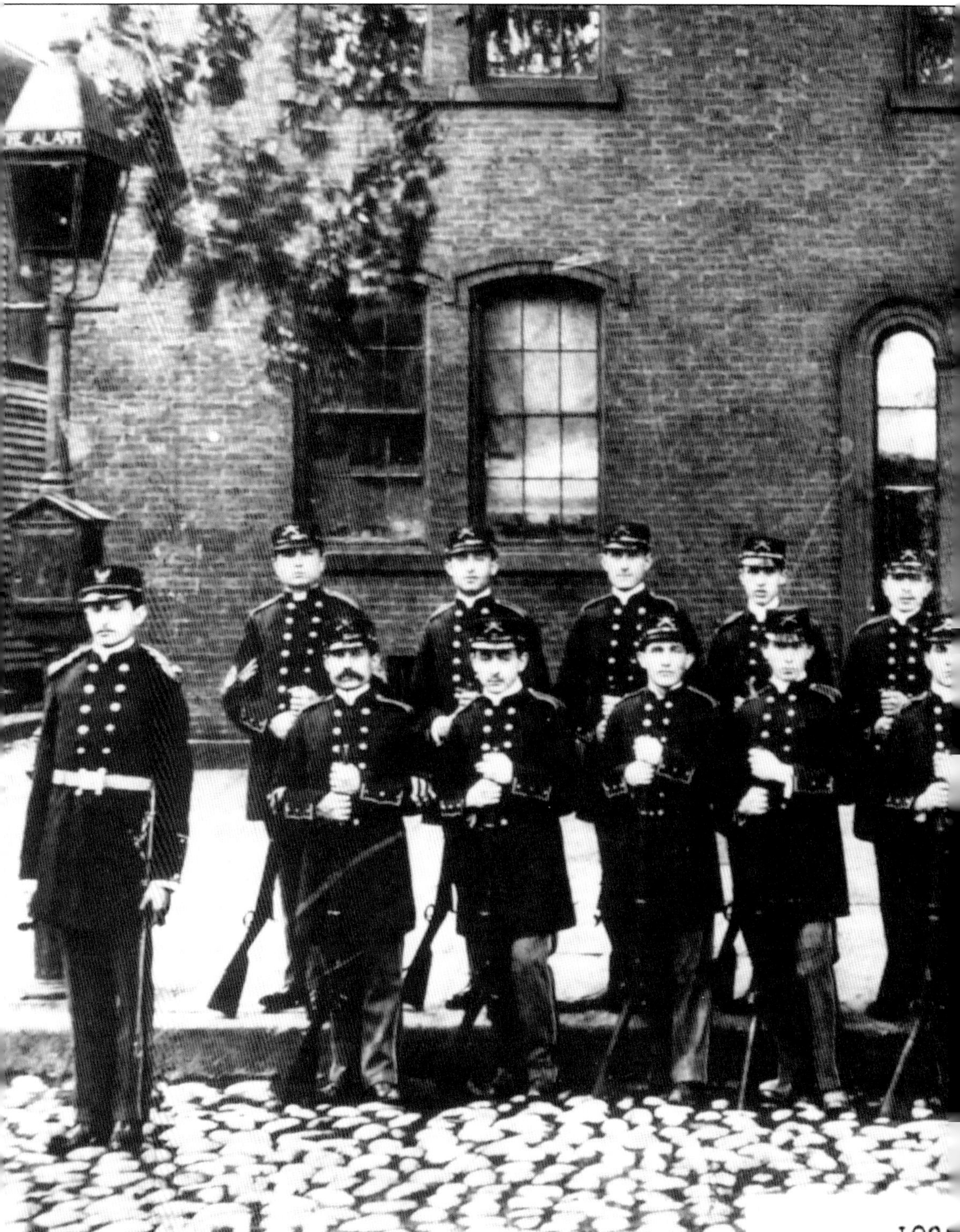

The Touro Guards, 1898, a Jewish volunteer military group who offered their services to Governor Elisha Dyer during the Spanish-American War. The war ended before they were

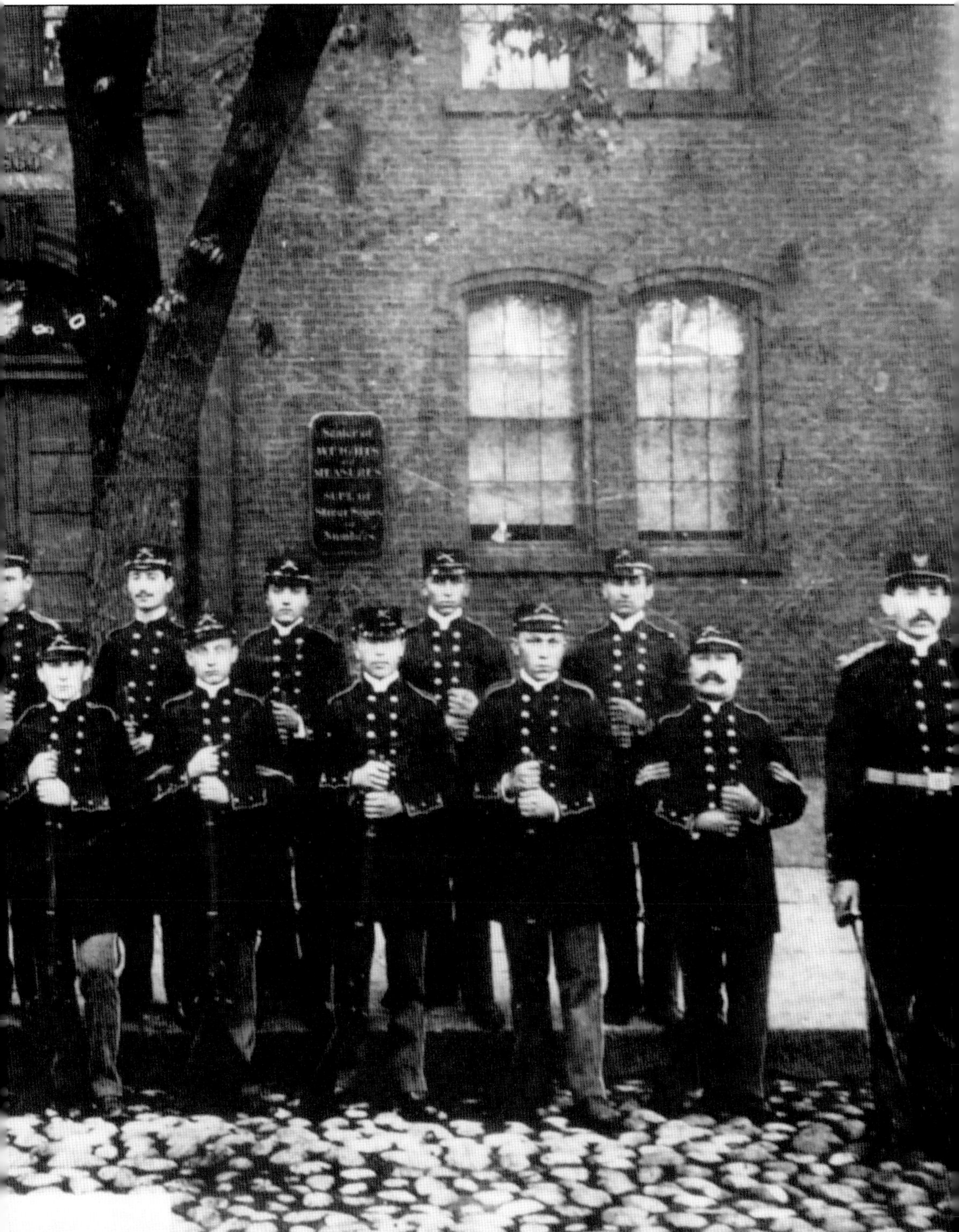

called up to participate.

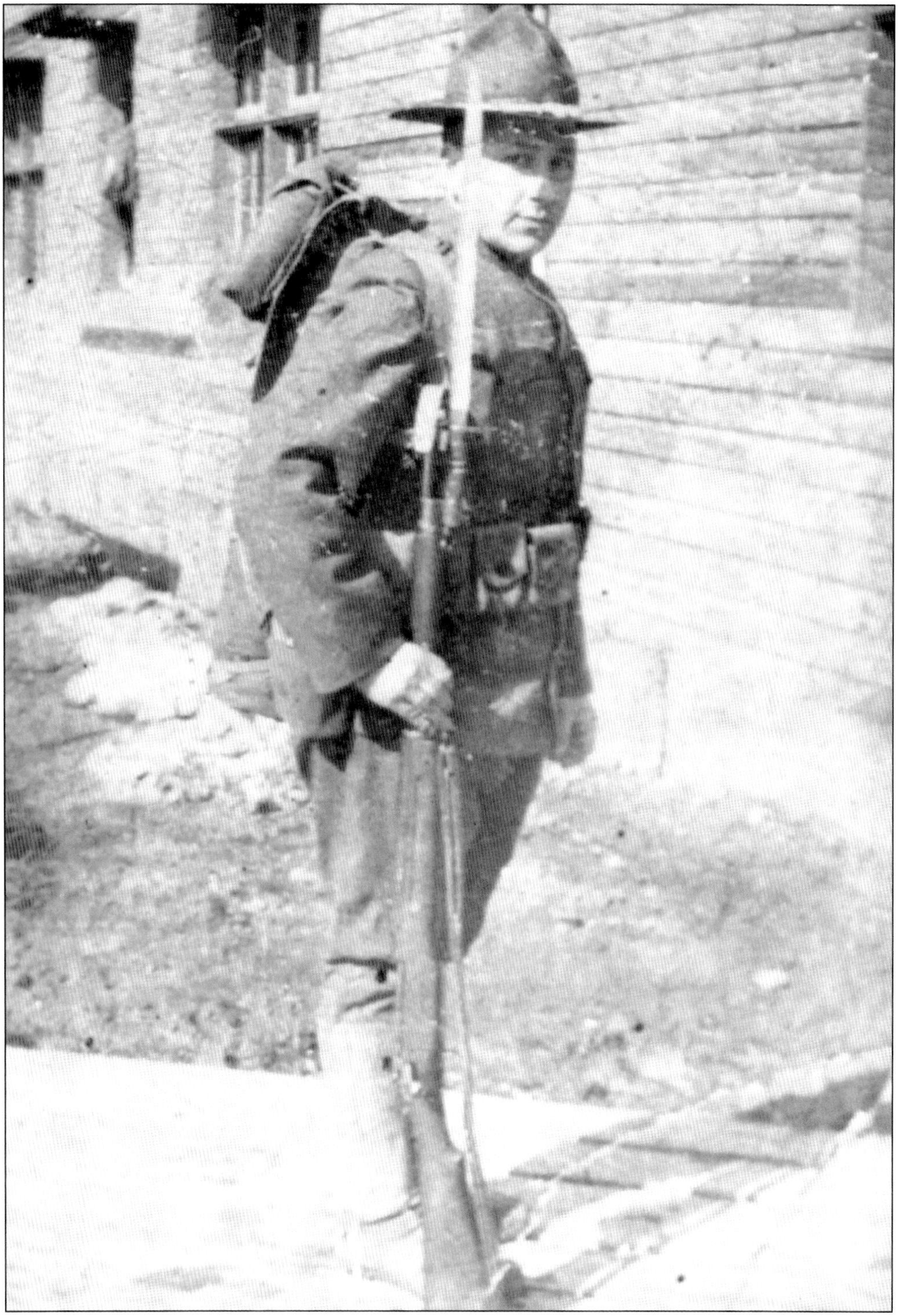

Charles Koffler, who served in the U.S. Army in 1917 and 1918, attached to Company C of the 302nd infantry. His father and brother were in the Austro-German Army (Charles had been born in Austria). Fortunately, he never met his father or brother in a combat situation.

Murray Shindler in his U.S. Navy uniform during World War I.

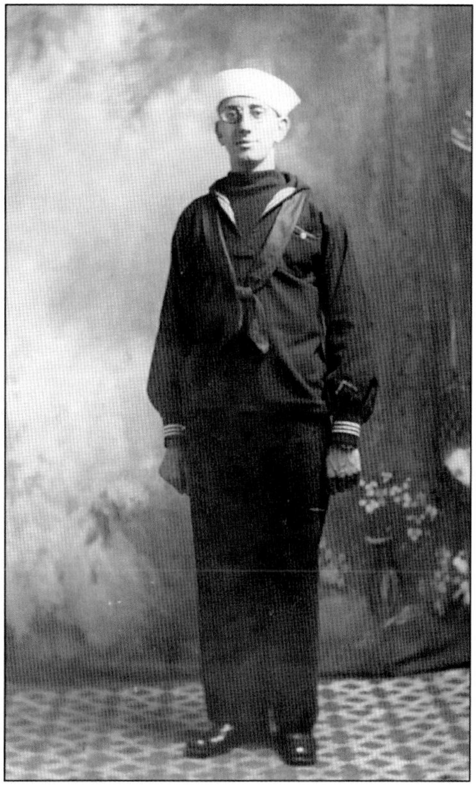

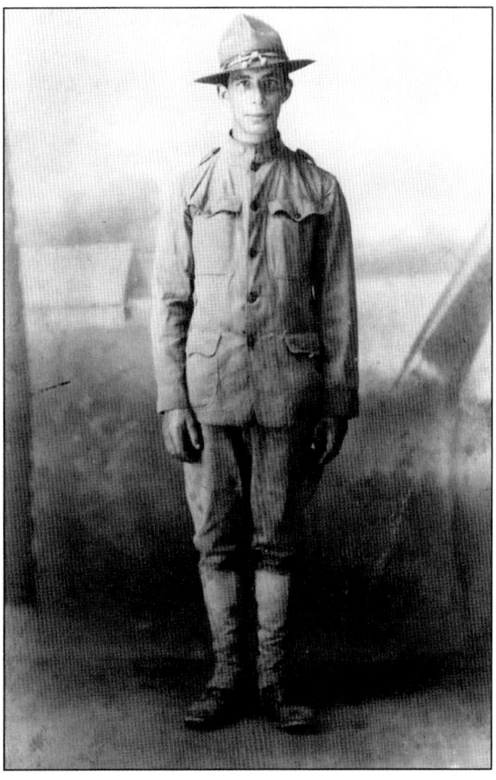

Louis Winnerman. Louis Winnerman served in the U.S. Army during World War I and World War II.

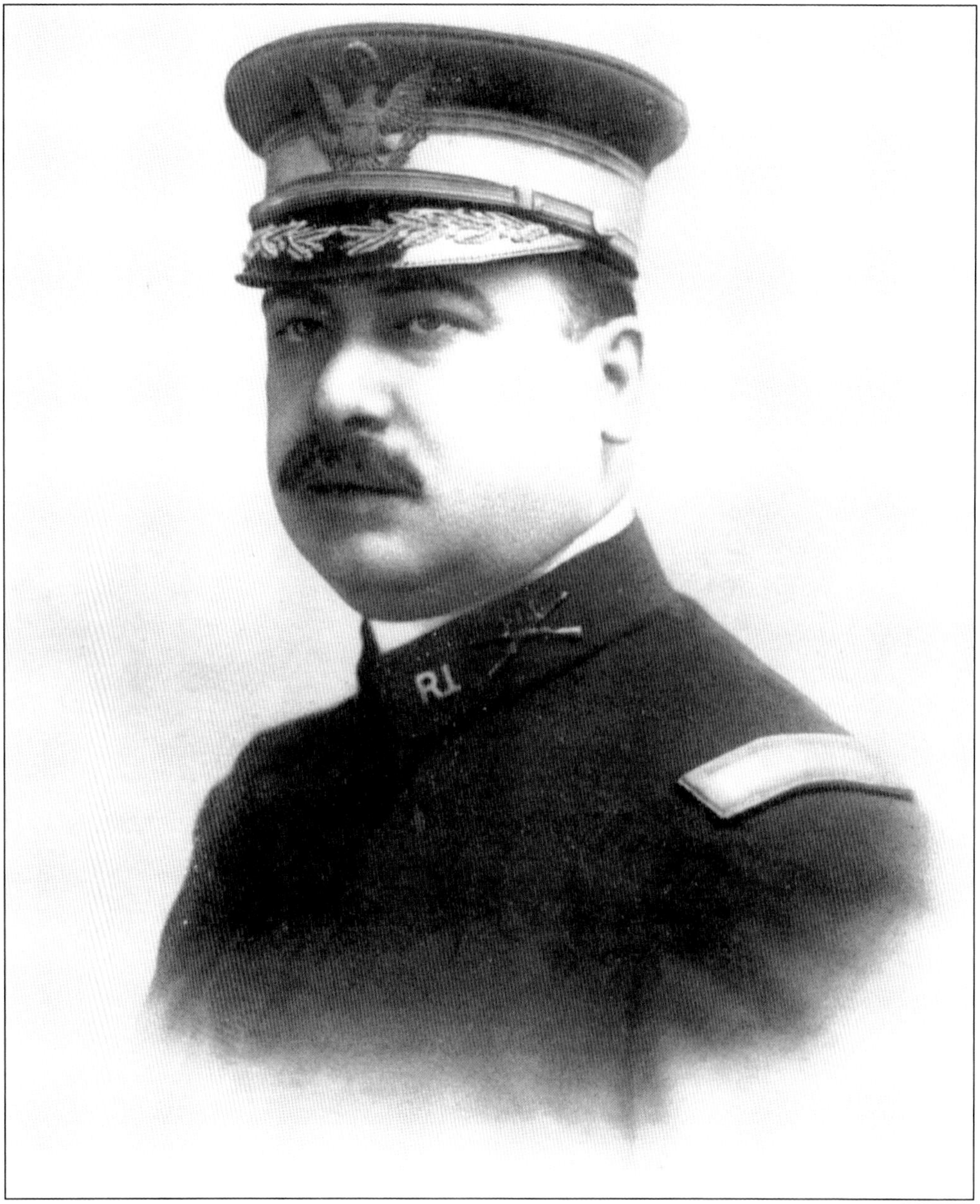

Colonel Harry Cutler. Colonel Cutler served in World War I with the Jewish Welfare Board. As chairman, he championed the rights of Jewish servicemen. He was asked by the secretary of war to represent the Jewish Welfare Board on the War Memorials Commission. His mission was to ensure that treaties be enacted to give equal rights—political, civil, and religious—to the Jews of all lands.

Jack Cleinman. Jack Cleinman was sent to active combat in France during World War I and was killed on October 20, 1918, at Bois des Loges during the Meuse Argonne Offensive. His grave marker with the Star of David is shown in a non-sectarian military cemetery. The Jack Cleinman Square at the corner of Hope and Olney Streets in Providence is named in his memory.

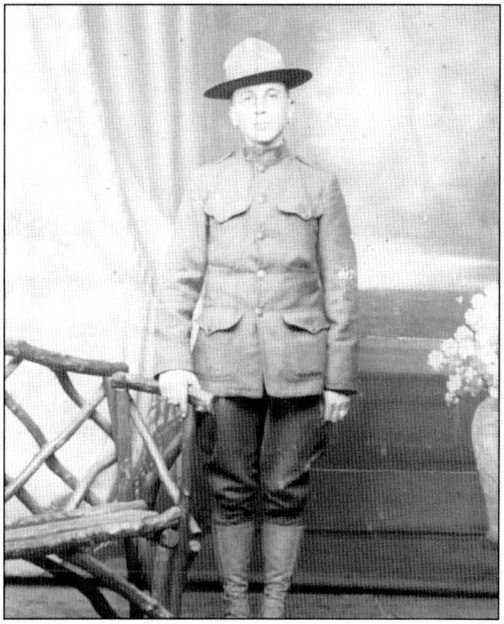

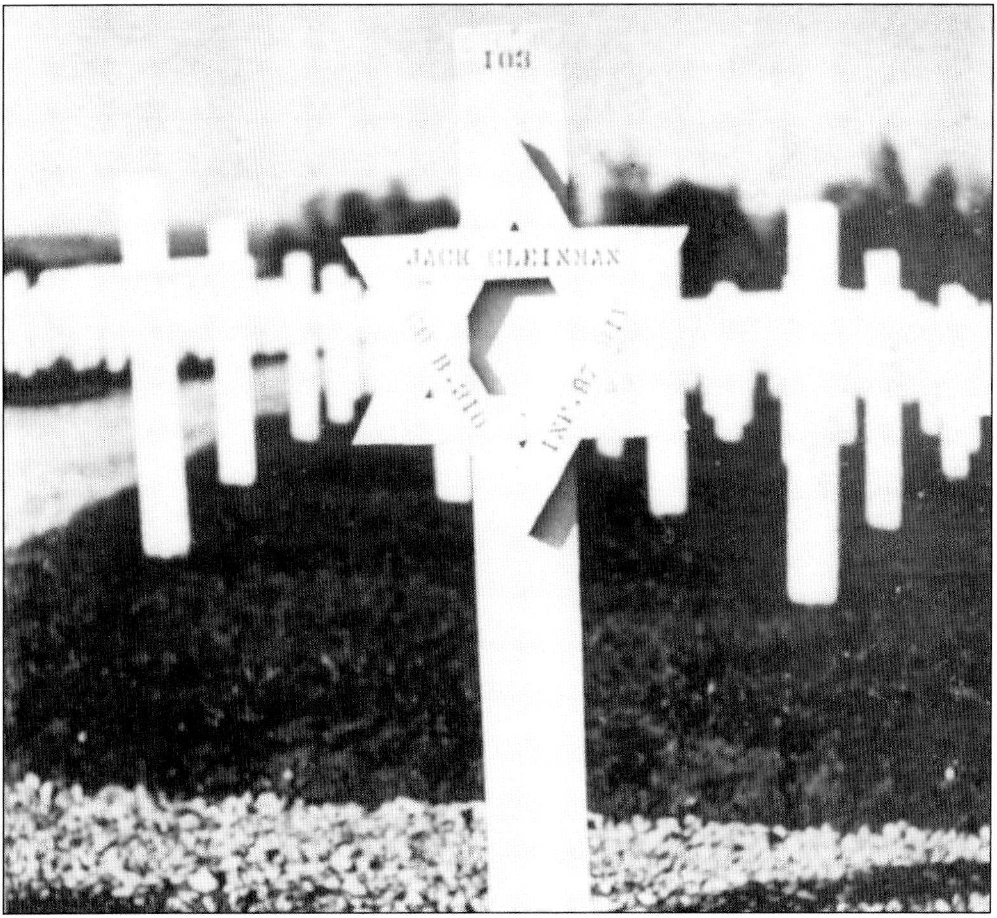

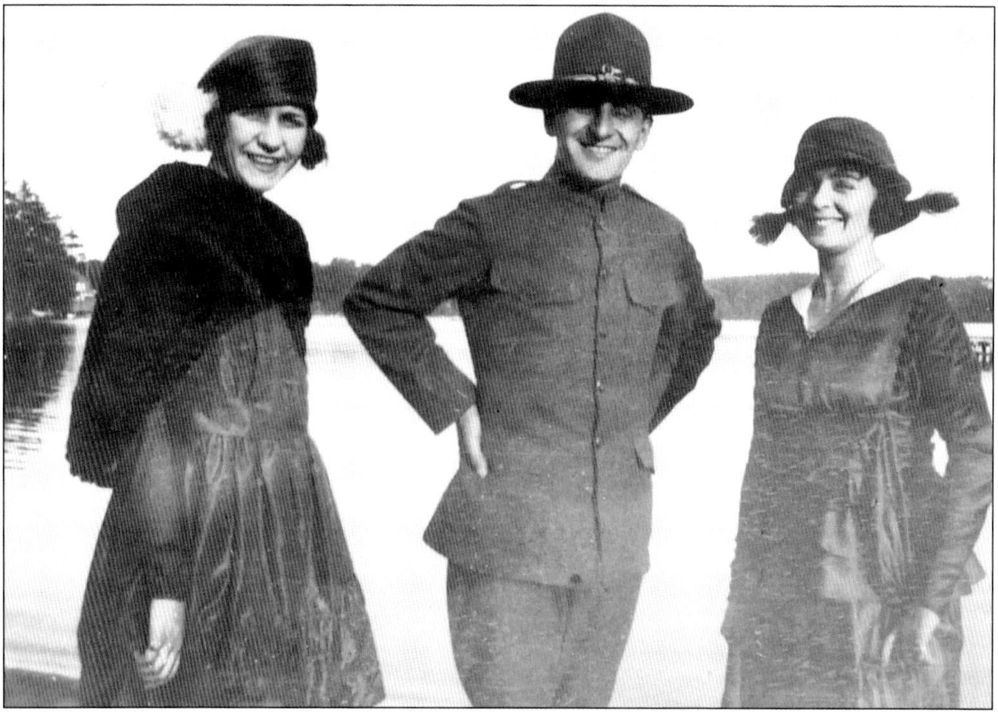

Esmond S. Borod. Esmond S. Borod served in World War I and is seen here with two lady friends in Germany in 1917.

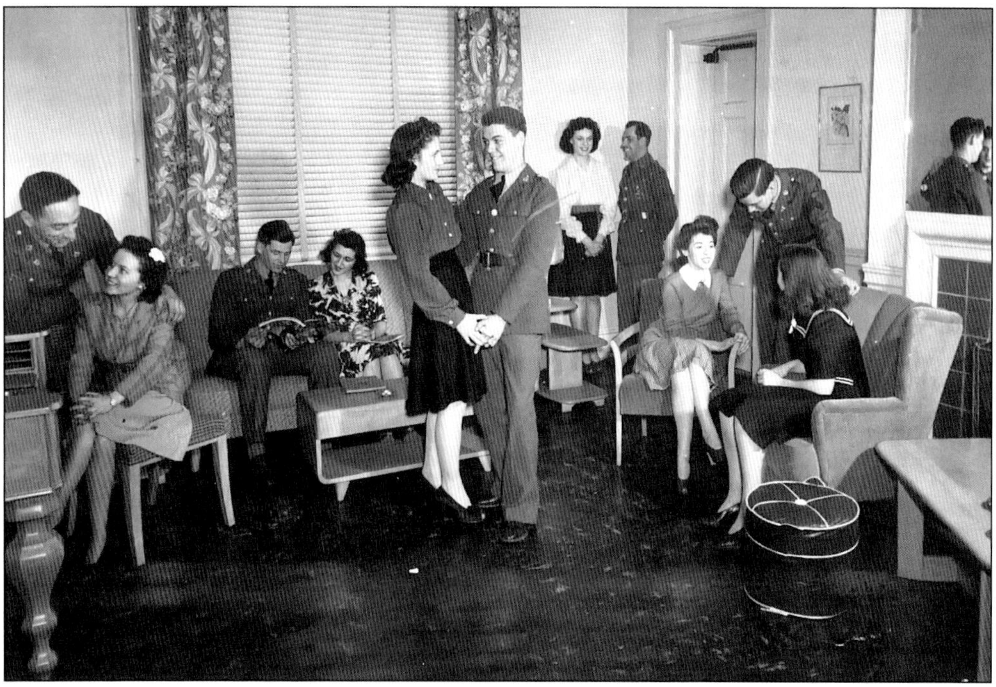

Preparing for a Saturday night dance. During World War II, the Jewish Community Center, Providence, held Saturday night dances for servicemen who were stationed in the Rhode Island area. Local girls volunteered as hostesses.

Jeanne Max (Miller). Many women from Rhode Island enlisted in the armed forces during World War II. Jeanne Max (Miller) served as a lieutenant in the U.S. Navy and was assigned to the staff of the chief of naval operations.

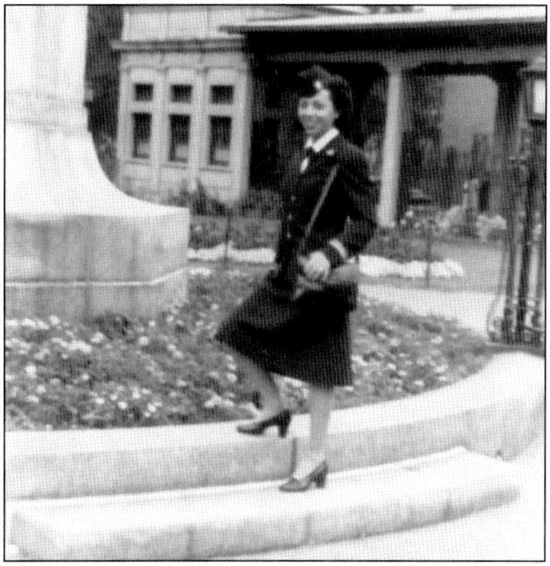

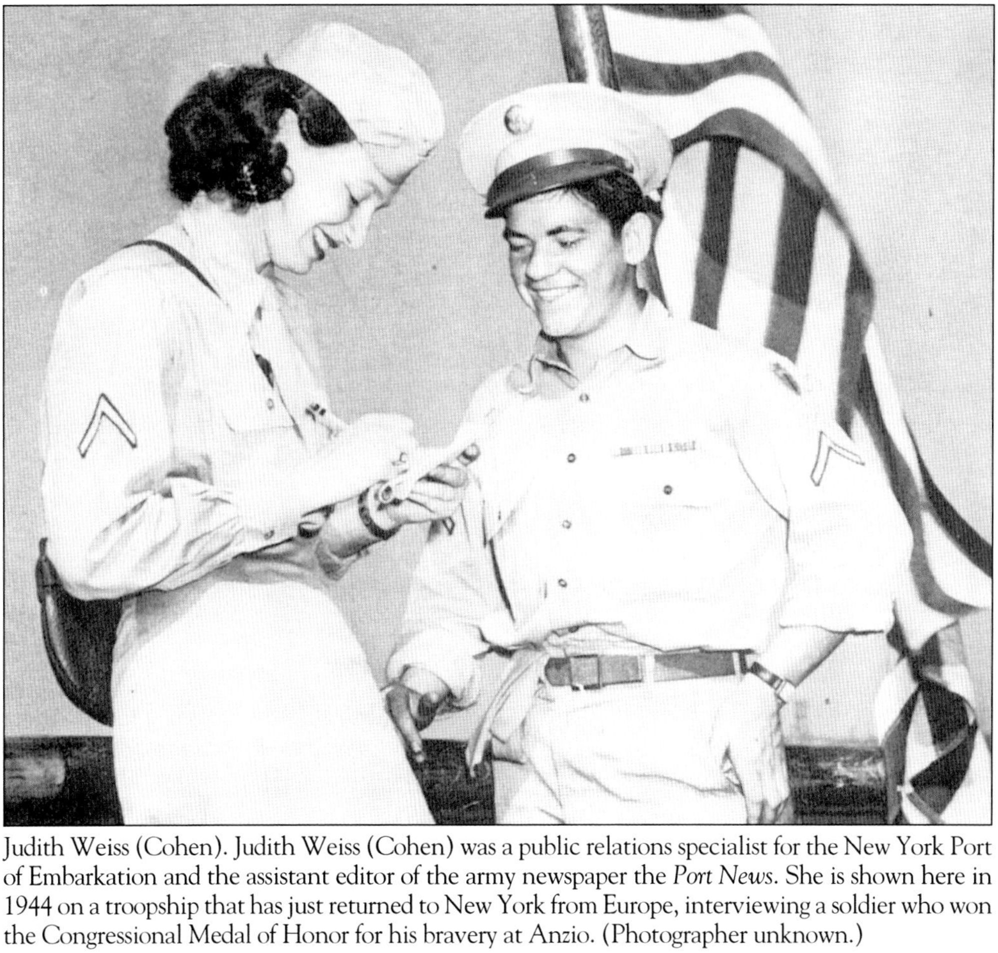

Judith Weiss (Cohen). Judith Weiss (Cohen) was a public relations specialist for the New York Port of Embarkation and the assistant editor of the army newspaper the *Port News*. She is shown here in 1944 on a troopship that has just returned to New York from Europe, interviewing a soldier who won the Congressional Medal of Honor for his bravery at Anzio. (Photographer unknown.)

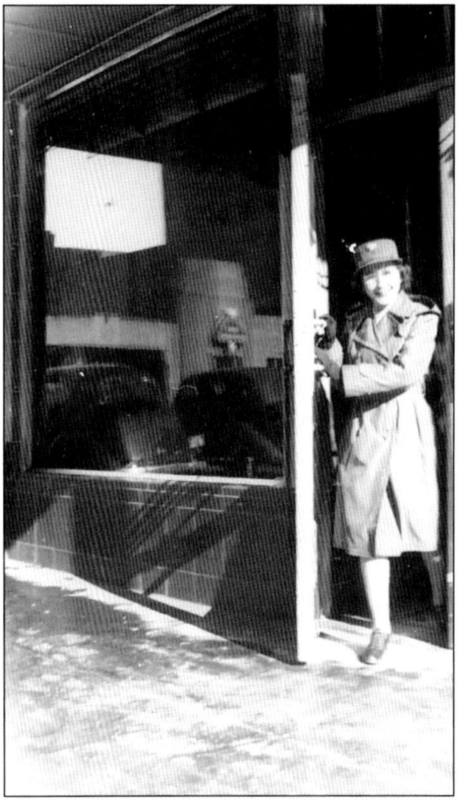

Charlotte Kwasha. In 1942, Charlotte Kwasha reported to a training area in Des Moines, Iowa, to join the Women's Auxiliary Army Corps (WAAC). She saw duty in the Philippines and in New Guinea.

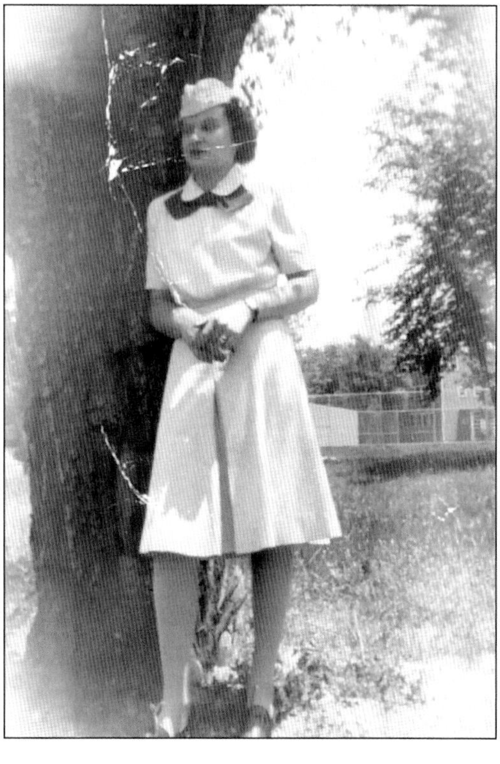

Hope Abrams (Mellion), yeoman first class. Hope Abrams (Mellion) served with the navy department in Washington from 1944 to 1946.

Merrill Percelay. Merrill Percelay graduated from the United States Merchant Marine Academy. He sailed in the Merchant Marine as a third officer, North Atlantic Theatre, during World War II. Crossings were made in convoys because of the constant threat of attack from enemy submarines. (Courtesy Merrill Percelay.)

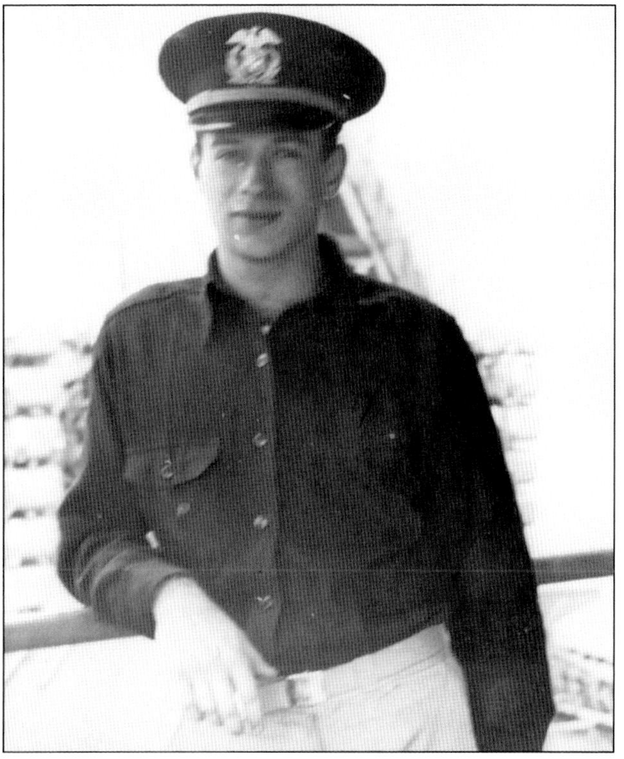

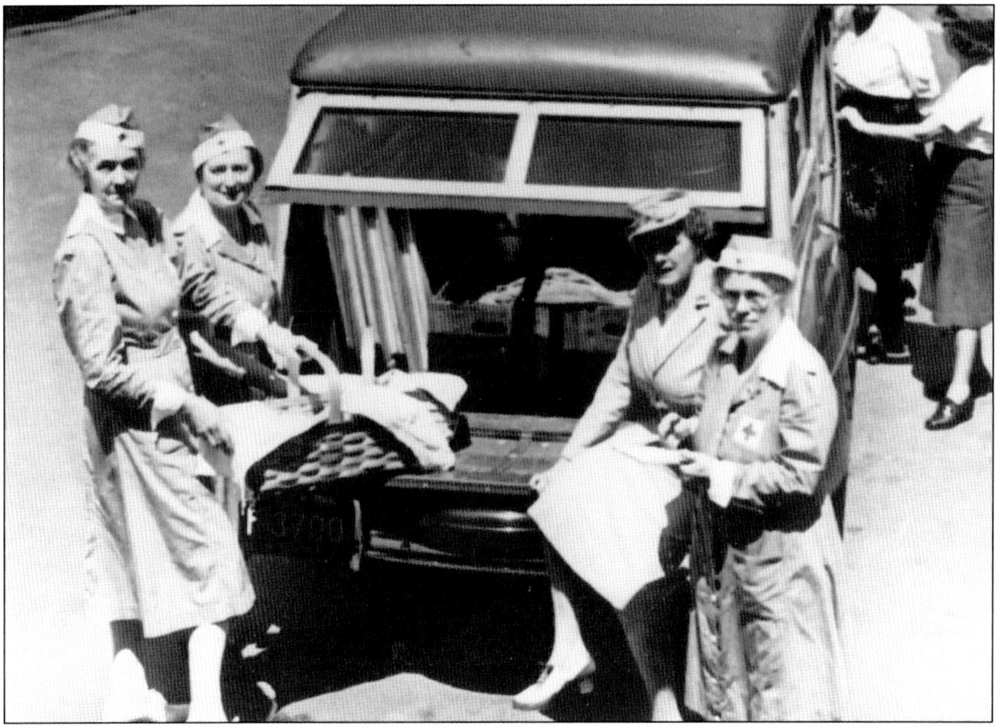

American Red Cross volunteers. Women from Rhode Island joined this valuable organization of workers. Shown second from the left is Minnie Seefer.

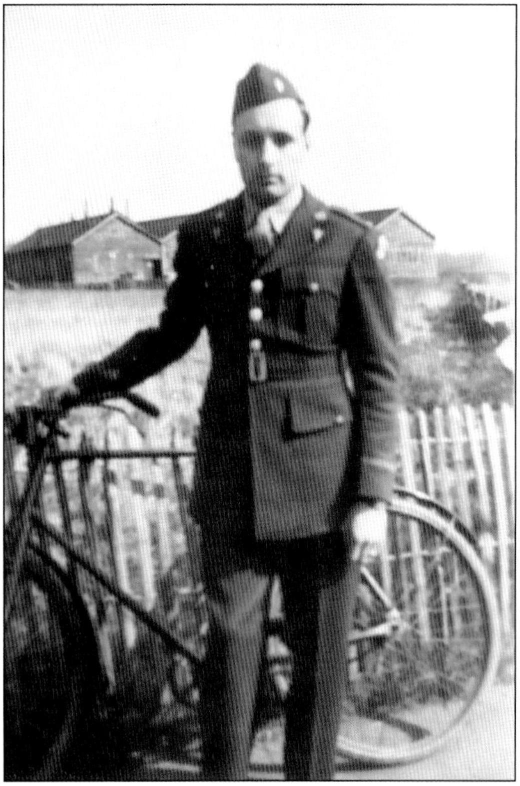

Captain Abraham Horvitz, surgeon with the Third Auxiliary Surgical Group, First Army. He took part in the invasion of the Normandy Landing on Utah Beach because surgeons were needed to take immediate care of the wounded.

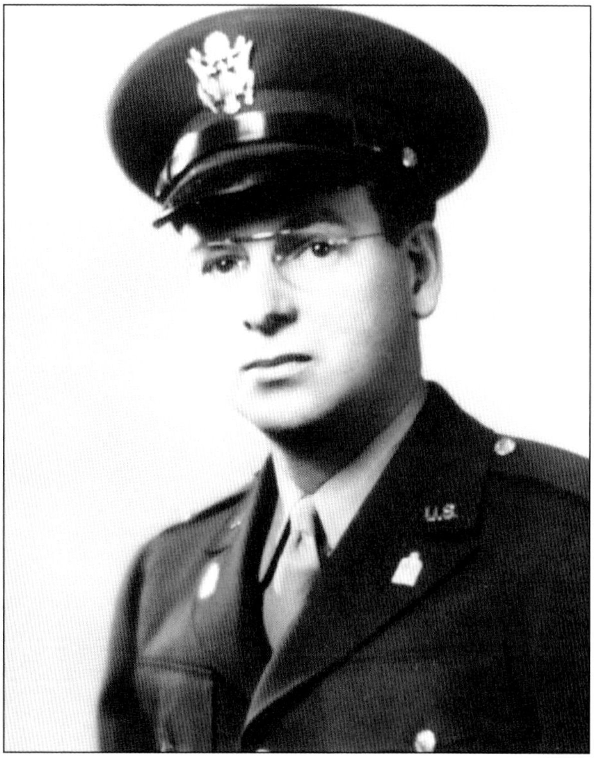

Rabbi Eli A. Bohnen. Rabbi Bohnen entered the U.S. Army in 1943. He was a chaplain with the 42nd (Rainbow) Infantry Division during the liberation of the Dachau Concentration Camp. He later served as an advisor to the United States military regarding displaced persons, helping them to regain a semblance of normality and assisting in their resettlement.

Hyman S. Banks. Hyman S. Banks was a recipient of the Purple Heart. He was killed in action during World War II.

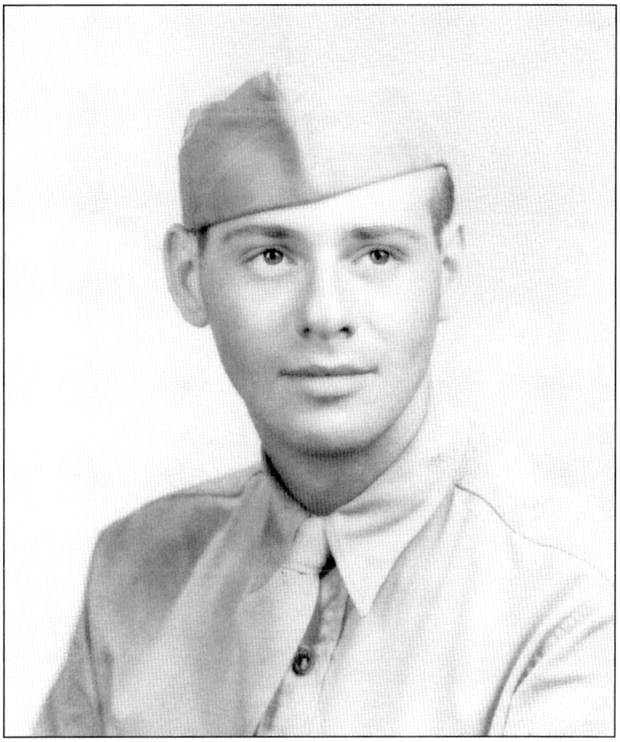

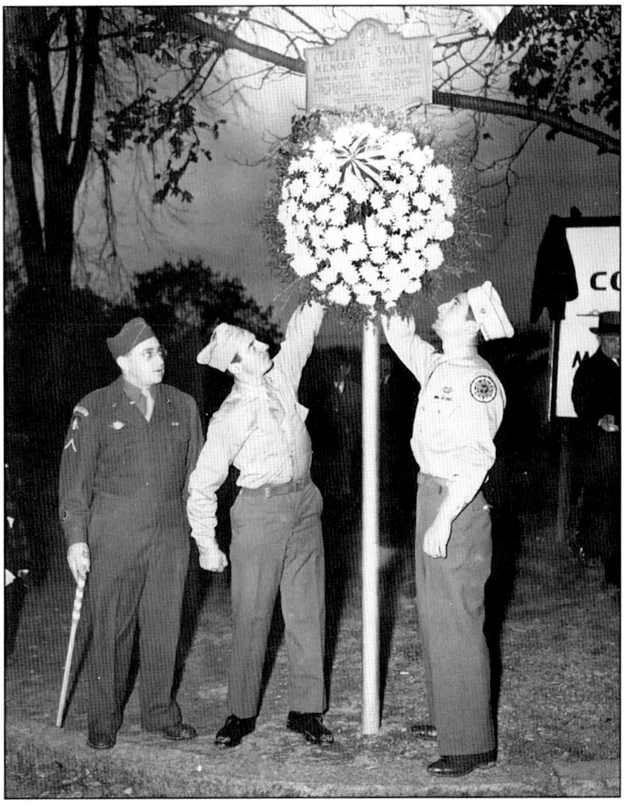


Squares dedicated to Jewish Rhode Island servicemen who died in World War II. This photograph shows a wreath being placed on one of the poles at the Cutler-Suvall Memorial Square. David B. Cutler was killed in action on December 26, 1944. Abner D. Suvall was killed in action on May 10, 1944, at Makin Atoll in the Gilbert Islands. The Silverman Brothers Jewelry

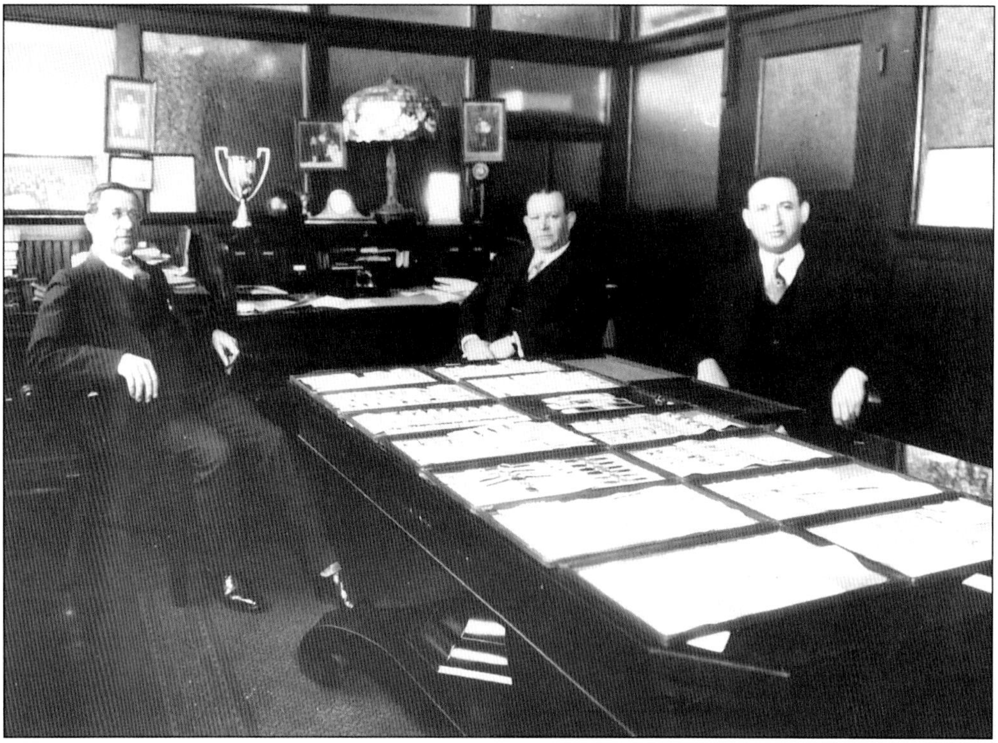

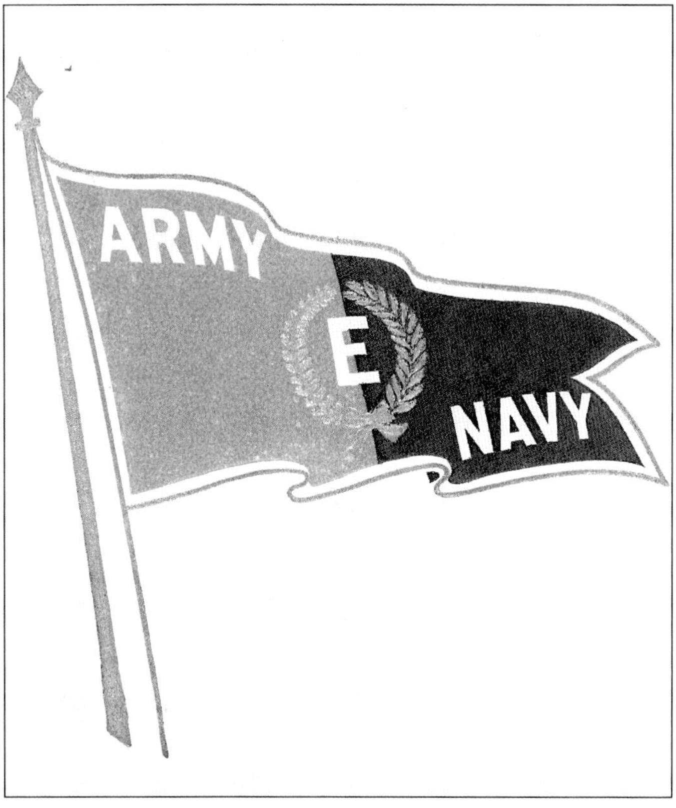


Factory. During World War II, the firm was awarded the U.S. Army-Navy "E" award for work in turning out surgical instruments and fine parts for torpedo and bomb war-heads. Shown here, from left to right, are Charles, Archibald, and John Silverman.

The Adolph Mellor Company. This company went to work for the government after the outbreak of World War II. They manufactured jewel bearings, tiny precious sapphire crystals that were used in the sighting devices of bombers and tanks. The company was given the Army-Navy "E" award for its wartime achievements.

Salomon Shuman. He served in the front lines during the Korean War with the 9th Infantry 2nd Division. (Courtesy of Salomon Shuman.)

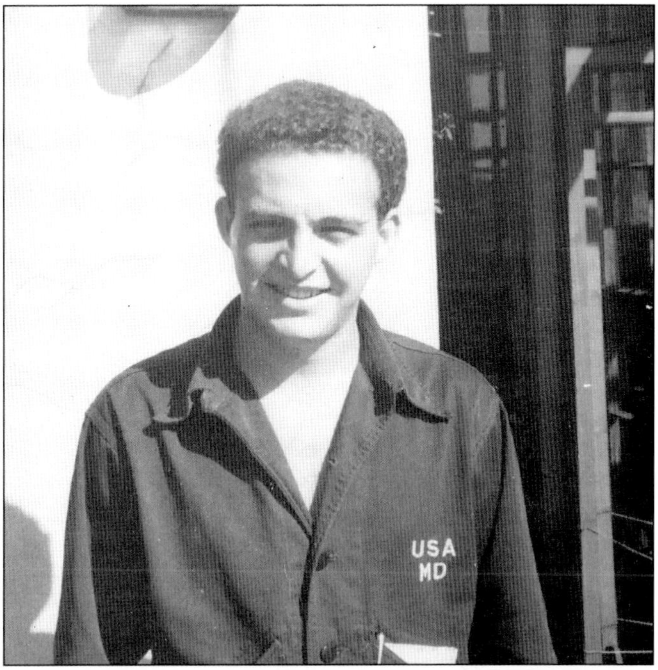


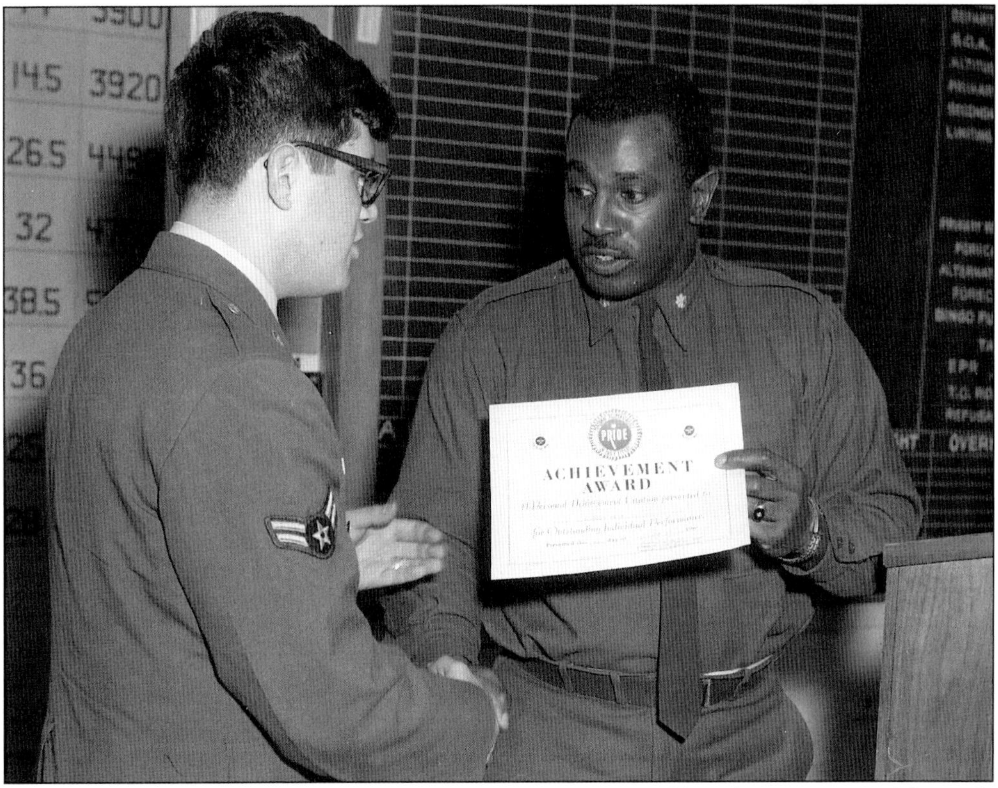


Gerald S. Sherman, an airman first class in the Vietnam War. Gerald S. Sherman received the Pride Achievement Award from Major Arthur Douglas, Quang Hai, Republic of Viet Nam, for his service from 1969–70. (Courtesy of Gerald Sherman.)

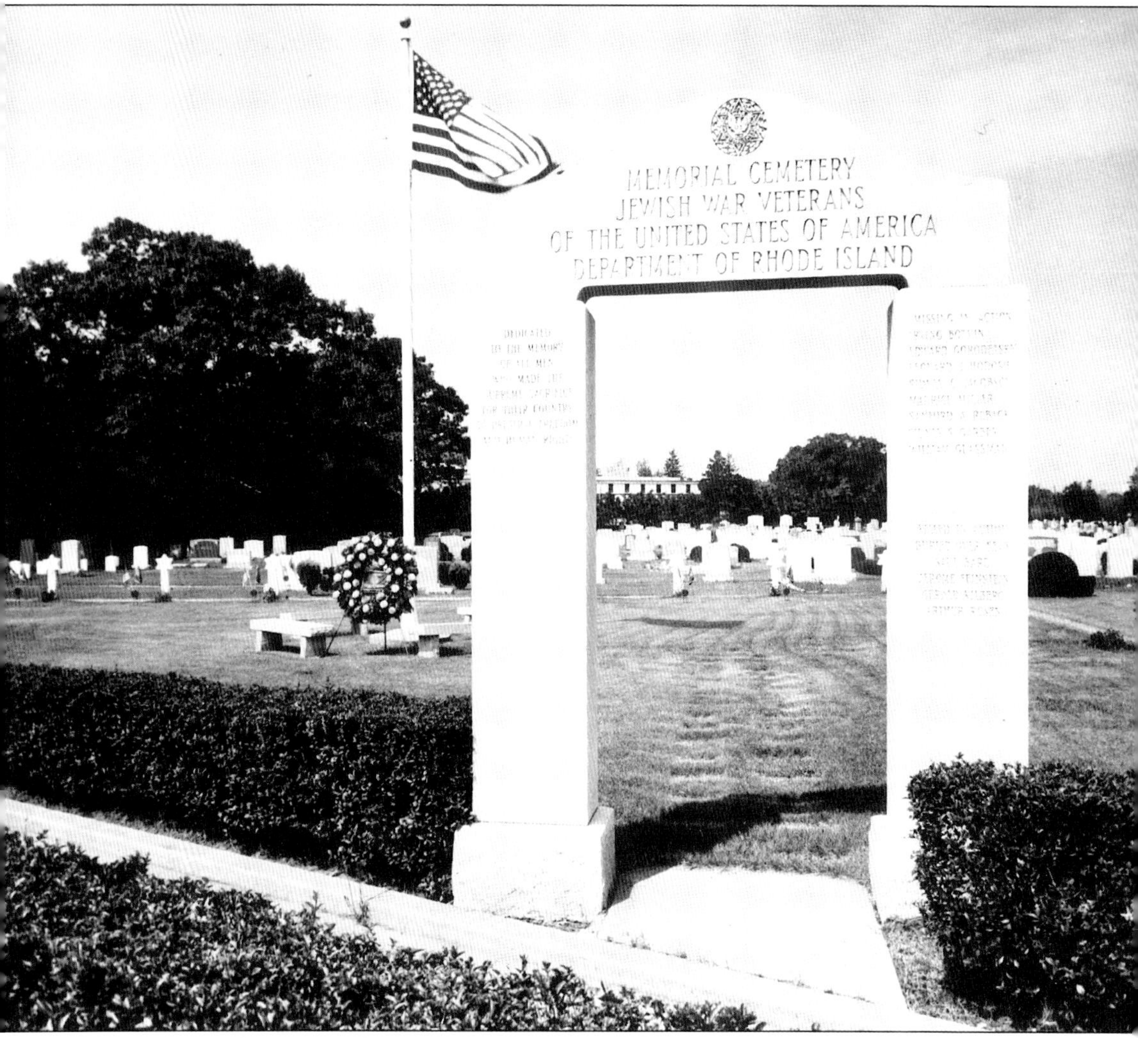


The memorial cemetery for Jewish Veterans of the United States of America, dedicated on November 11, 1951, in Lincoln Park Cemetery. A service is held annually for Jewish soldiers killed in war.

## EPILOGUE

In August 1747, there was recorded in several publications a list of those who were taken prisoner in the French and Indian Wars. They were sent to Boston and there set free. One of these prisoners was Jacob Judah, "A Jew Boston" of Rhode Island. Since the French and Indian Wars, our country has been involved in many other conflicts.

*Six*

# A Tradition of Giving

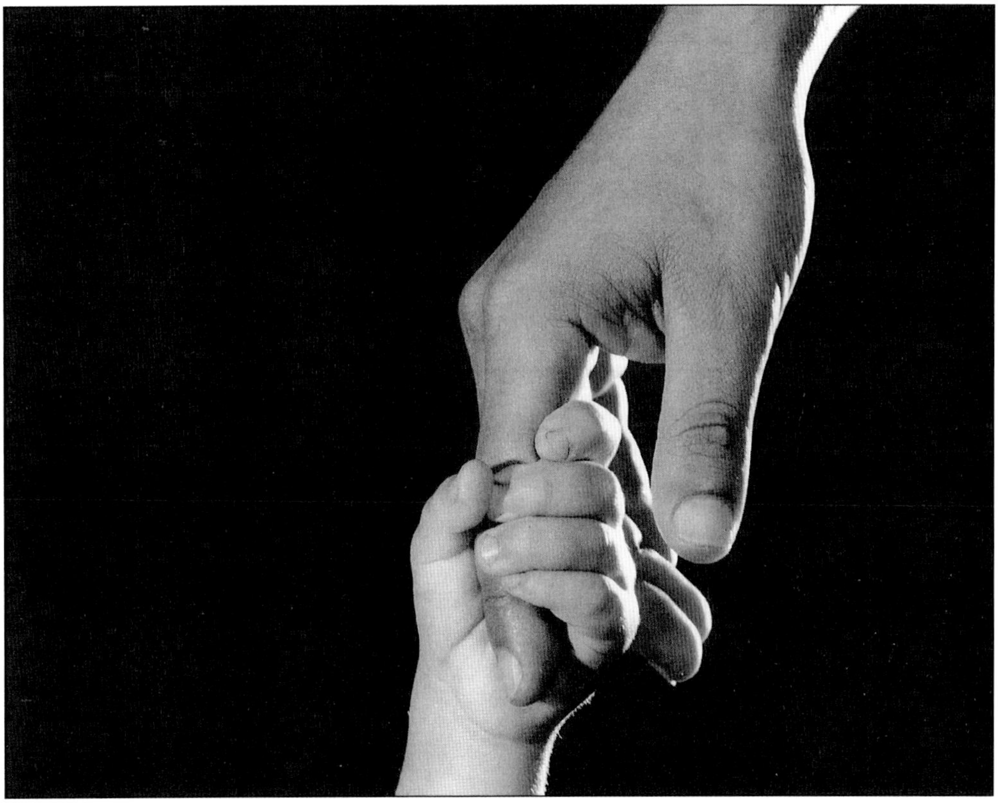

Tzedaka. In the Jewish lexicon, the word used to denote charity or philanthropy; "tzedaka" properly means righteousness. It is a derivation of the word for justice. Assisting the needy is therefore considered more than an act of kindness; it is a moral duty, an act of justice. Whether on an individual or community basis, generations of Jewish men and women have reached out to their neighbors of all ethnic origins to offer a helping hand to those in need. (Courtesy of the Jewish Book Council; photograph by Bill Aron.)

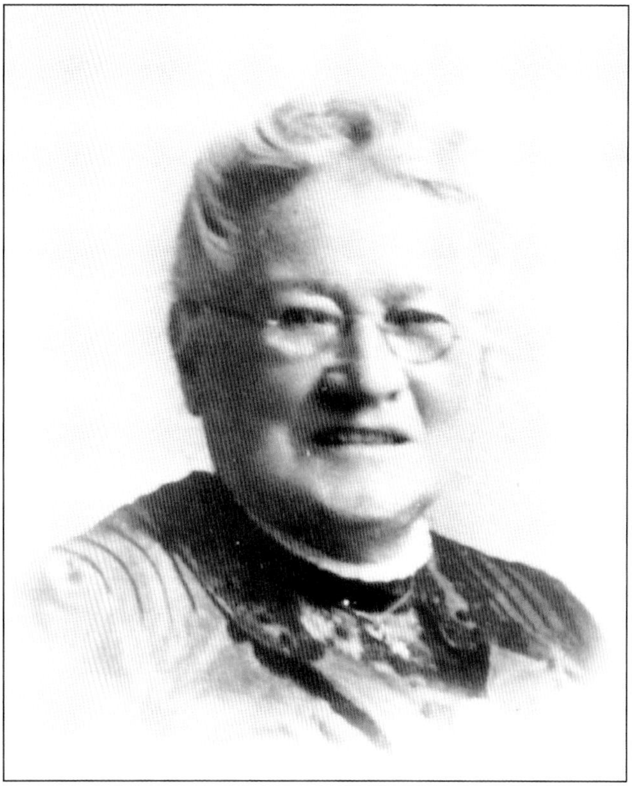

Amelia Rodenberg, a founding member of Montefiore Lodge and its charity committee. Amelia and her fellow committee members were charged with dispensing aid to the applicants. Funds were raised through balls, cake sales, raffles, and the like, as well as by fines levied against lodge members absent from meetings without cause or derelict in their duties. Prior to her marriage, Mrs. Rodenberg had served as a nurse at the Battle of Antietam.

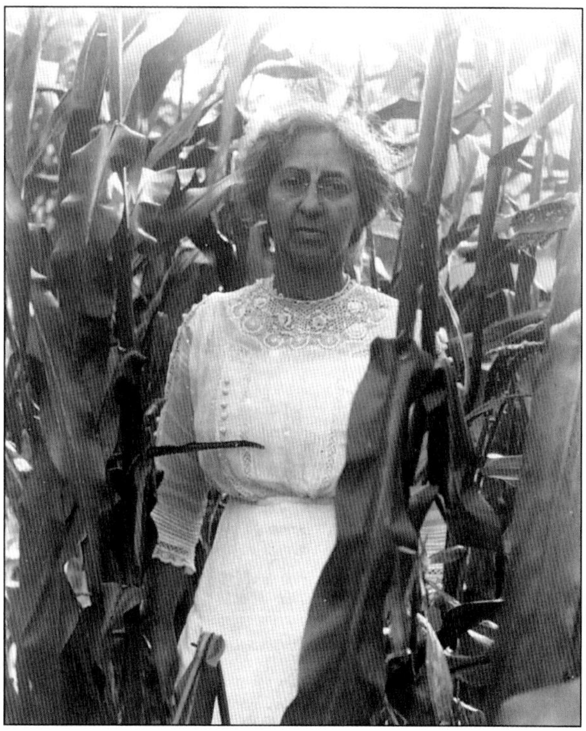

Estelle Rosenfeld Einstein, a member of the charity committee for 27 years. During her term of service she performed all the duties of a volunteer social worker in the entire Jewish community. She furnished liaison between the lodge and Jewish and non-Jewish organizations in similar fields of activity as well as with governmental agencies.

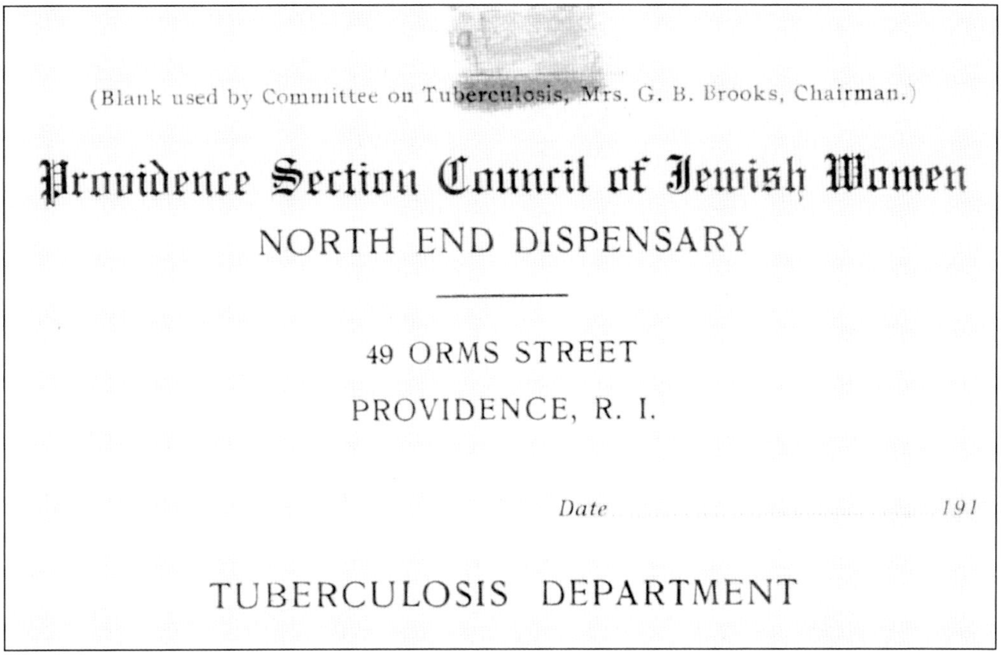

(Blank used by Committee on Tuberculosis, Mrs. G. B. Brooks, Chairman.)

Providence Section Council of Jewish Women

NORTH END DISPENSARY

49 ORMS STREET

PROVIDENCE, R. I.

*Date*............................................191

TUBERCULOSIS DEPARTMENT

North End Dispensary, chartered in 1911 and sponsored by the Providence section of the National Council of Jewish Women. Marion Misch brought the need for a clinic in the North End of Providence to the attention of the council. It was decided by the executive board to rent rooms in the North End Working Girls Home, located at 49 Orms Street, and to provide "medical aid and surgical treatment for the sick and needy of all denominations."

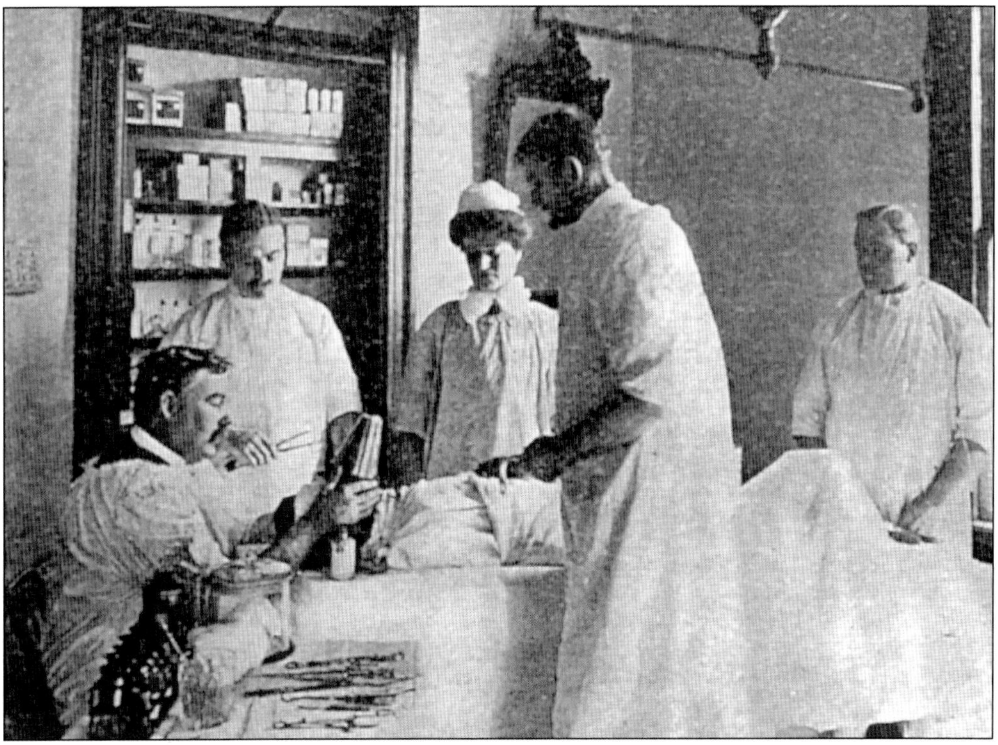

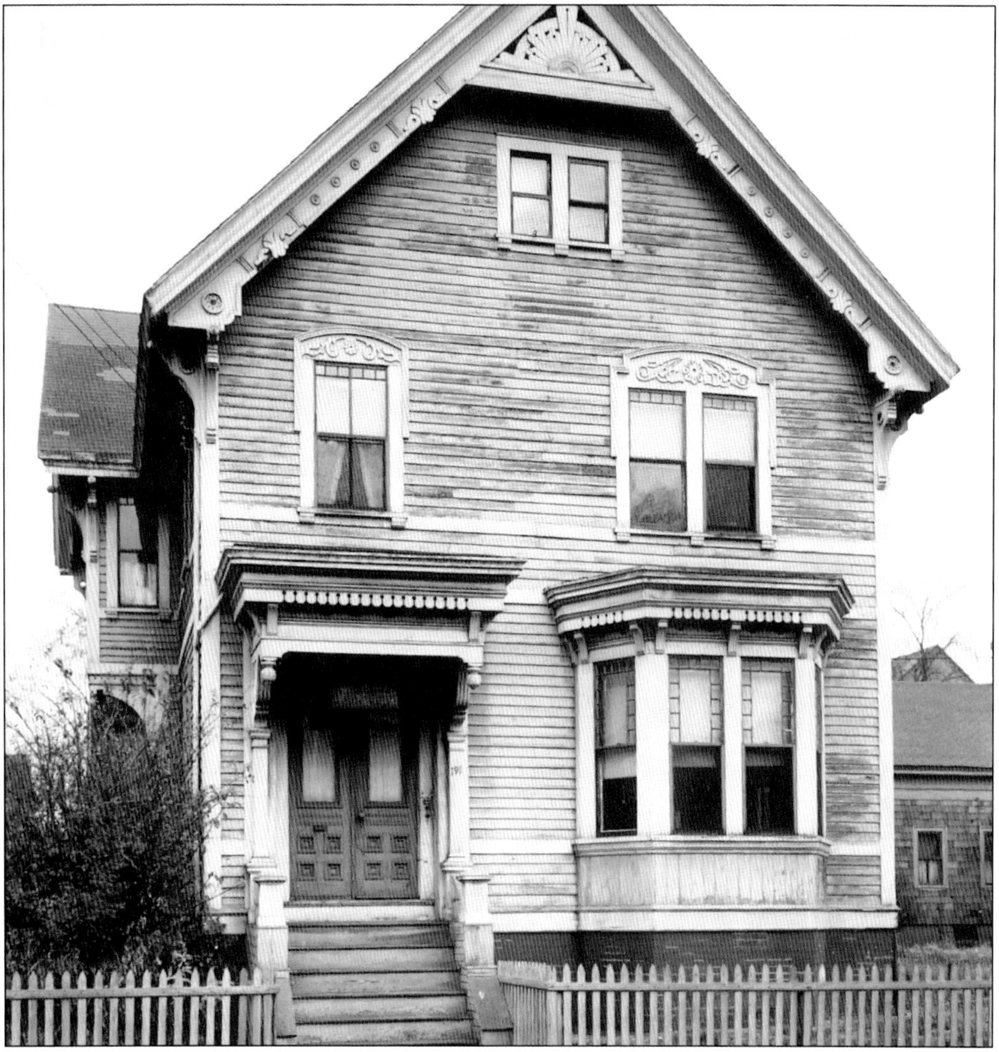

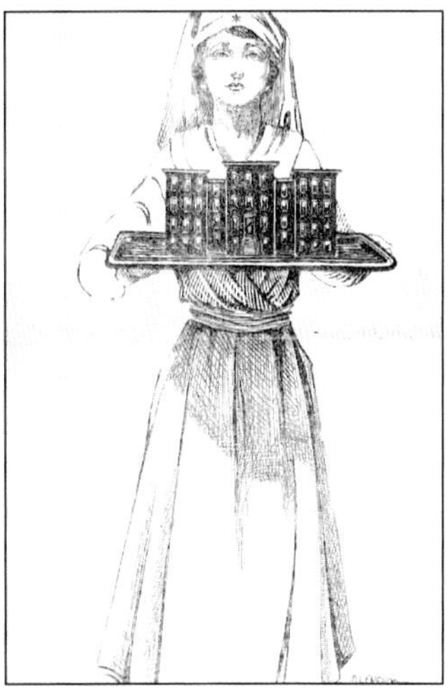

The first permanent Jewish Home for the Aged, located 191 Orms Street. The Ladies Hebrew Union Aid Association, based in the North End of Providence, sponsored many charitable endeavors, including visits to the Jewish indigent and ill in various state facilities. There they learned of the plight of elderly Jews, alone and unable to speak the language. They resolved to provide a home. With $165 and donated furnishings, they rented a house and then purchased the one pictured above.

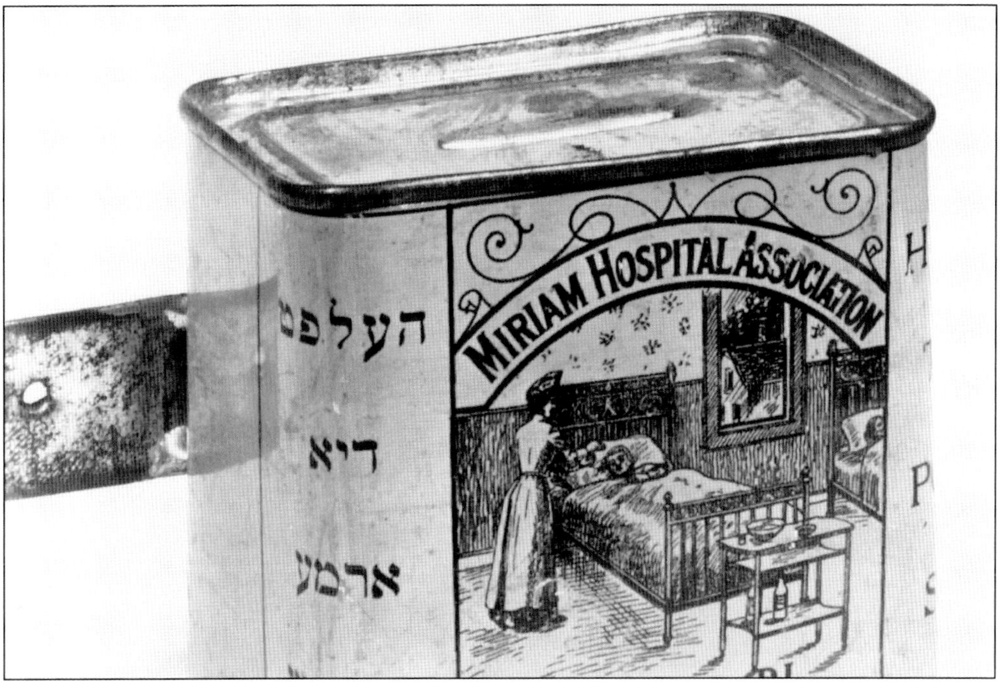


A collection box, 1914, distributed by the Miriam Hospital Association, previously owned by Sarah Smith. The boxes were distributed to homes throughout the city to raise funds for a proposed hospital. The association grew out of a women's lodge with a mission to visit the sick in hospitals, fund hospital stays for the needy, provide medical assistance, and ultimately to establish a Jewish hospital.

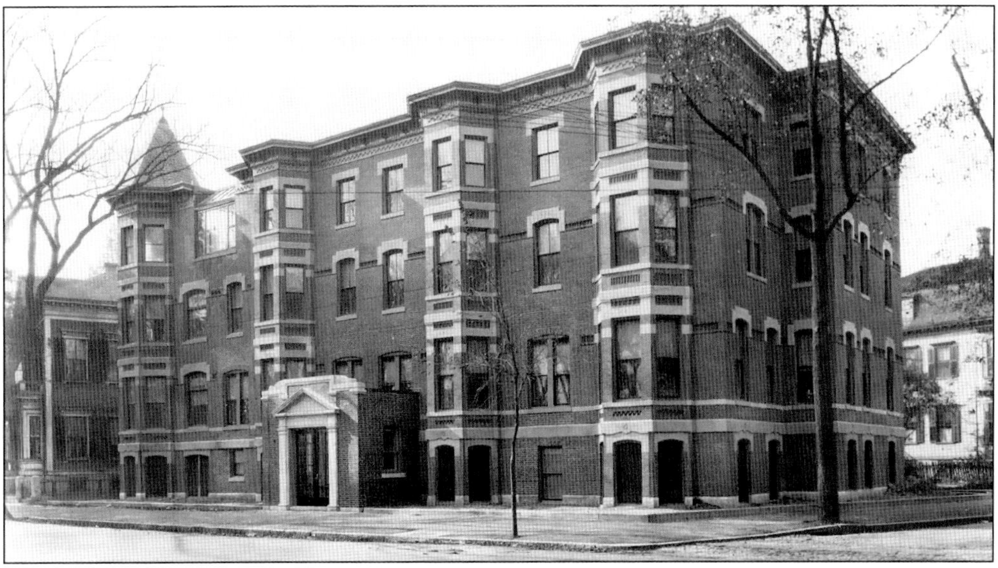

Miriam Hospital, Parade Street, 1924. Under the leadership of Mary Grant, the women raised the funds and purchased these buildings. However, when it became necessary to raise larger sums of money than they were able, they relinquished the leadership to a mens' organization. The women continued to be involved in the day-to-day activities of the hospital, providing special services to make patients' stays more pleasant.

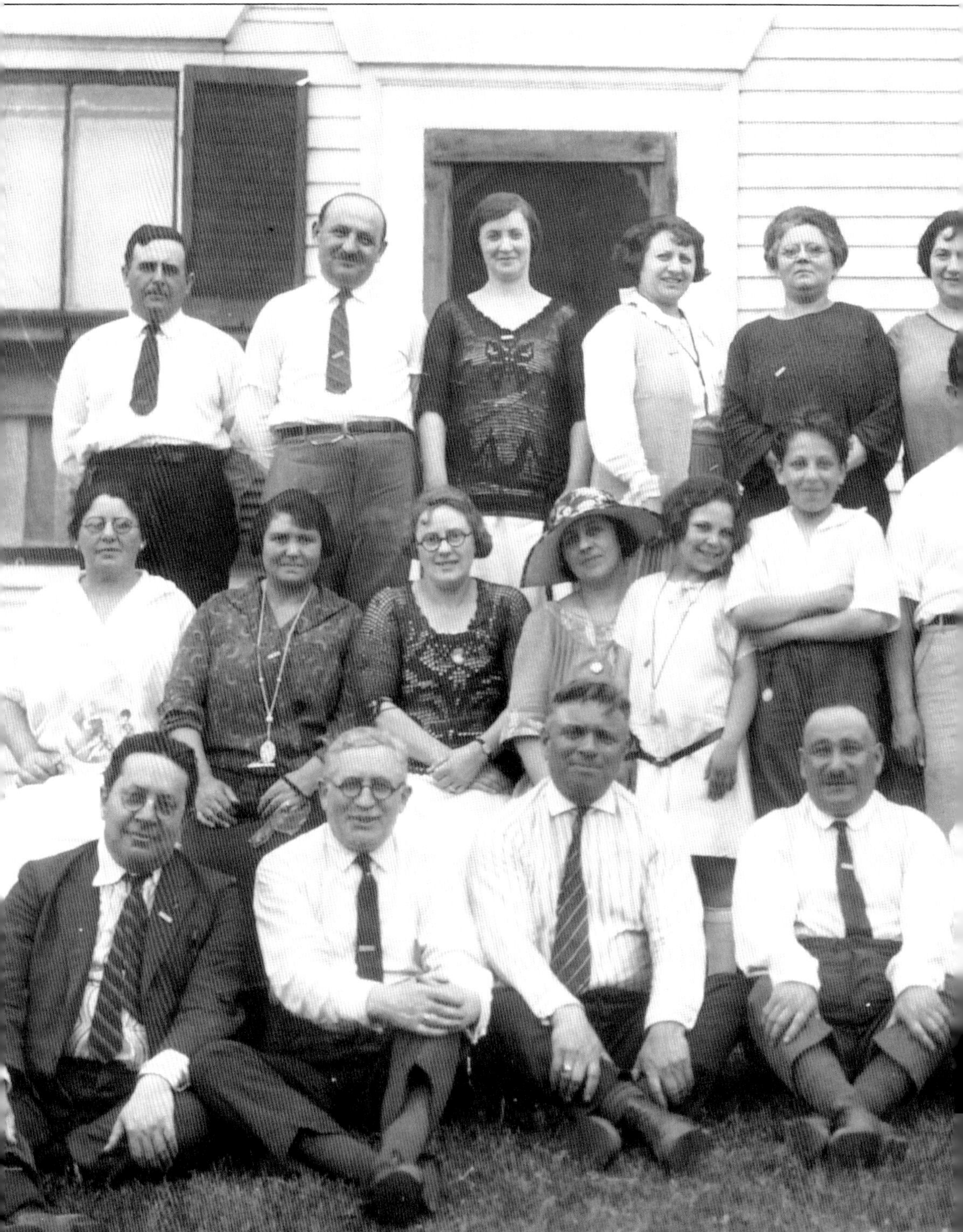

A meeting in behalf of the Palestine Foundation Fund, 1928. The fund, which later became part of United Palestine Appeal, brought together Zionist organizations such as the Zionist Organization of

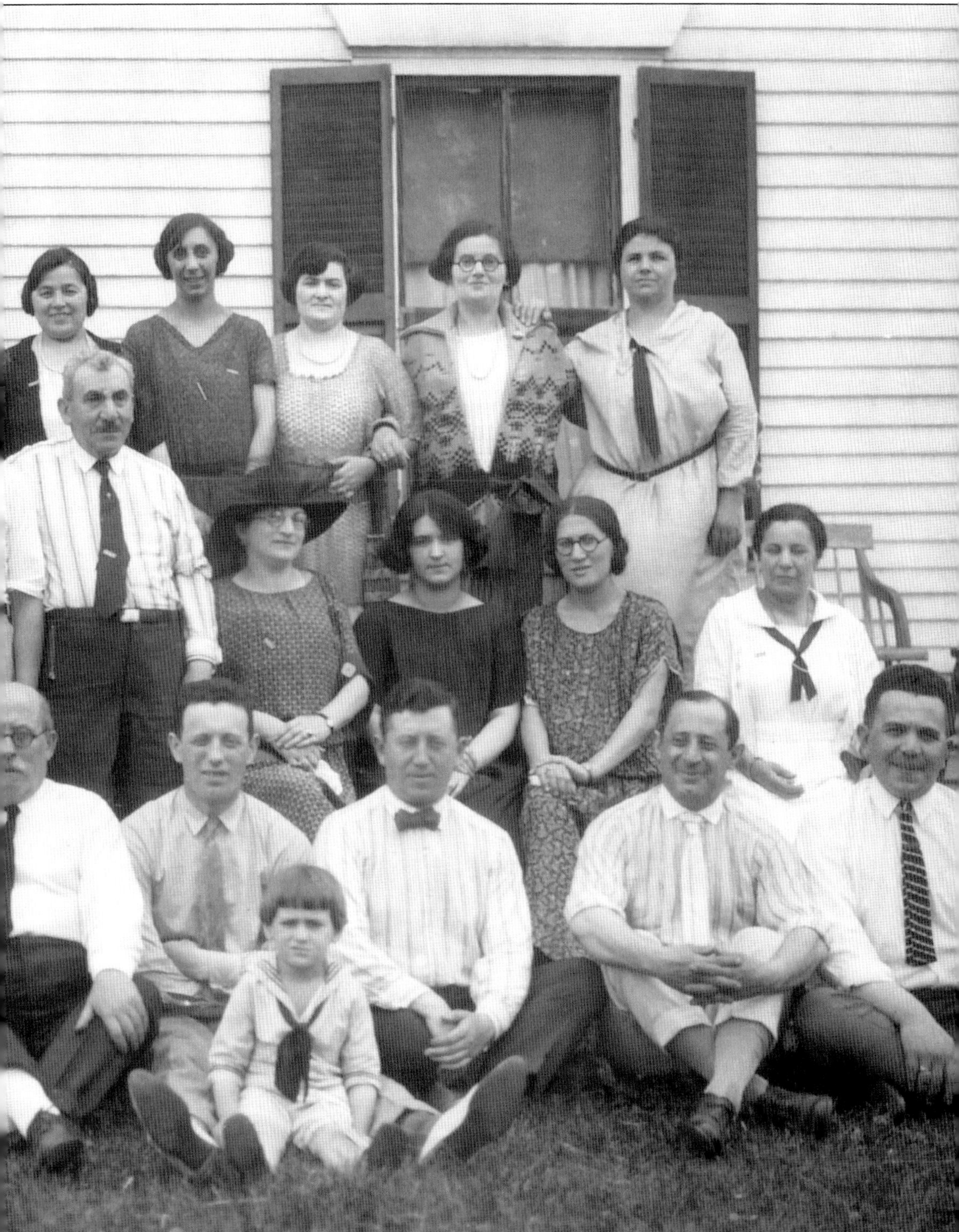

America, Labor Zionists, Hadassah, and Pioneer Women with non-Zionists to support, on a non-profit basis, immigration and settlement in Palestine.

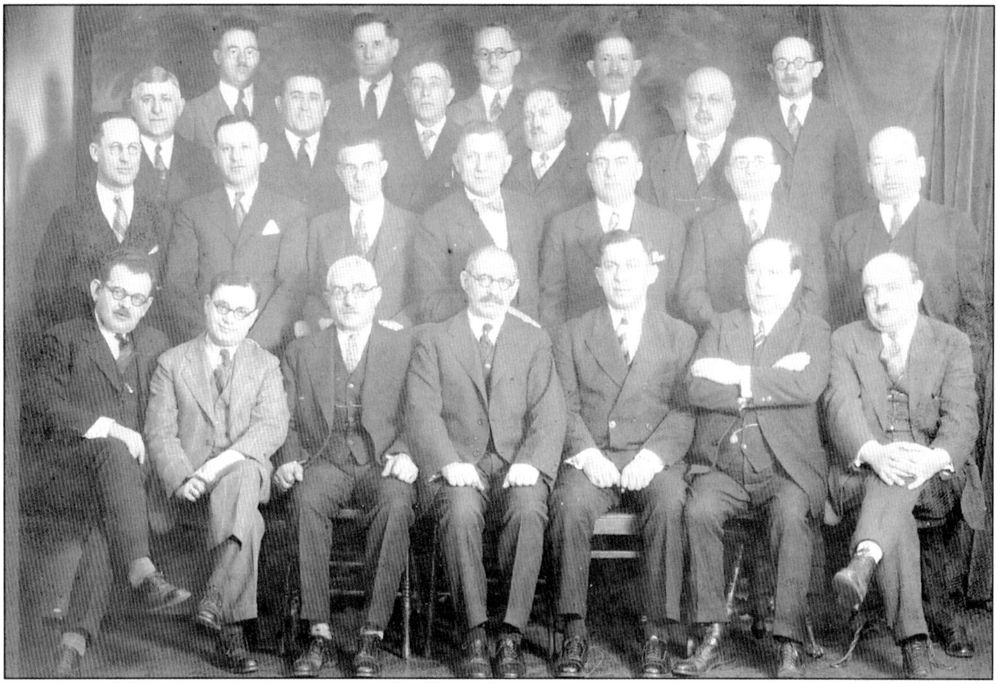

The Hebrew Free Loan Society Board of Trustees, 1928. The society, funded by dues and voluntary contributions, offered interest-free loans. All that was required for the loan was the signature of the borrower and a co-signer. There were four such agencies in Rhode Island: Woonsocket, Pawtucket/ Central Falls, South Providence, and the one pictured above in the North End of Providence.

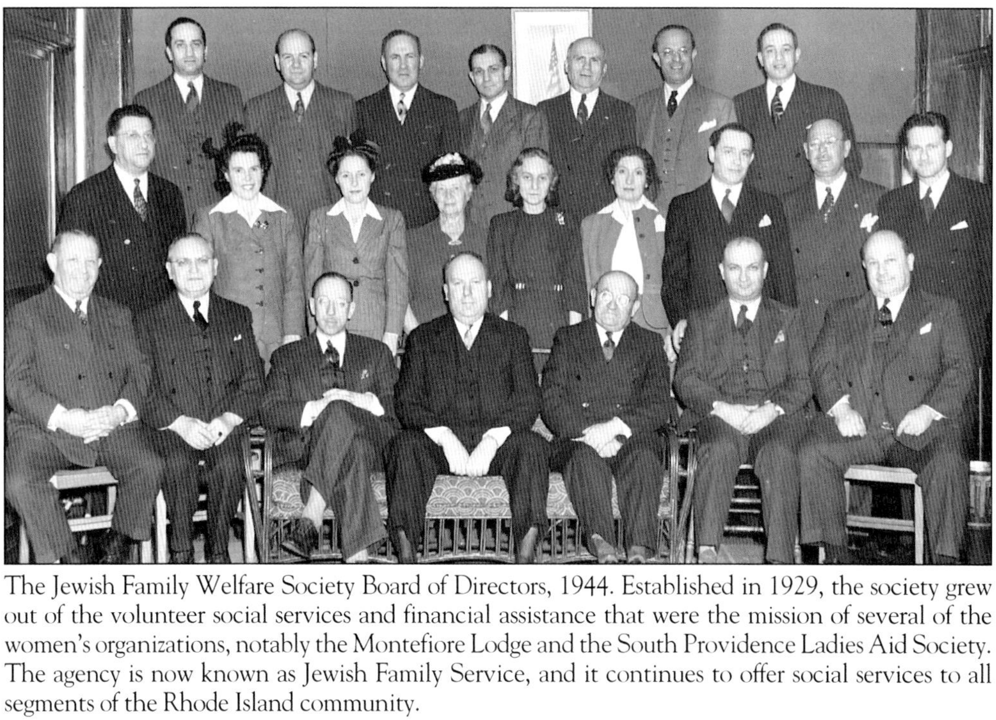

The Jewish Family Welfare Society Board of Directors, 1944. Established in 1929, the society grew out of the volunteer social services and financial assistance that were the mission of several of the women's organizations, notably the Montefiore Lodge and the South Providence Ladies Aid Society. The agency is now known as Jewish Family Service, and it continues to offer social services to all segments of the Rhode Island community.

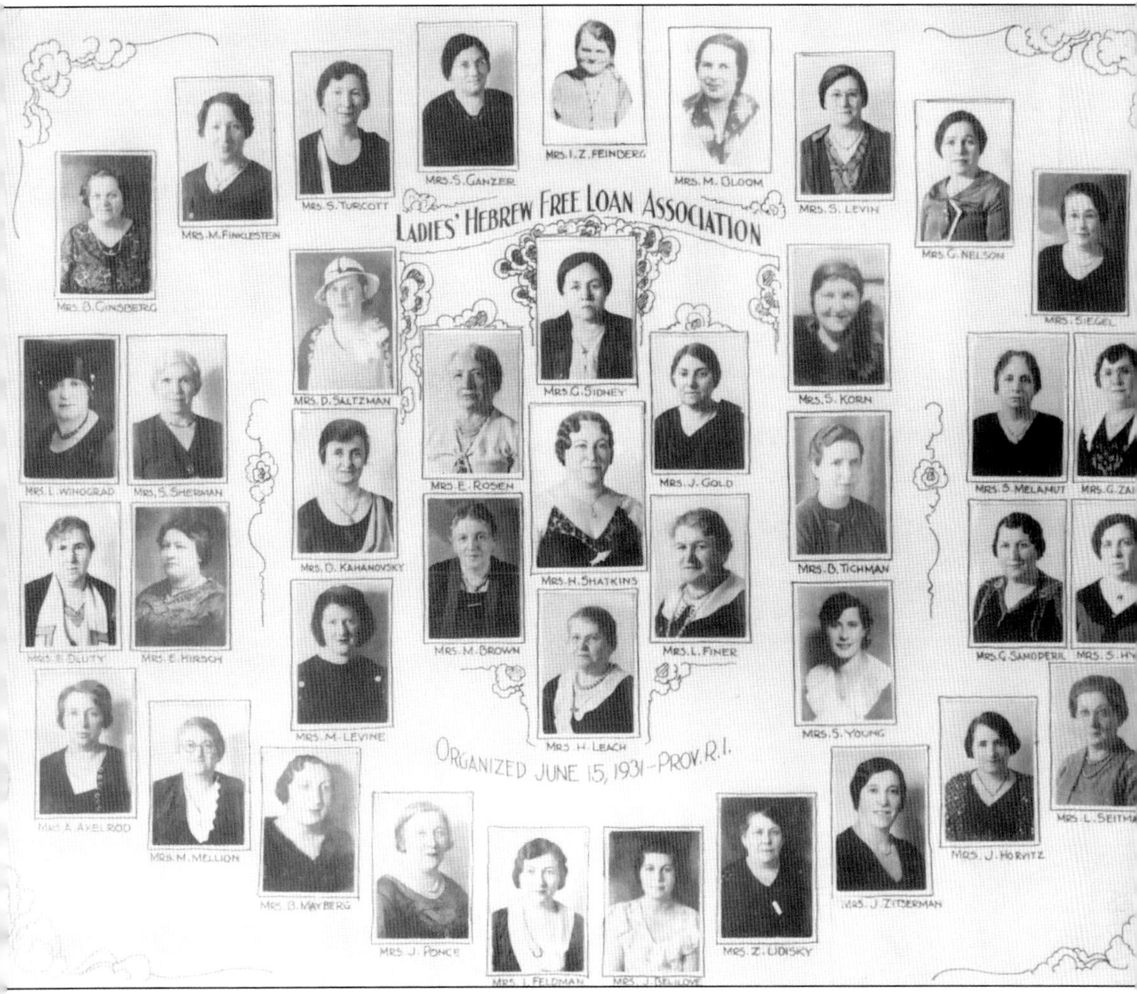


The Ladies Hebrew Free Loan Association. Since there was no mechanism for women to borrow small sums of money for temporary family needs, a group of concerned women formed a free loan association. A borrower was assured of confidentiality when she applied for her interest free loan on her signature and that of a co-signer. The association ceased operations in 1958 as their function within the community was no longer needed. The funds remaining in the treasury were donated to several philanthropic organizations.

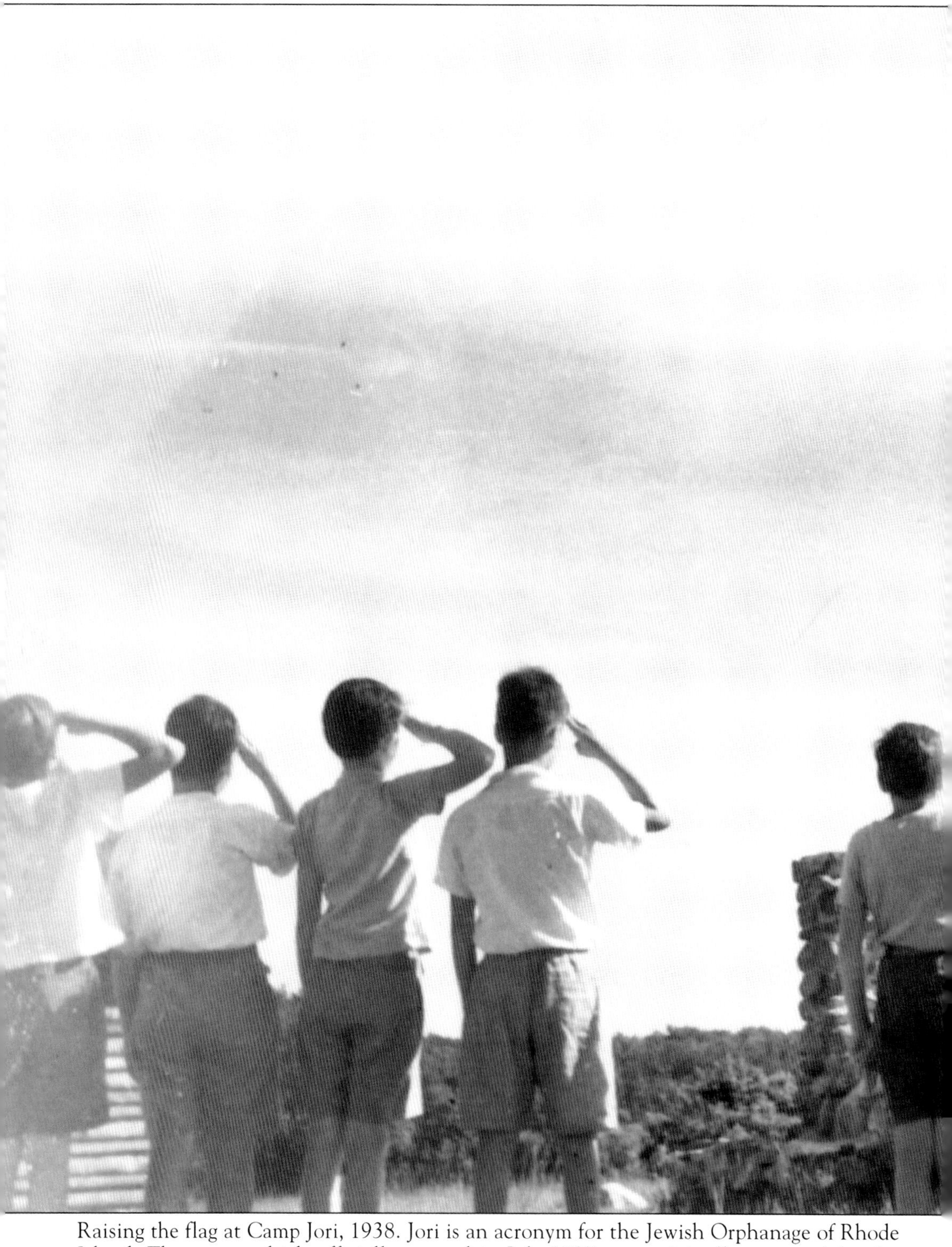

Raising the flag at Camp Jori, 1938. Jori is an acronym for the Jewish Orphanage of Rhode Island. The camp, which officially opened in July 1937, was originally proposed for the residents of the orphanage. When the dwindling population of the facility and foster home

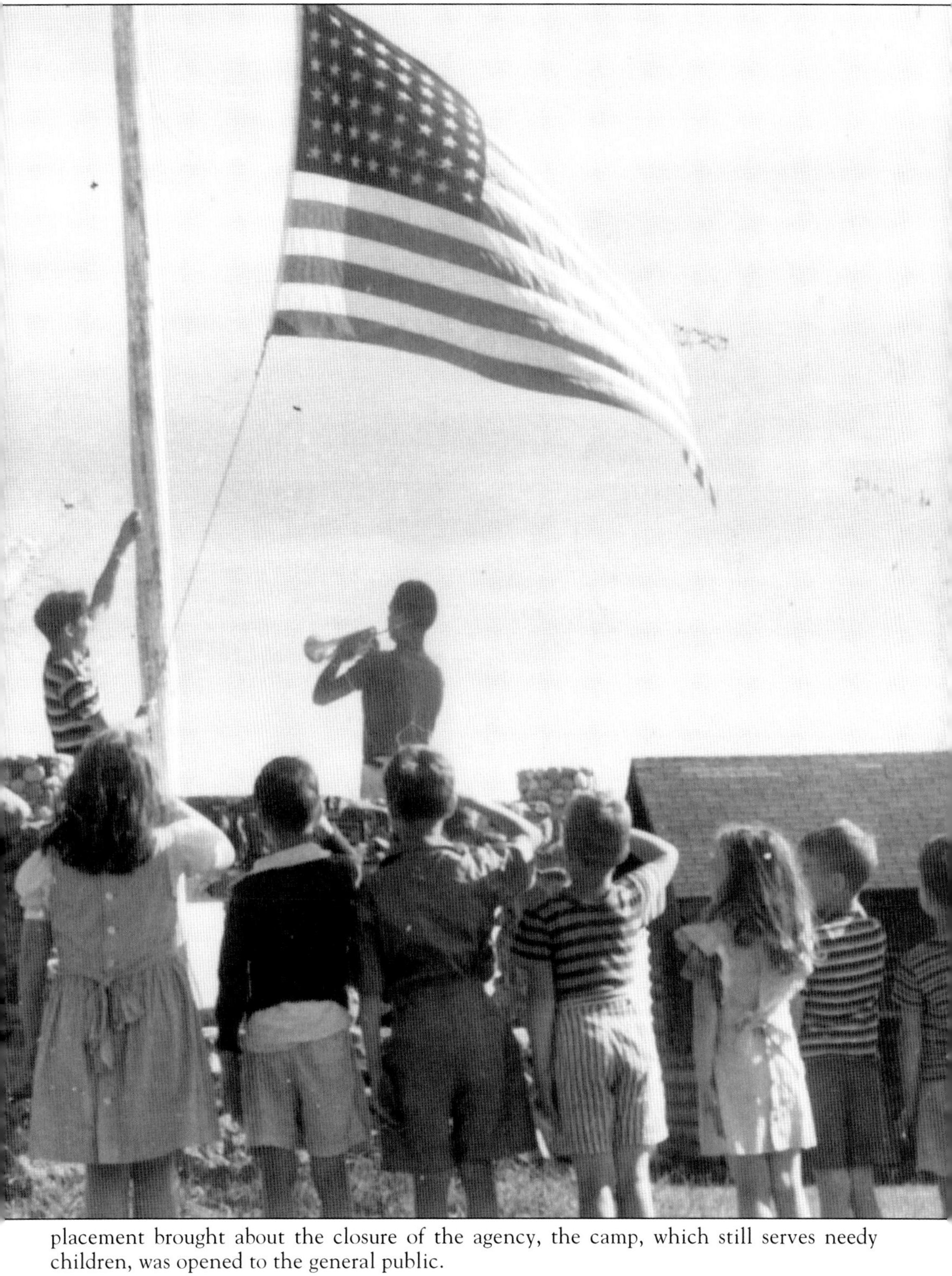

placement brought about the closure of the agency, the camp, which still serves needy children, was opened to the general public.

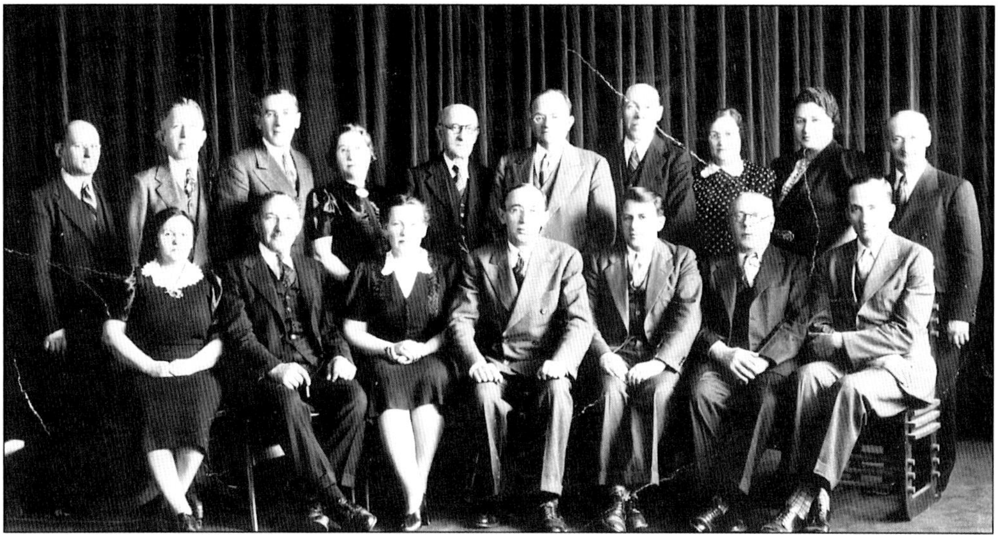

The Workmen's Circle School Board of Directors, 1930. The Workmen's Circle was a progressive fraternal and educational organization with branches in Providence and Pawtucket. At its height, the Workmen's Circle sponsored two afternoon/Sunday schools in Providence. Yiddish was the basic language of instruction. The curriculum also included art, music, dramatics, and Yiddish literature.

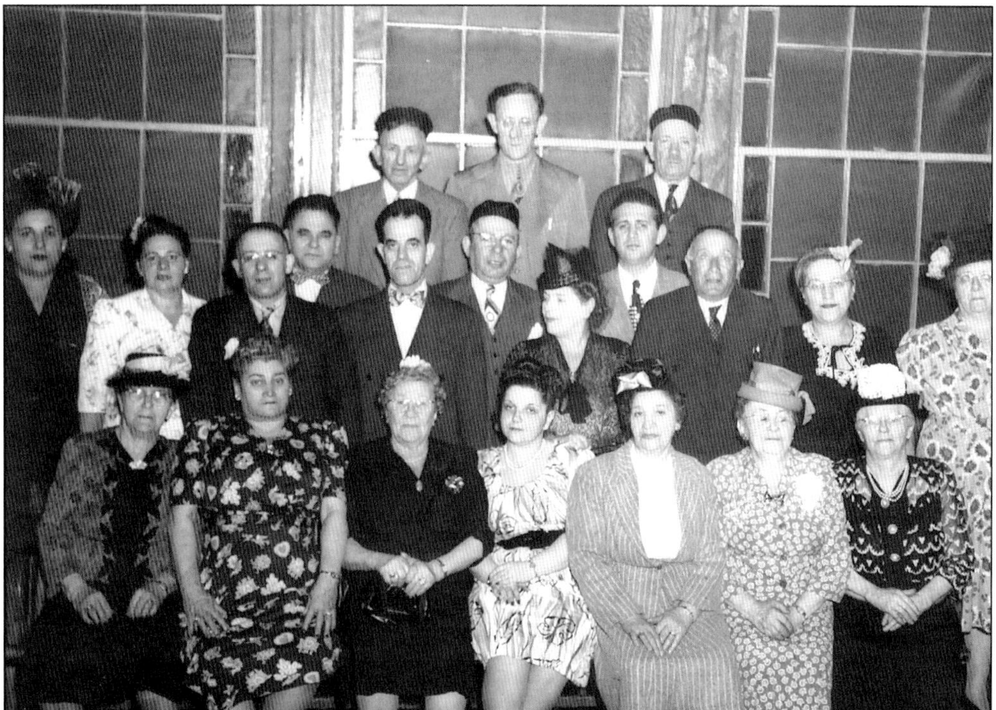

The Providence Hebrew Sheltering Society Board of Trustees, *c.* 1938. The society maintained a house on Jefferson Street in the North End of Providence, where it provided temporary shelter and meals to itinerants, immigrants, stranded travelers, and the dispossessed. During World War II, it served Kosher meals to Jewish servicemen in the Newport Naval Hospital.

Henry Hassenfeld, president (left), and Joseph Levy, campaign chairman, of the General Jewish Committee of Rhode Island, 1957. As early as 1895, Rabbi David Blaustein of the Congregation Sons of Israel and David proposed the formation of United Hebrew Charities to systematize the distribution of community funds to avoid duplications. It took 50 years for a similar agency, the General Jewish Committee (GJC), to come into being. The GJC, now the Jewish Federation of Rhode Island, expanded its fund-raising/allocations role to establish the Bureau of Jewish Education, the Community Relations Council, and Community Planning.

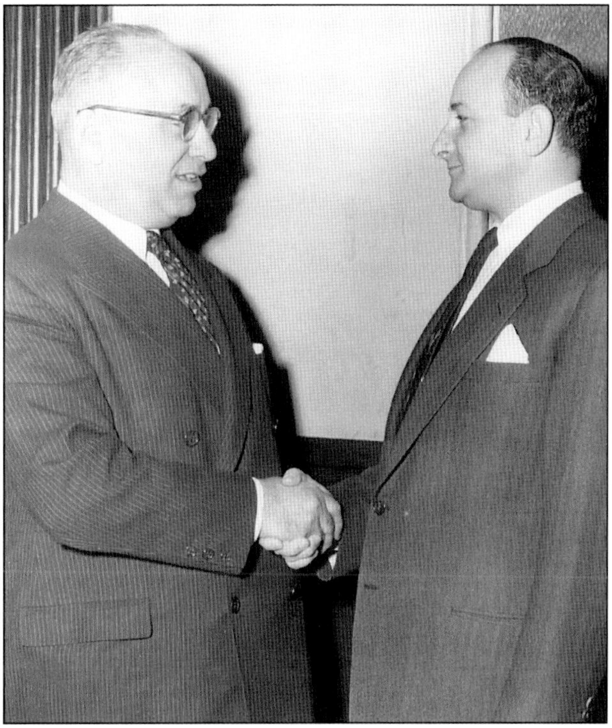

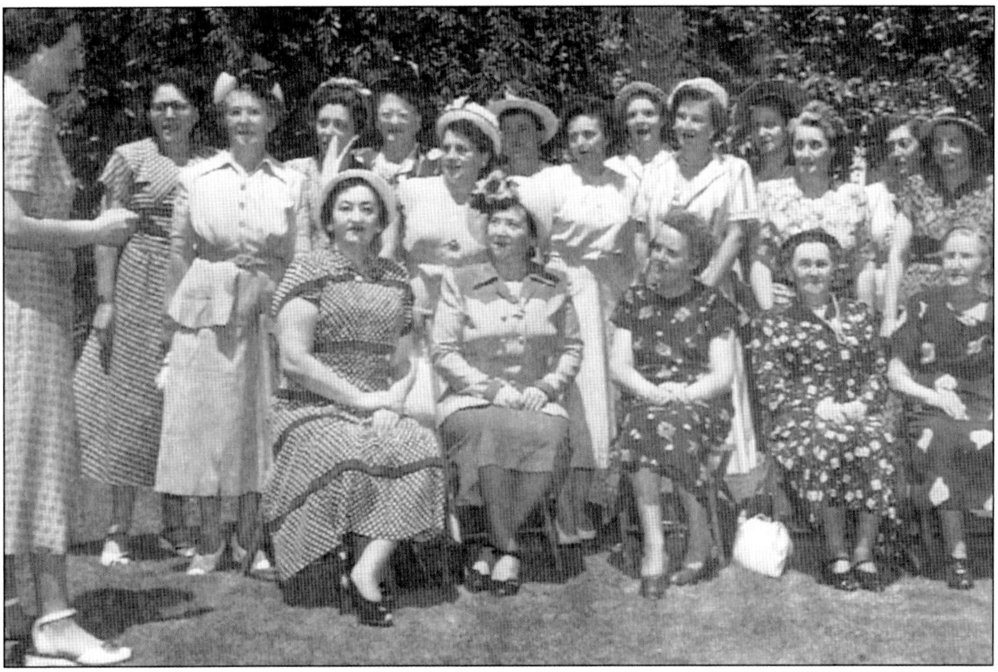

The presidents of the women's organizations in Providence. These women were brought together by Selma Pilavin (Robinson), one of the founders of the Women's Division of the GJC, who sought their aid in raising funds. Included were the heads of Sisterhoods; Zionist groups such as Pioneer Women, Hadassah, and Mizrachi; Veterans Auxiliaries; and the various organizations serving as social agencies in the community.

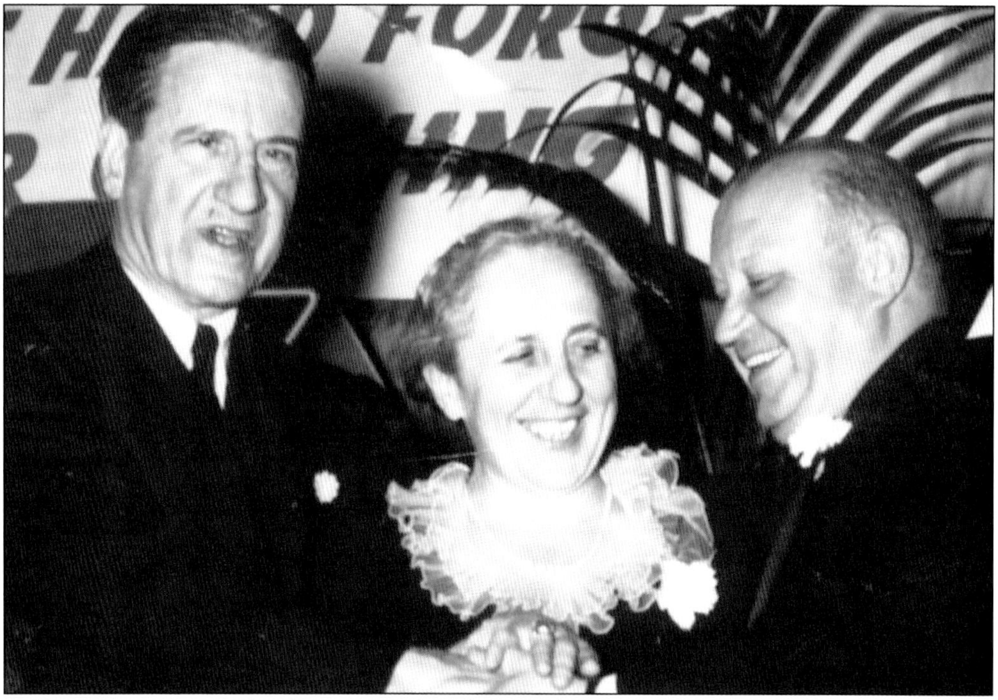

Rabbi Steven S. Wise, Ida Silverman, and Archibald Silverman (from left to right).

Outstanding within a community known for its generosity toward the needy were the Silvermans, Ida and Archibald. Both had been penniless immigrants from Russia around 1890, who met in Providence and married in 1900.

Archie became a wealthy business man, who gave both money and personal effort to aid the needy in Rhode Island.

Ida raised a family and in the 1920's became an ardent worker in the Zionist cause. She travelled world wide (Central Europe, England, Australia, North and South America, etc.) speaking eloquently to raise both interest and money for the establishment of a Jewish state. She was a friend of Justice Louis Brandeis, Ben Gurion, and Chaim Weizman.

Archie supported Ida both morally and monetarily, She could not have succeeded in her work without his help.

# *Seven*

# Making a Living

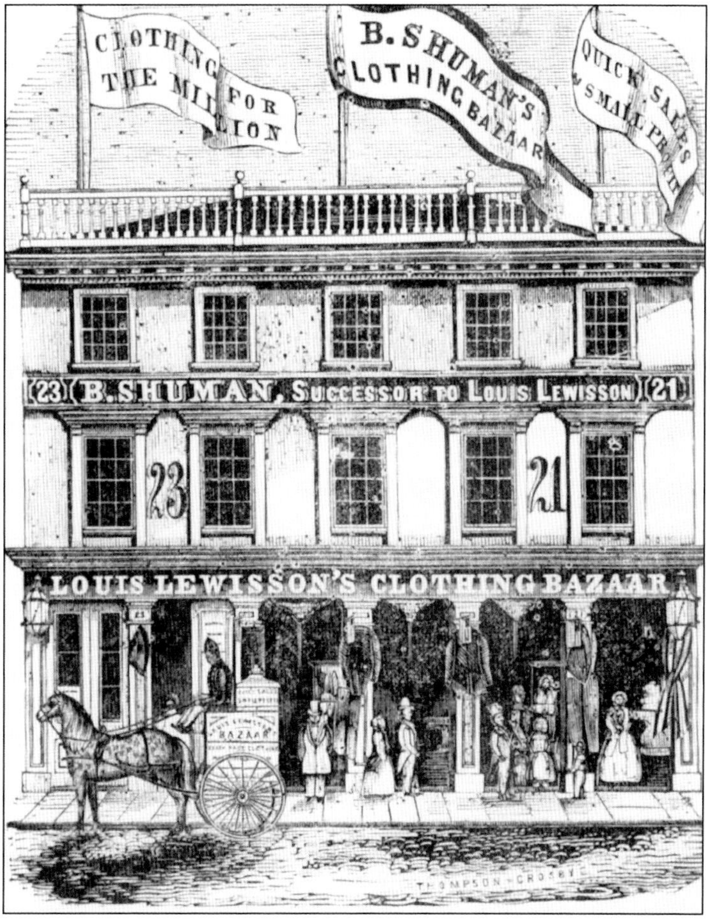


A print of the B. Shuman Co., 1862. The earliest Jewish settlers who arrived in Rhode Island between 1838 and the Civil War possessed some capital and mercantile experience. They opened stores associated primarily with dry goods or clothing. In Providence they had to compete with long-established merchants who catered to and monopolized the "carriage trade," as well as competing among themselves for the available customers. (Courtesy of Rhode Island Historical Society.)

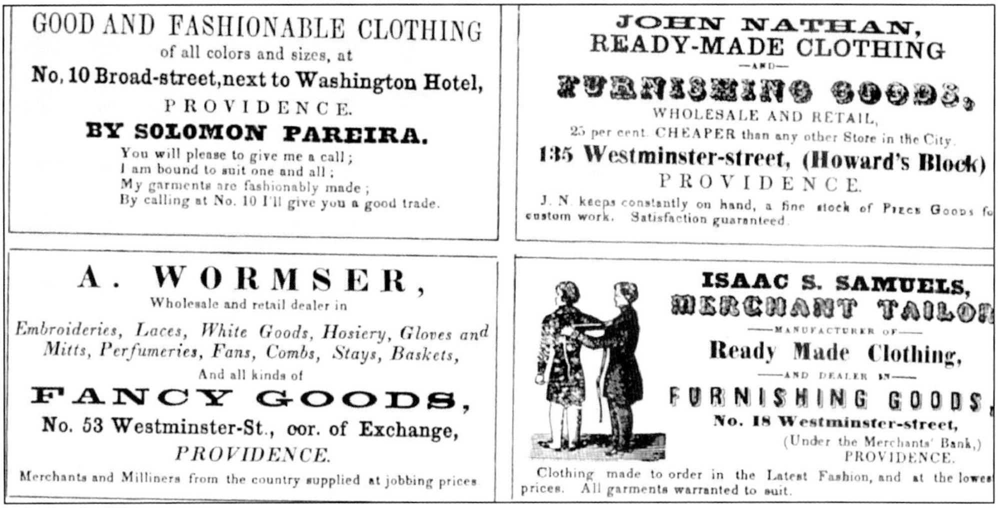


Business advertisements of Jewish firms found in the *Providence Journal.* Advertisements in the newspapers of this era attest to the vigorous attempts of the Jewish merchants to attract trade. In addition to the fierce competition, they had to weather frequent "panics" and financial depressions. Not all the businesses survived; many changed locations frequently or moved elsewhere. (Courtesy of Rhode Island Historical Society.)

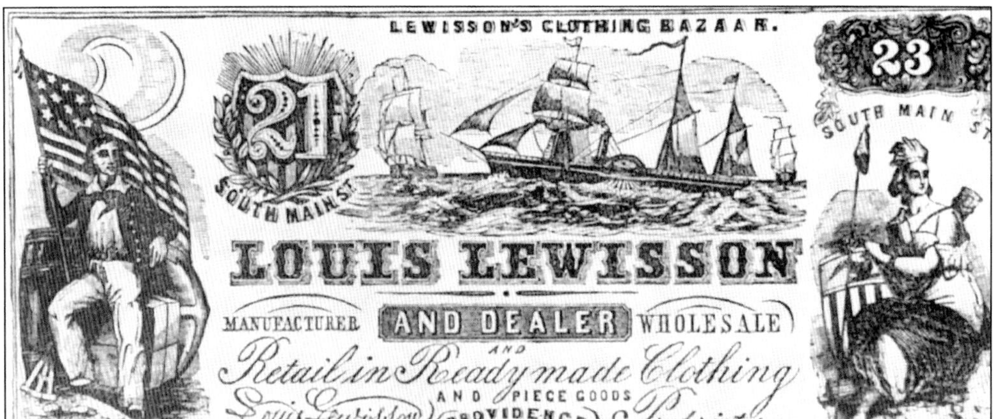


An advertisement of Louis Lewisson, clothier, 1852. Louis Lewisson was one of the most flamboyant of the advertisers and businessmen. Each Thanksgiving he issued his annual proclamation inviting the poor of the city to present themselves at his clothing bazaar and receive a "good substantial Thanksgiving dinner." For those too ill to come themselves he would send dinner via his own delivery wagon. Lewisson, who was born in Prussia, was the first Jew naturalized in Providence (1851). (Providence City Tax Book; courtesy of Rhode Island Historical Society.)

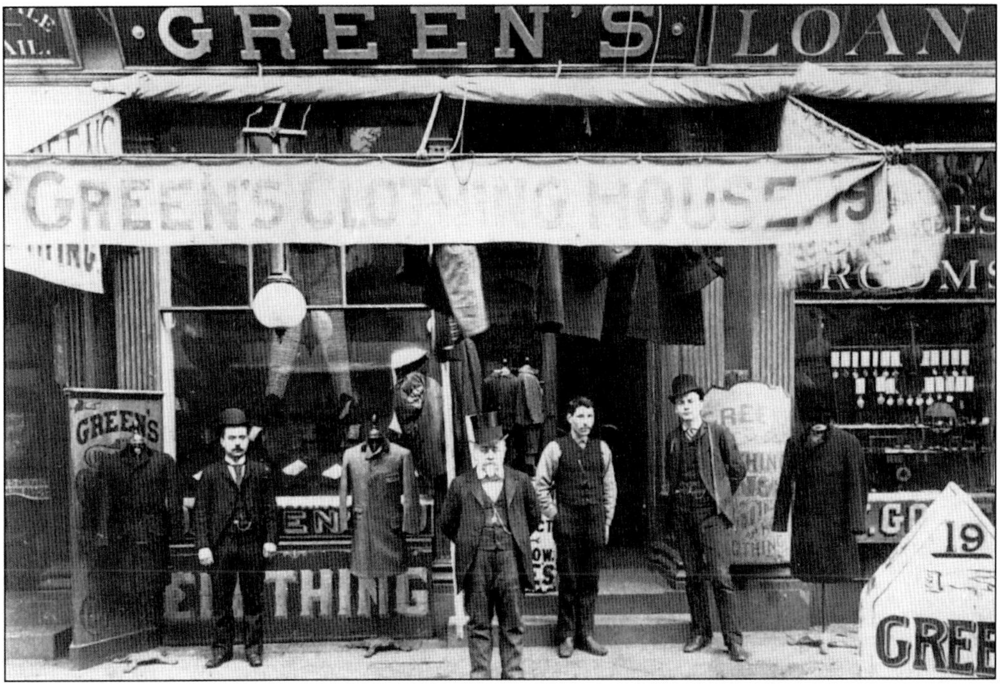


Henry Green (wearing the top hat) in front of his clothing store, Providence, *c.* 1870. Henry Green, who came to Providence in 1856, opened his first store, a tailor shop, on North Main Street. Over the years he changed his line of business to mens' clothing and in the process moved his establishment several times to locations on North Main Street, to Market Square, and finally to Dorrance Street near city hall. (Courtesy of Temple Beth El Archives.)

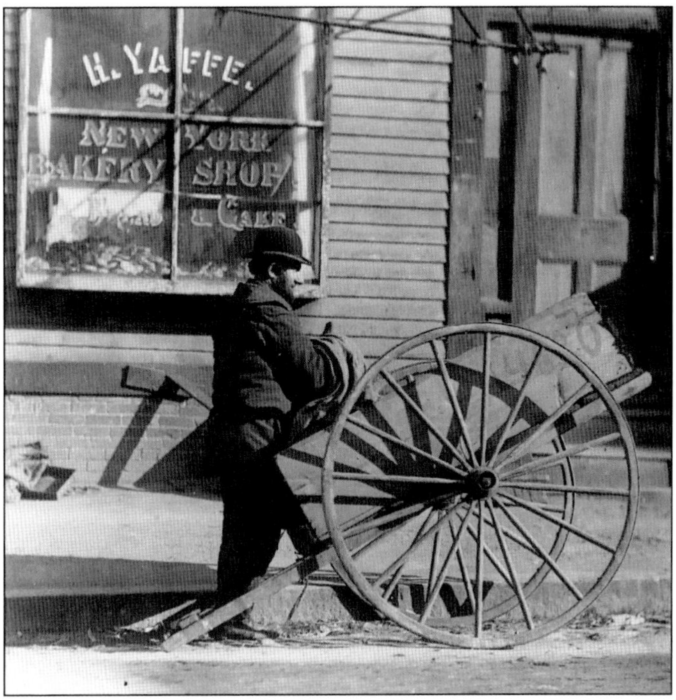


An unidentified peddler passing in front of the bakery of Hyman Yaffee, Providence. As the number of poor immigrants from the small towns and villages of Eastern Europe swelled, so did the number of peddlers. The image of a man with a pushcart or basket of goods for sale, wending his way from house to house, was a familiar one in the landscape of Providence and of other cities and towns of that era. Also familiar on urban streets was the cry of the peddler seeking rags, bottles, and cast-offs. (Courtesy of Rhode Island Historical Society.)

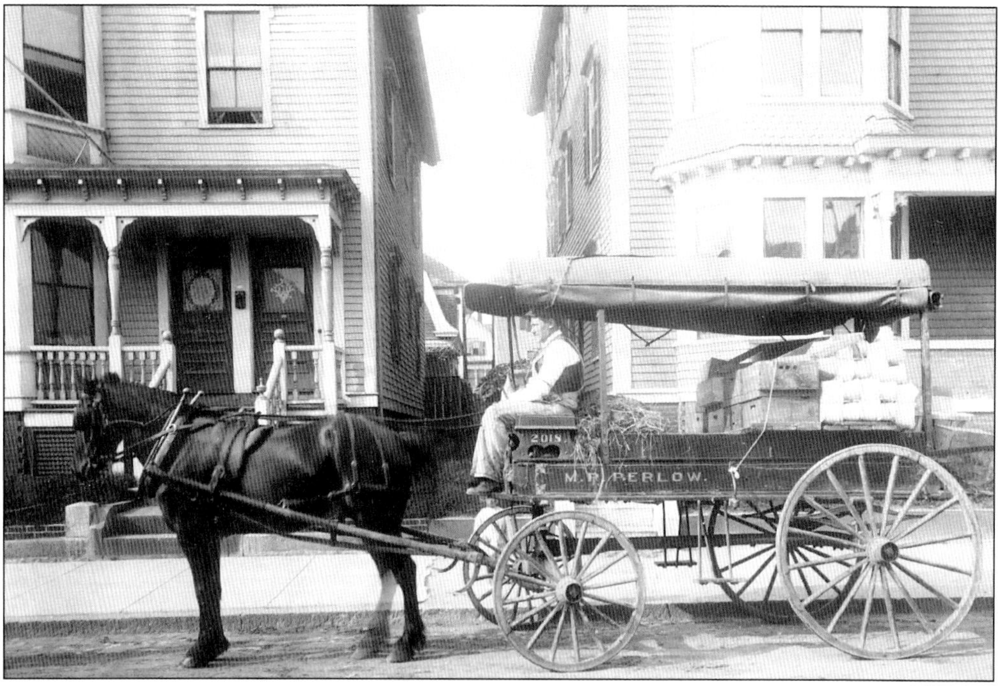


M. Perlow, fruit and vegetable peddler. Peddling required little capital. With a few dollars borrowed interest-free from one of the Hebrew Free Loan societies, one could become an "entrepreneur." In time, perhaps, the peddler could accumulate the capital to open a store of his own.

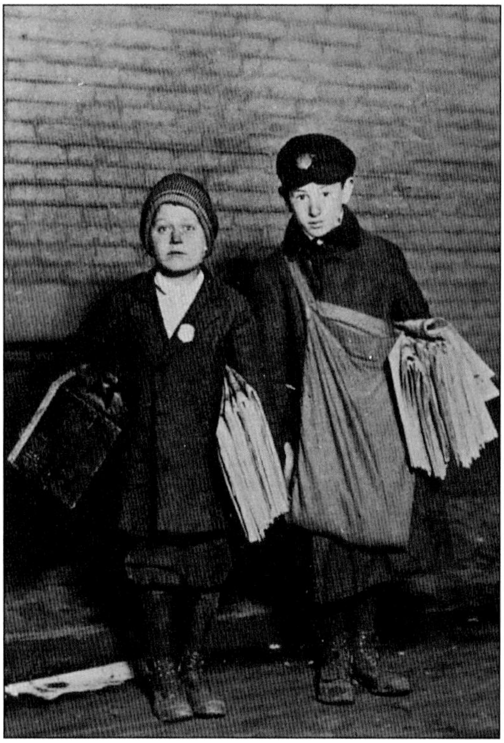

Two paperboys. It was very common for Jewish youngsters to become newsboys or newsgirls to augment the family's meager income. In the years before World War I, according to one source, the majority of young people selling newspapers were Jewish. (Courtesy of Rhode Island Historical Society.)

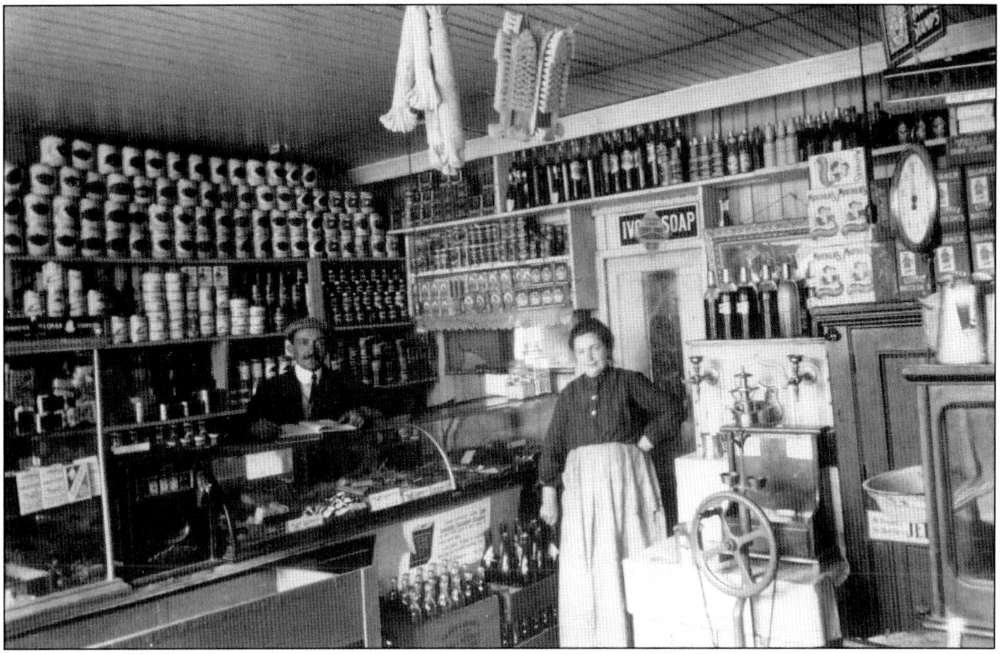


Adelson's Market, Newport, 1902. Elix and Dora Adelson owned a grocery store located at Thames Street and Narragansett Avenue. They settled in Newport before the turn of the century, a part of the re-emerging Jewish community of the area.

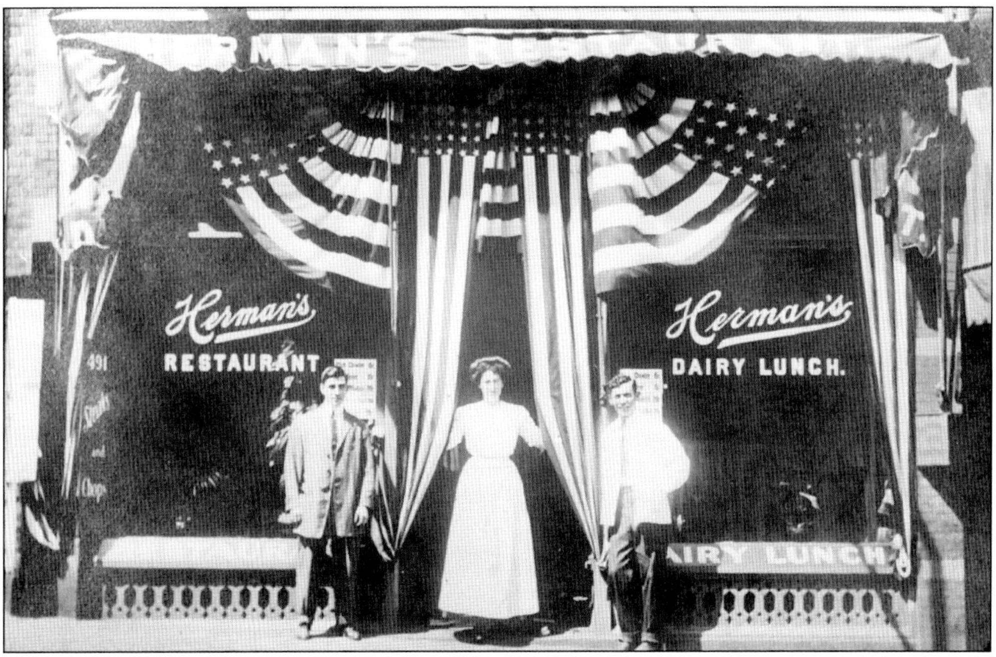


Herman's Lunch, Providence, 1907. The dairy restaurant, located in the lower North End, was owned by two gentlemen with the first name of Herman—Herman Swartz and Herman Komensky. The restaurant was decorated in celebration of Old Home Week, a city-wide festivity.

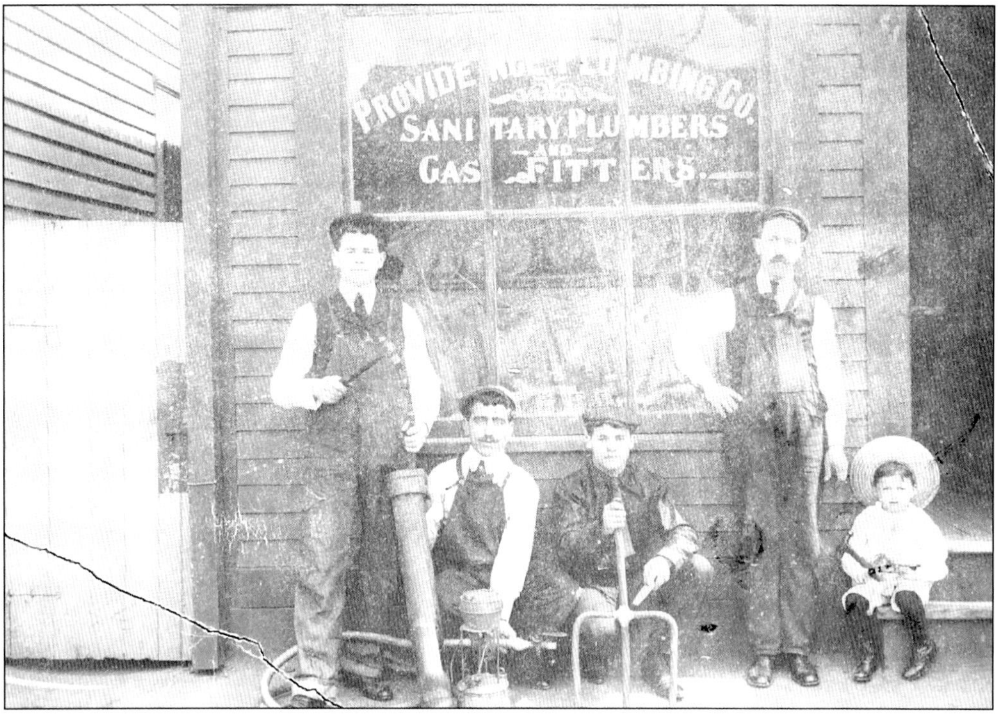


Providence Plumbing Co., 351 Point Street, Providence, 1904. Standing in front of the shop are, from left to right, Abe Rotman, Maurice Rotman, unidentified, Frank Scoliard, and his son Elisha.

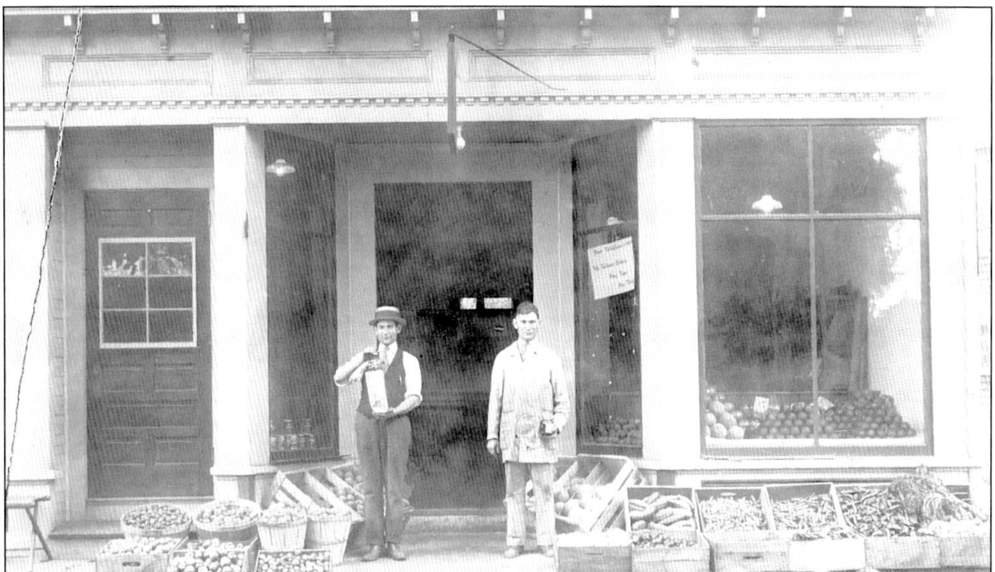

Samuel (left) and David Weisman, Weisman's Fruit Store, corner of Prairie and Willard Avenues. Rivaling the North End as a major center of Jewish activity, South Providence attained a vitality and character all its own. The area was settled by East European Jews later than the North End, and it never attained the population or size of the older neighborhood.

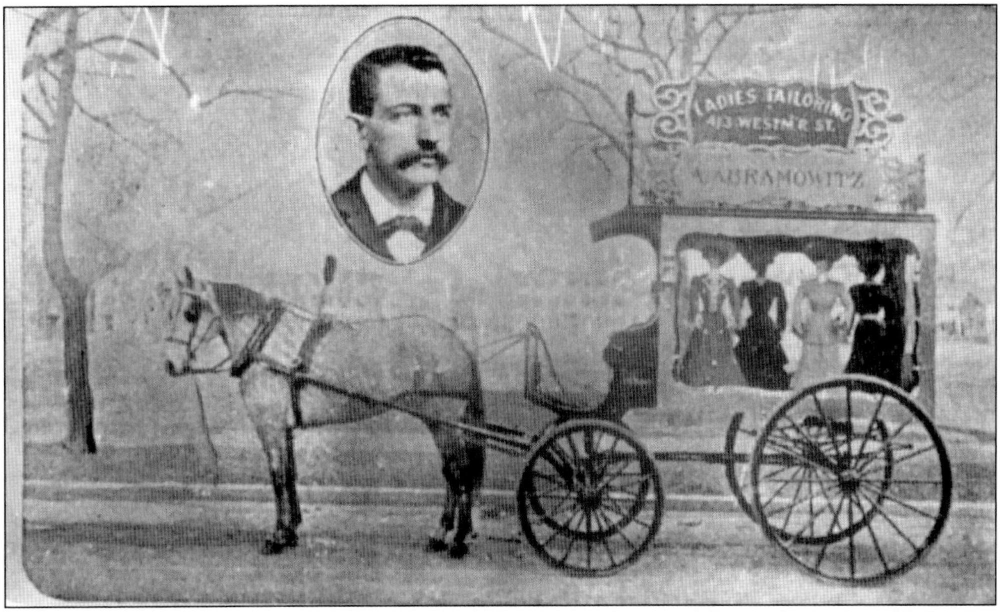


A business card of A. Abramowitz. Mr. Abramowitz advertised his tailoring establishment by means of business cards and a wagon containing four wax female dummies, as pictured on the card. Each dummy wore an intricately detailed garment that showcased Mr. Abramowitz's craftsmanship. The wagon also participated in parades held in Providence.

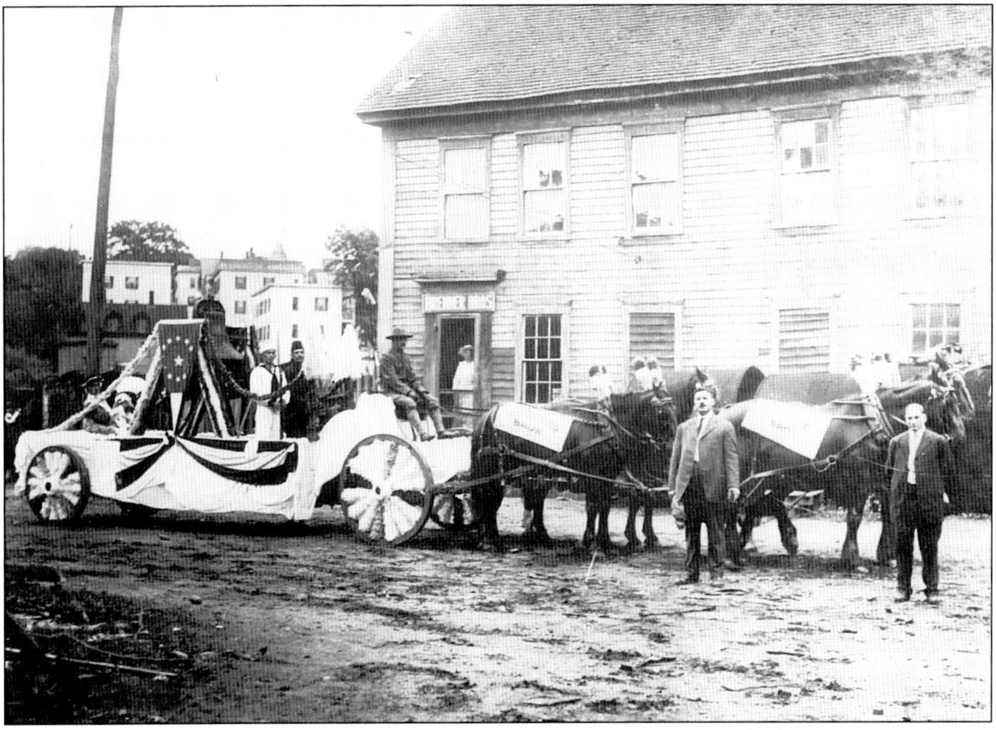


A parade float by Brenner Bros., Woonsocket. The Brenner Bros. were dealers in junk and scrap metal. The firm grew from a small business into a major concern. For Woonsocket celebrations, they decorated one of their wagons and showed their civic pride.

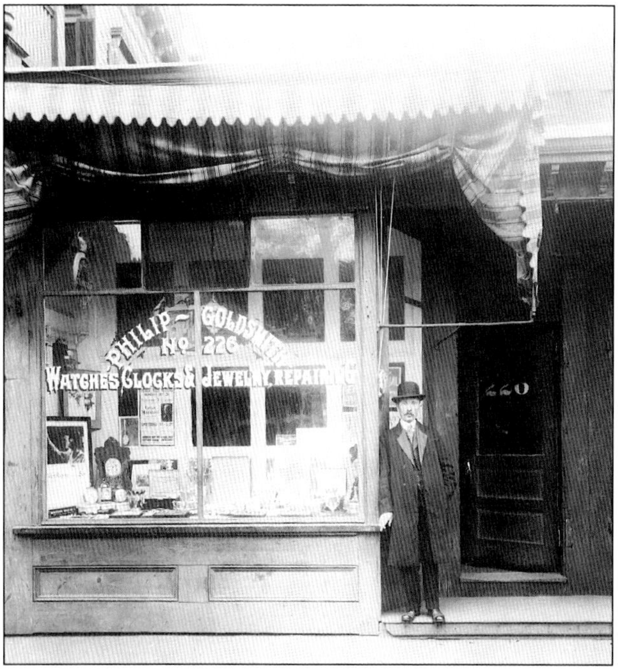


Philip Goldsmith in front of his jewelry store on Prairie Avenue. Philip Goldsmith sold and repaired jewelry and watches. The major item in his stock, however, was silver-plated flatware. To own such a set for use on special occasions and holidays was the dream of many an immigrant family. The younger Goldsmith siblings, though still in grammar school, helped in the store. It was not uncommon for children of their age to work after school at their parents' place of business.

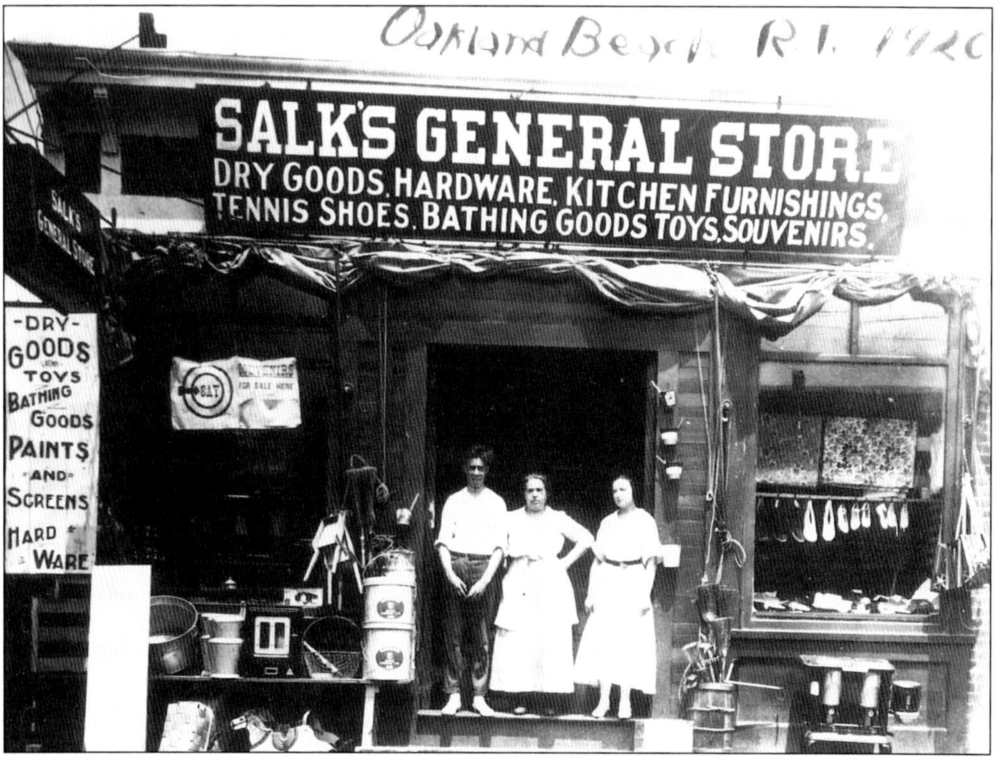


Salk's General Store, Oakland Beach, 1920. Founded by Hyman Salk in 1917, the store was opened to fill the need for such a business in the shore community. Salk also had a dry goods store in South Providence. Shown above are, from left to right, Samuel Salk; his mother, Mrs. Hyman Salk; and his aunt, Mrs. Lena Port Zinn.

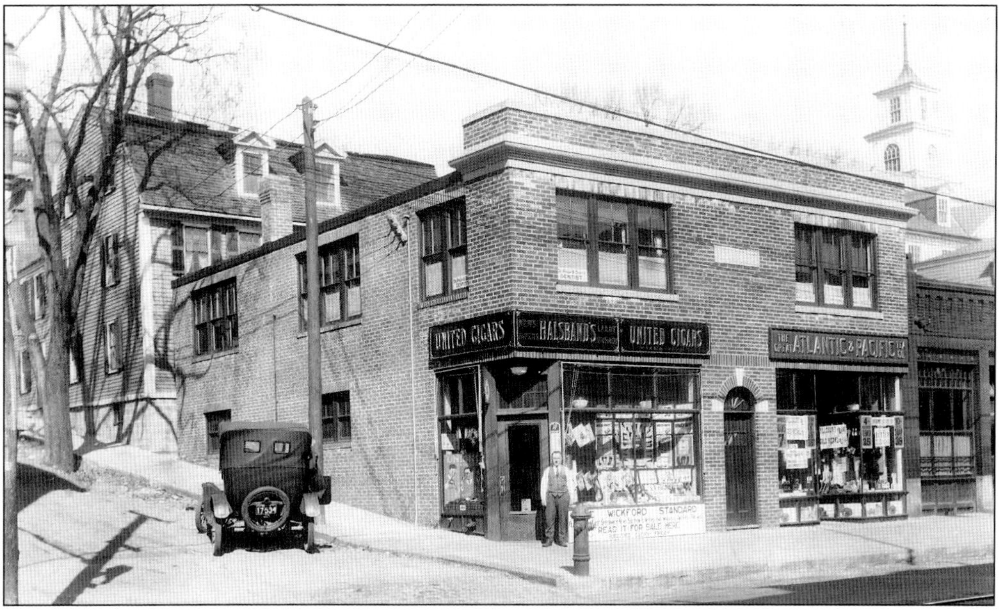


Halsband's News Stand/Tobacconist Shop, Main Street, East Greenwich. Joseph Abrams, who had settled in Wickford, urged his sister and brother-in-law, Mary and John Halsband, to open a business in East Greenwich, where they could earn a good living, perhaps even $5 per week. Halsband established his original store on Main Street in 1908 and moved to his own building in 1928.

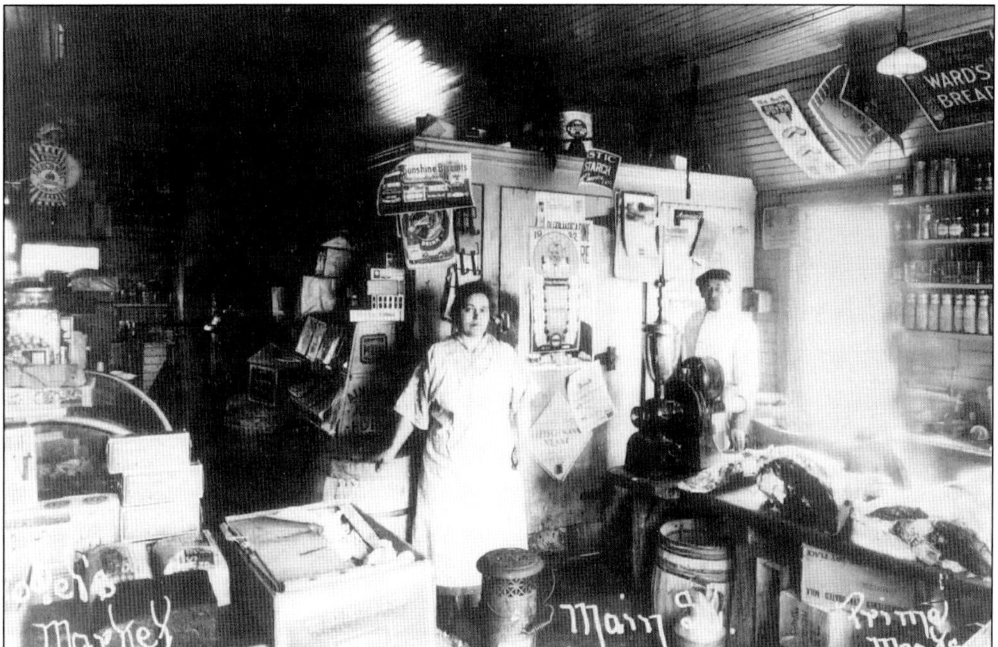


Herman Fogel's Market, Main Street, East Greenwich. Herman and Fannie Fogel also heeded their brother's advice and opened a market on Main Street in 1912. The store is now the site of a dry cleaning business founded by their son and daughter-in-law, Joseph and Lillian Fogel, after World War II, and now owned by grandson Herbert and his wife, Judith.

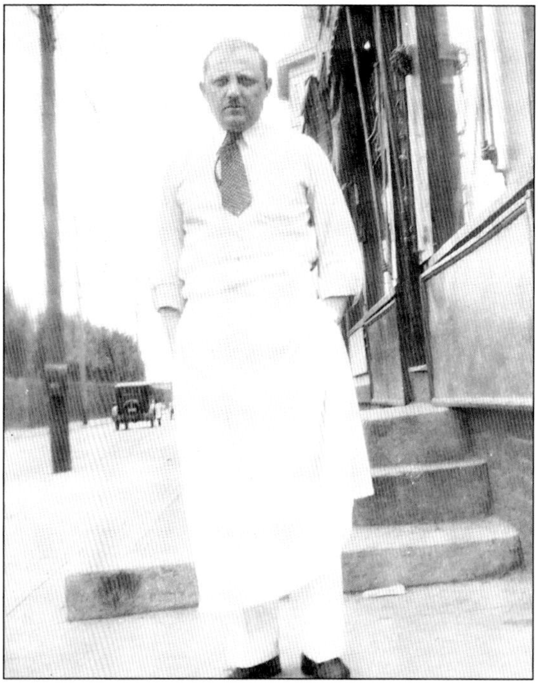

Joseph Teller in front of his market on Lonsdale Avenue, Central Falls. Central Falls was the first home of many Jews who later moved to Pawtucket. They came to the town because a relative or a friend from the old country told them that it was a good place to live. Central Falls also had a busy shopping area with kosher meat markets and grocery stores.

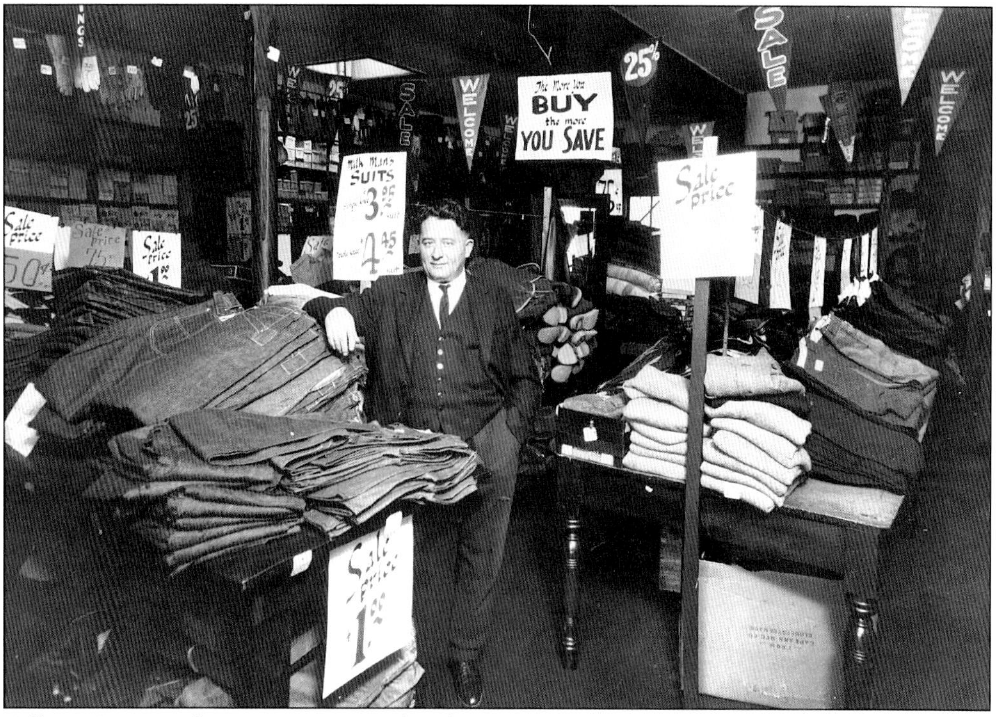


Adler's Army and Navy Store, Wickenden Street, Providence, 1924. Fred Adler was an engraver who worked in the jewelry industry. Since this work was seasonal and unpredictable, he opened a clothing store. During the Depression years, Adler went to the jewelry factories seeking engraving work, which he would bring back to his store to complete when not waiting on trade.

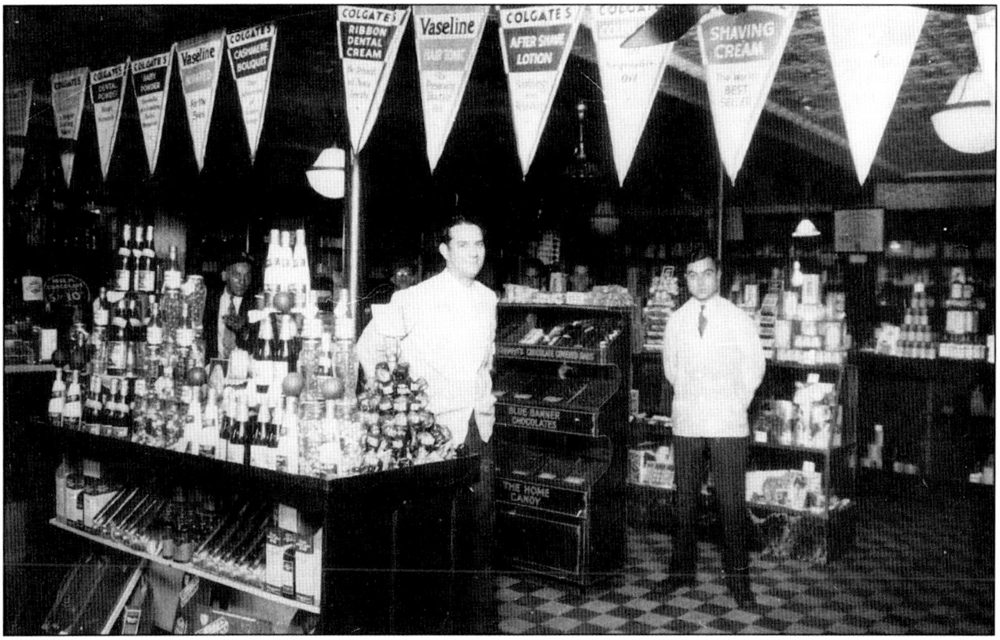


The Olneyville Square Pharmacy, Olneyville Square. The Sklut family were one of several Jewish families with businesses in the Olneyville area. The elder Mr. Sklut had a tailor shop on the second floor of a building facing the square. Harry Sklut (right) and his partner, Paul Rouslin, acquired the pharmacy soon after graduating from the Rhode Island College of Pharmacy.

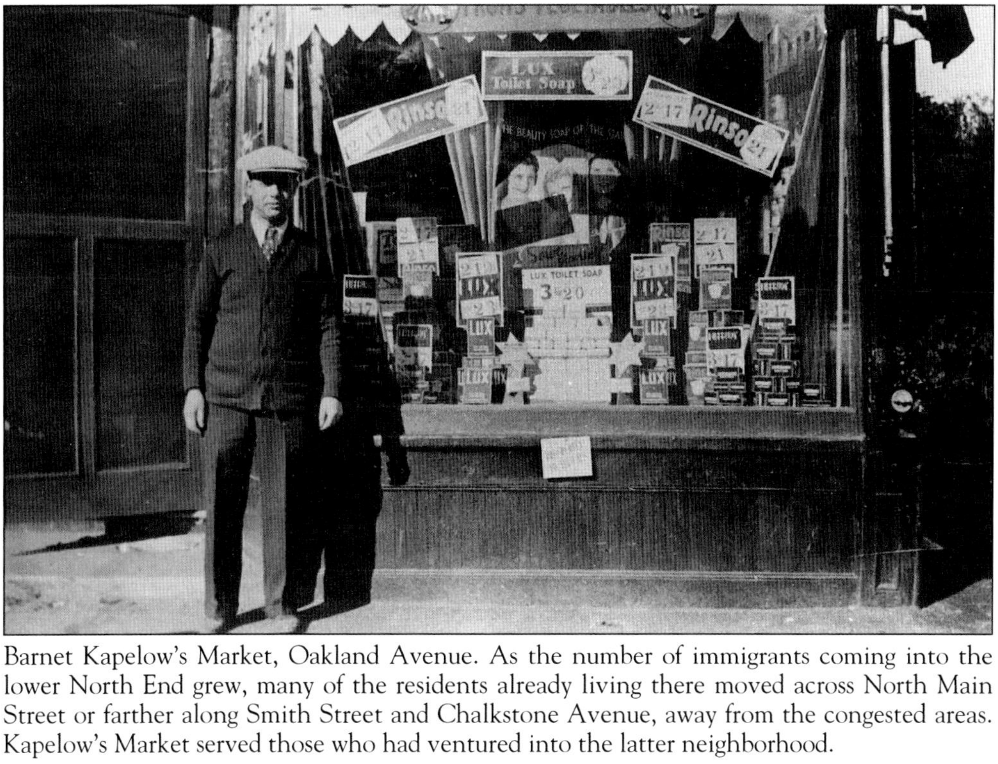


Barnet Kapelow's Market, Oakland Avenue. As the number of immigrants coming into the lower North End grew, many of the residents already living there moved across North Main Street or farther along Smith Street and Chalkstone Avenue, away from the congested areas. Kapelow's Market served those who had ventured into the latter neighborhood.

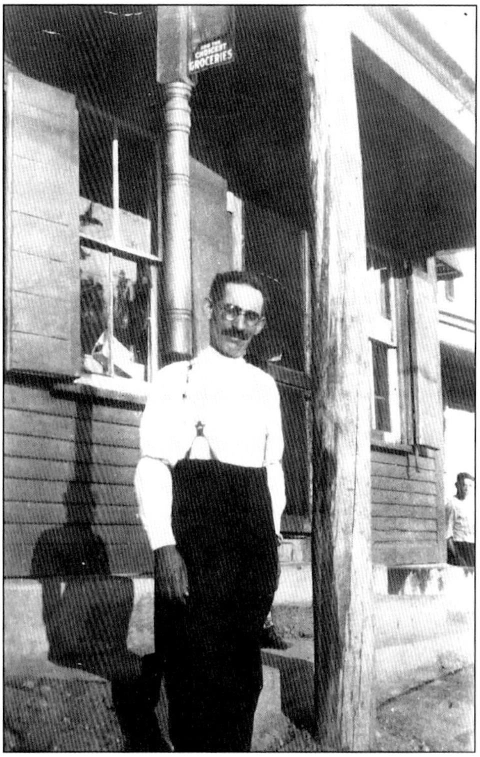

Rosenberg's Grocery and General Store, Chepachet. In 1919, Nathan Rosenberg read an advertisement offering a grocery and general merchandise store in the village of Chepachet. The business and the area appealed to him because it held the promise of independence and the freedom to make a life for himself and his family in America.

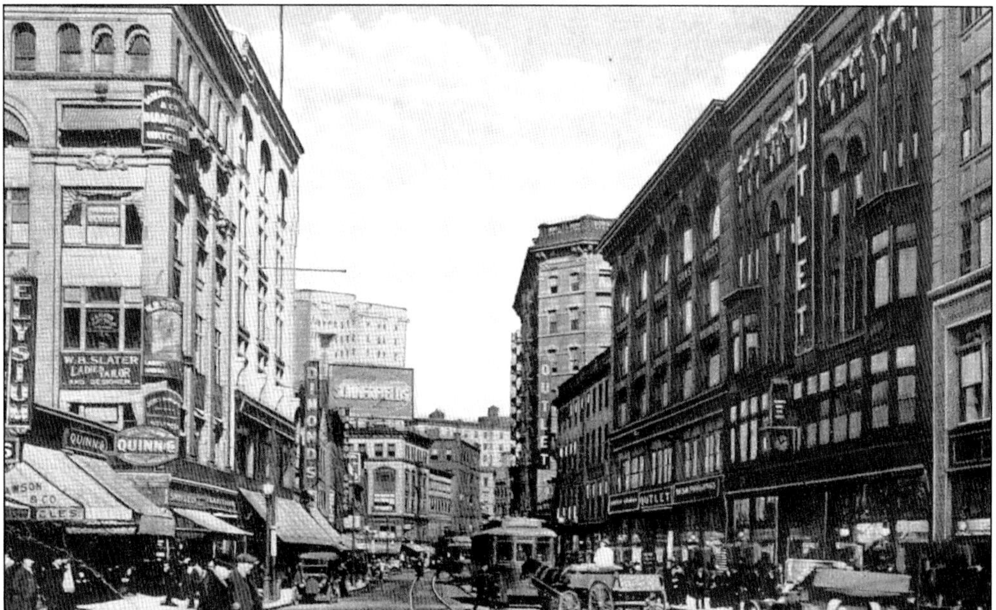


Lower Weybosset Street. After the Civil War, the German-Jewish merchants began to prosper, as did the general population. In Woonsocket, Solomon Treitel owned a highly successful men's clothing business. The Bee Hive in Westerly, the New Idea Store (later Shartenberg's) in Pawtucket, the Dimond Store, the Manufacturer's Outlet (later the Outlet Co.), and later the Caesar Misch Co. became major retailers.

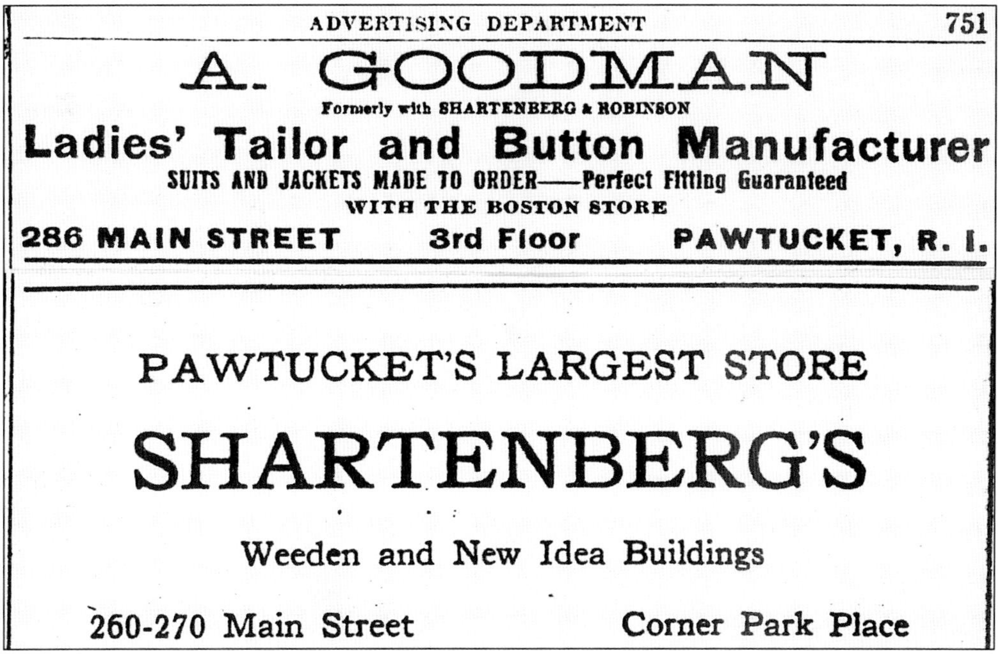

ADVERTISING DEPARTMENT 751

# A. GOODMAN

Formerly with SHARTENBERG & ROBINSON

**Ladies' Tailor and Button Manufacturer**

SUITS AND JACKETS MADE TO ORDER——Perfect Fitting Guaranteed

WITH THE BOSTON STORE

**286 MAIN STREET** **3rd Floor** **PAWTUCKET, R. I.**

PAWTUCKET'S LARGEST STORE

# SHARTENBERG'S

Weeden and New Idea Buildings

260-270 Main Street Corner Park Place

Advertisements, Pawtucket, *c.* 1936. The *Pawtucket Times Special Anniversary and Industrial Edition*, 1906, described the Shartenberg and Robinson Department Store (later Shartenberg's) as having a branch post office, saving bank, optician, photographer, and hairdresser, and its own electrical plant for lighting the store. As with many major retailers, a number of the departments in the store were leased. Joseph Elowitz leased the appliance department in Shartenberg's from 1933 to 1938, later adding radios and phonograph records to his stock. (Courtesy of City Directory.)

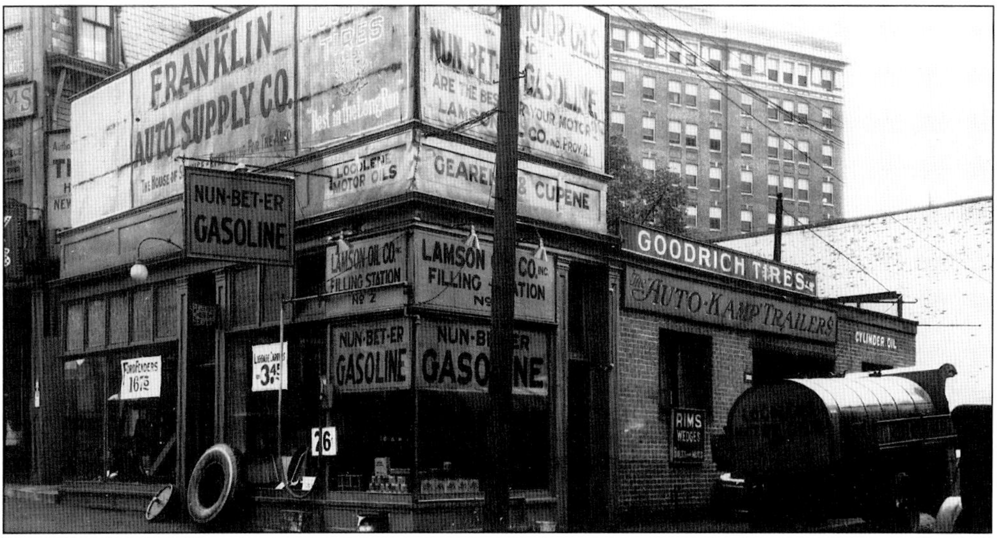


The Franklin Supply Co., Hoyle and Franklin Streets, 1921. As the immigrants became more at ease in their new home, they began to look for business opportunities where, with a great deal of vision and hard work, a willingness to take risks, and some luck, they could create a niche for themselves in the economy of Rhode Island. The Franklin Supply Co., owned by Max and Harry Rosen, was one such success story.

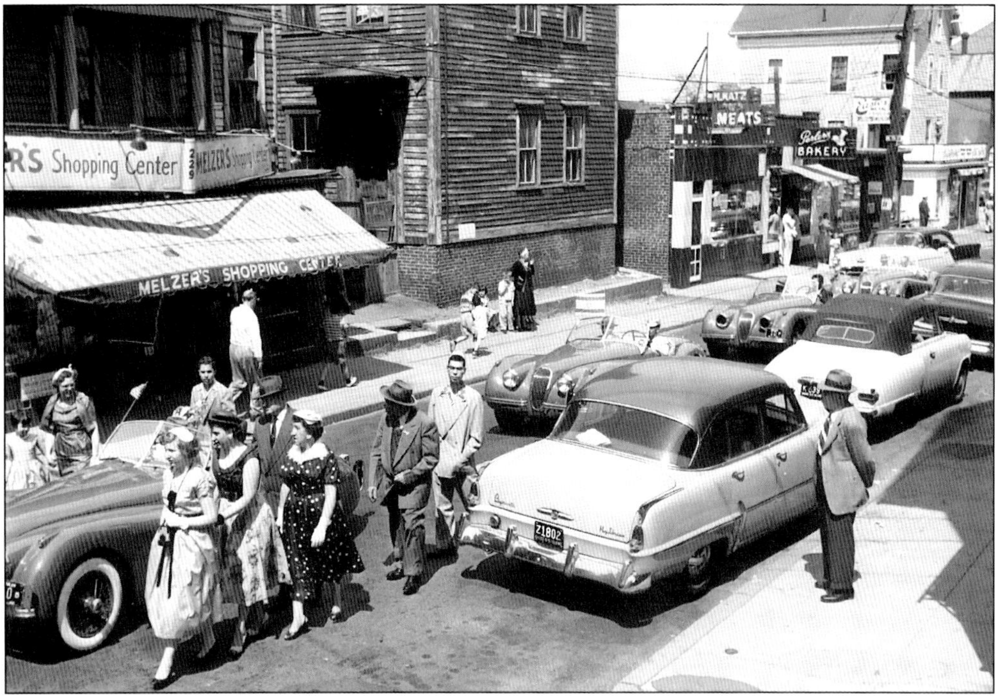


The Willard Avenue Shopping Area. It was a popular shopping center for the residents of South Providence.

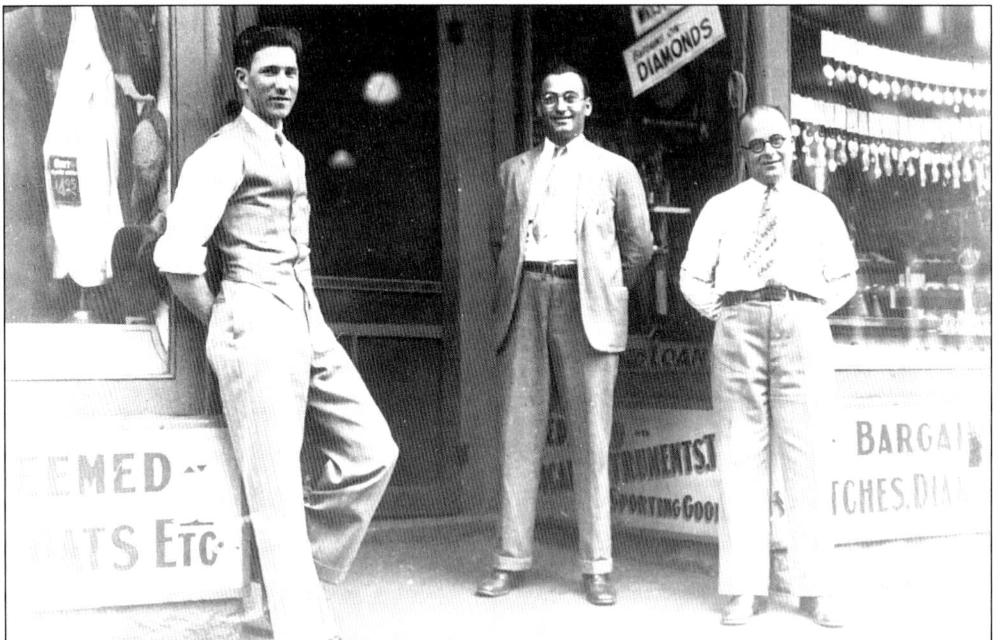


The Standard Loan Co., 129 South Main Street, *c.* 1928. Standing in front of the store are, from left to right, Harold Davis, an unidentified individual, and Harry Kotlen. Kotlen began with a men's clothing store on Charles Street. In time his business interests evolved into a pawn shop specializing in second-hand merchandise, particularly jewelry.

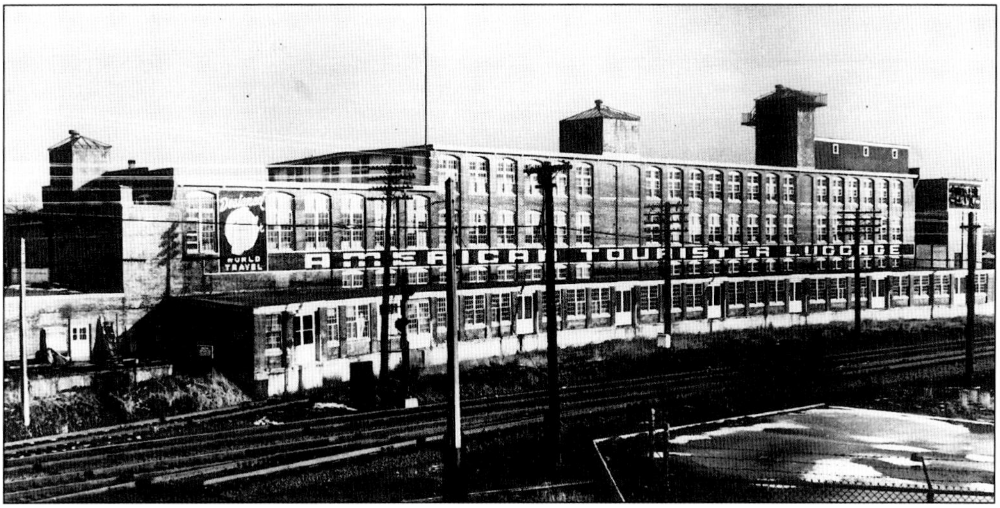


The American Tourister Co., Warren, 1933. Founded by Sol Koffler, this was the first company to manufacture molded luggage.

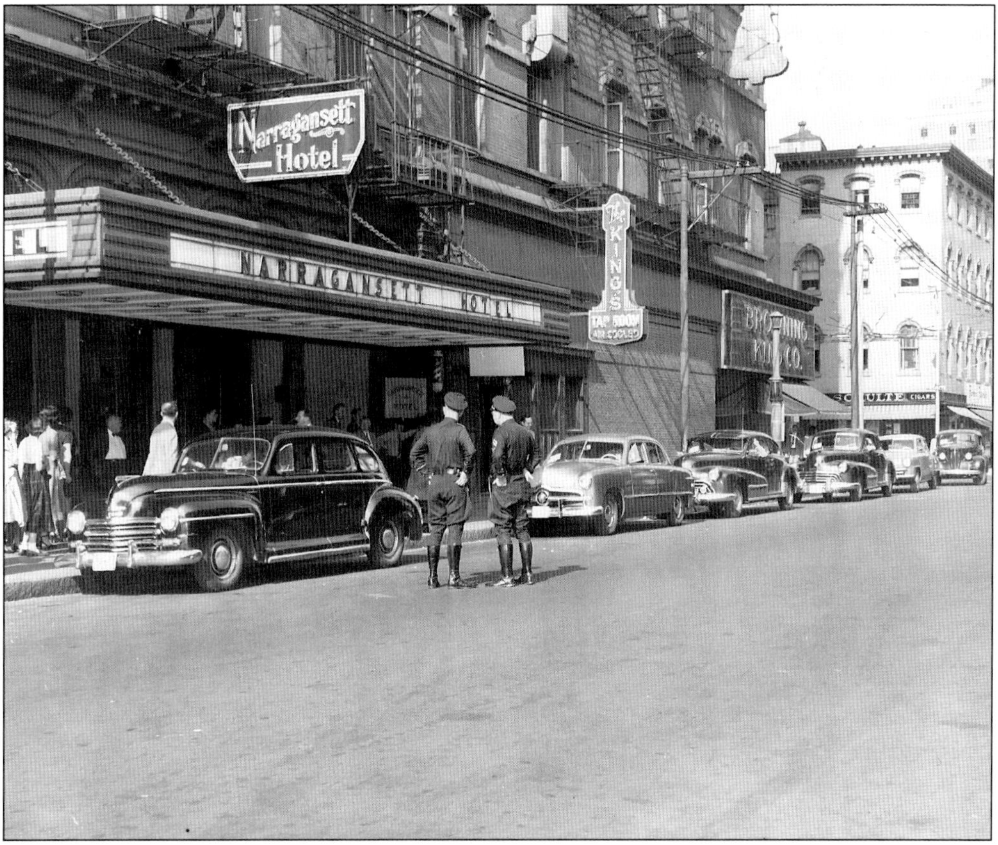


Narragansett Hotel, Providence. Located at the corner of Dorrance and Weybosset Street and completed in 1878, this hotel was purchased in 1924 by Edward Radding and Charles Brown. Max Zinn became a part owner. The hotel had kosher banquet facilities and was the scene of many important events in the Jewish community.

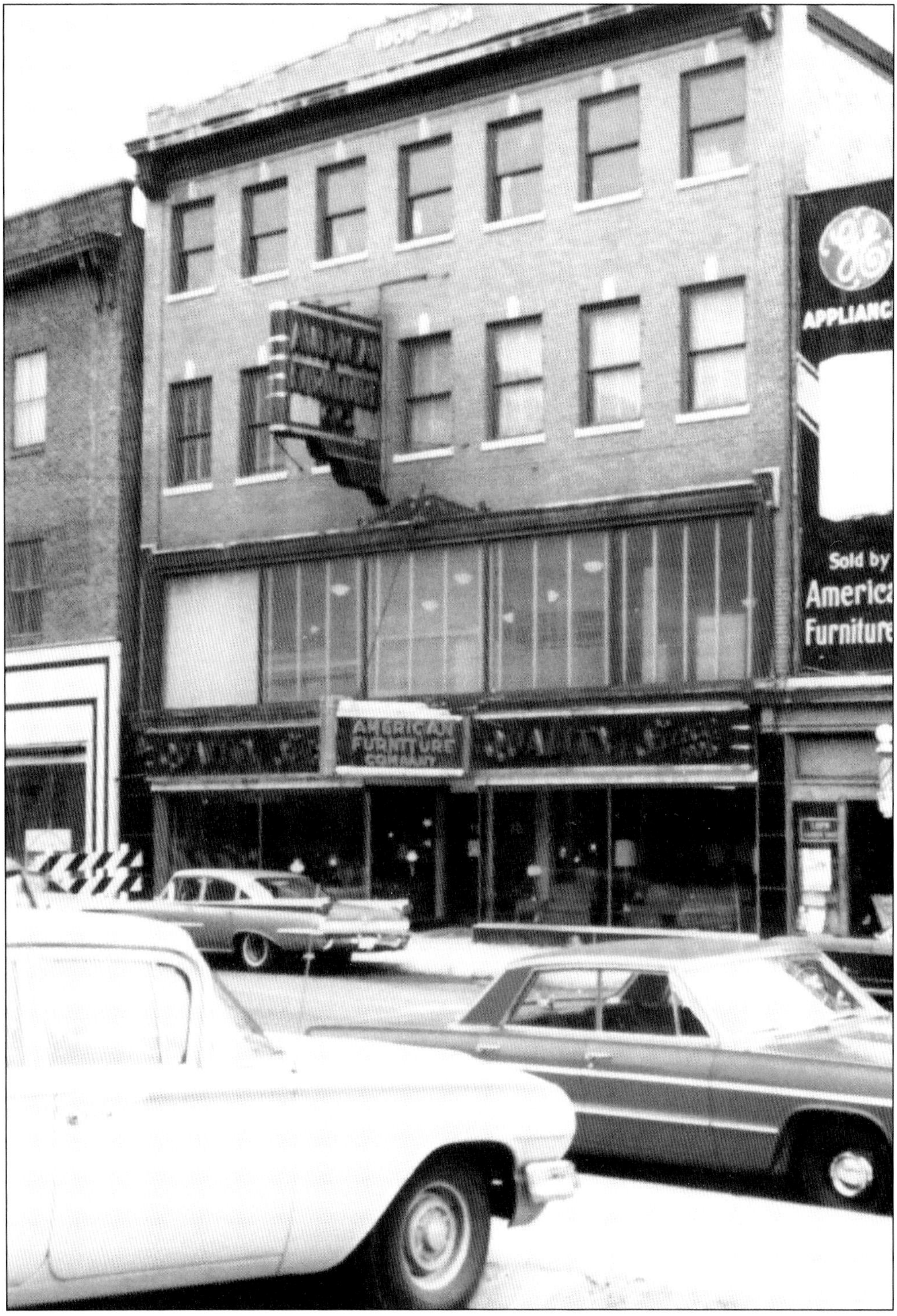


The American Furniture Co., East Avenue, Pawtucket. The American Furniture Co., established by Isaac and Sam Cokin, grew out of a junk business that began to specialize in buying used furniture and reselling it. It became a major retailer on East Avenue.

*Eight*

# Professions

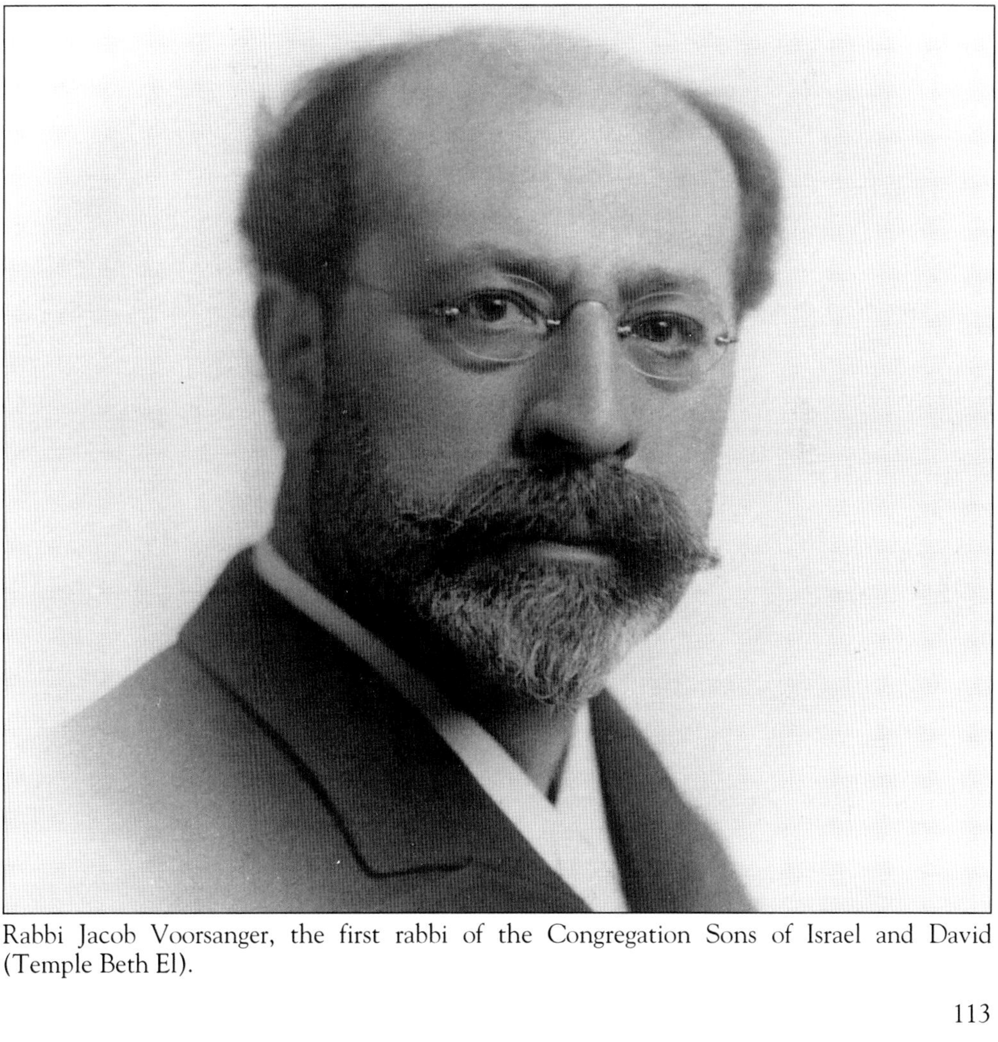

Rabbi Jacob Voorsanger, the first rabbi of the Congregation Sons of Israel and David (Temple Beth El).

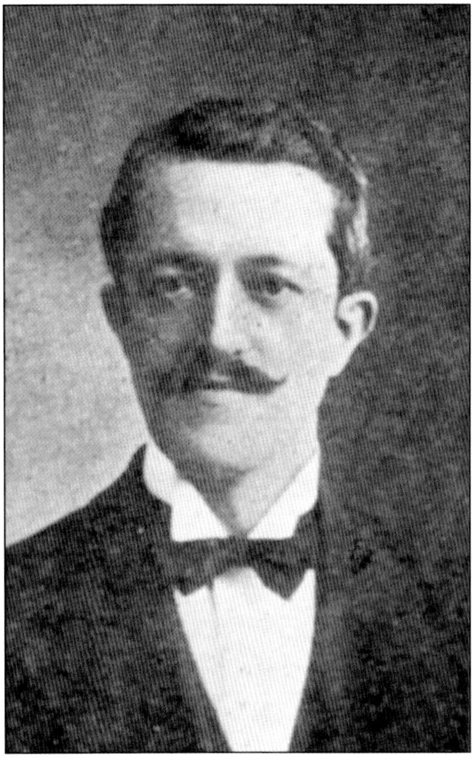

Jacob Eaton, politician. Made a member of the Republican Third Ward Committee in 1901, Jacob Eaton served as the chairman of that district from 1903 until his death in 1921.

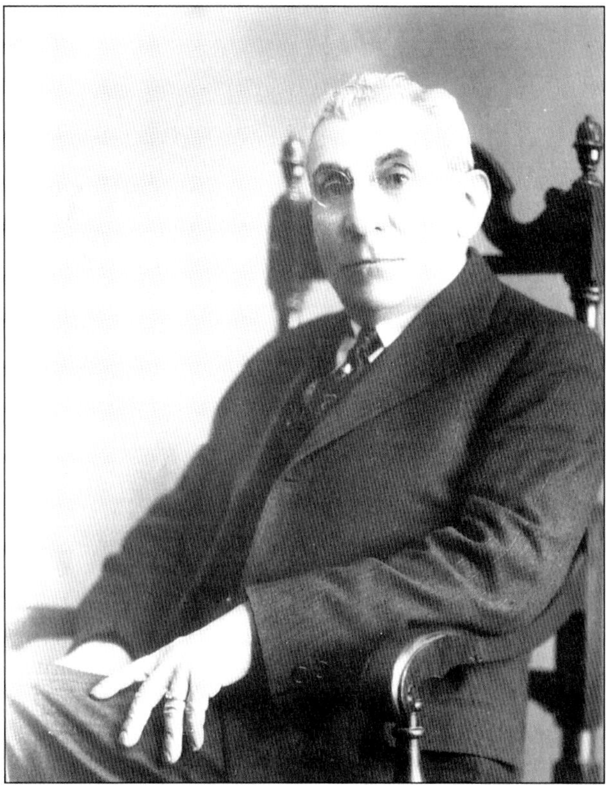

Bernard Manuel Goldowsky, private detective. Owner of the National Detective Agency (1906–1936), he handled civil, criminal, and industrial problems.

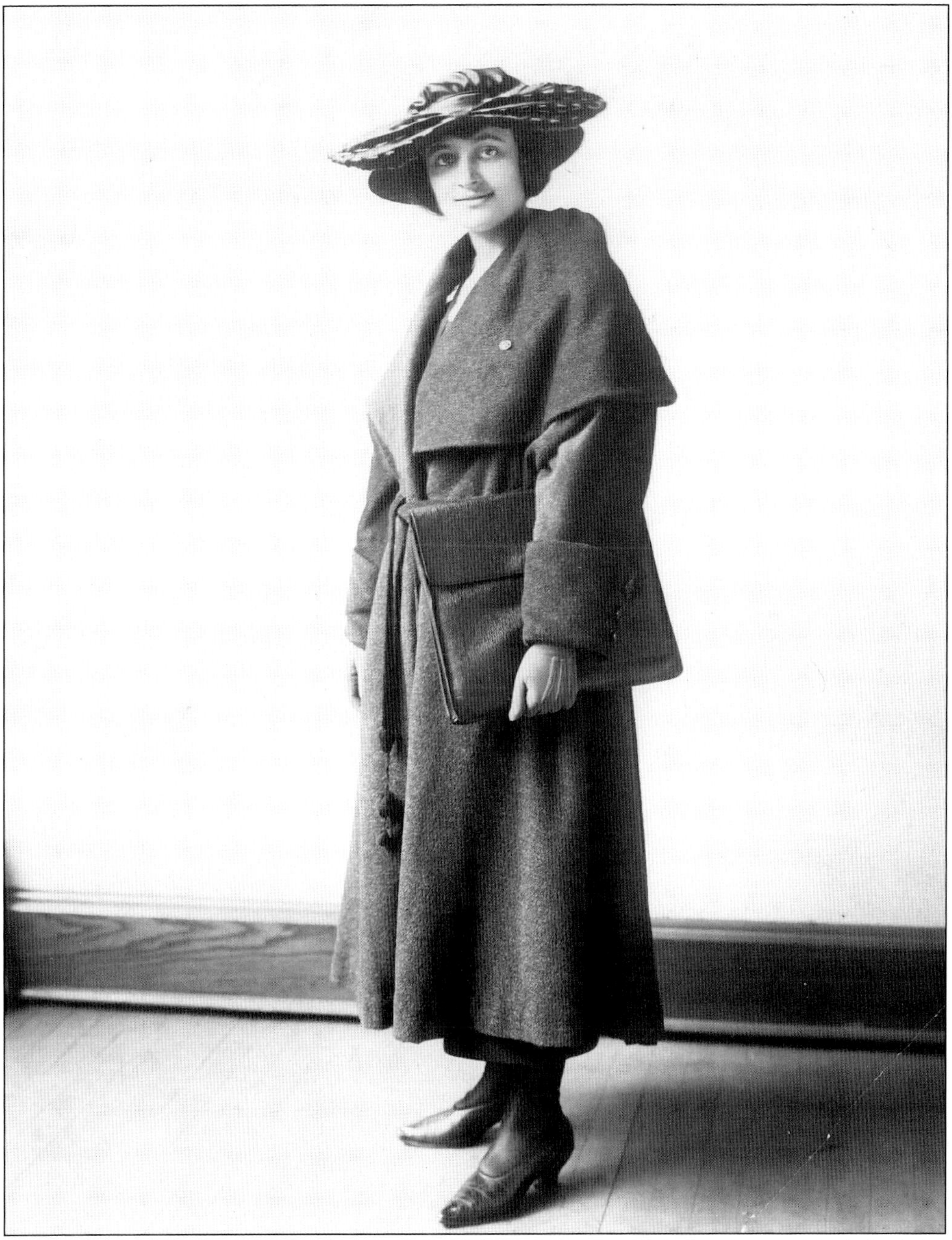

Mamie Brown Block, c.1915, advertising and businesswoman. Mamie Brown Block had the distinction of traveling as a field representative for an advertising firm, a unique position for a woman of her time.

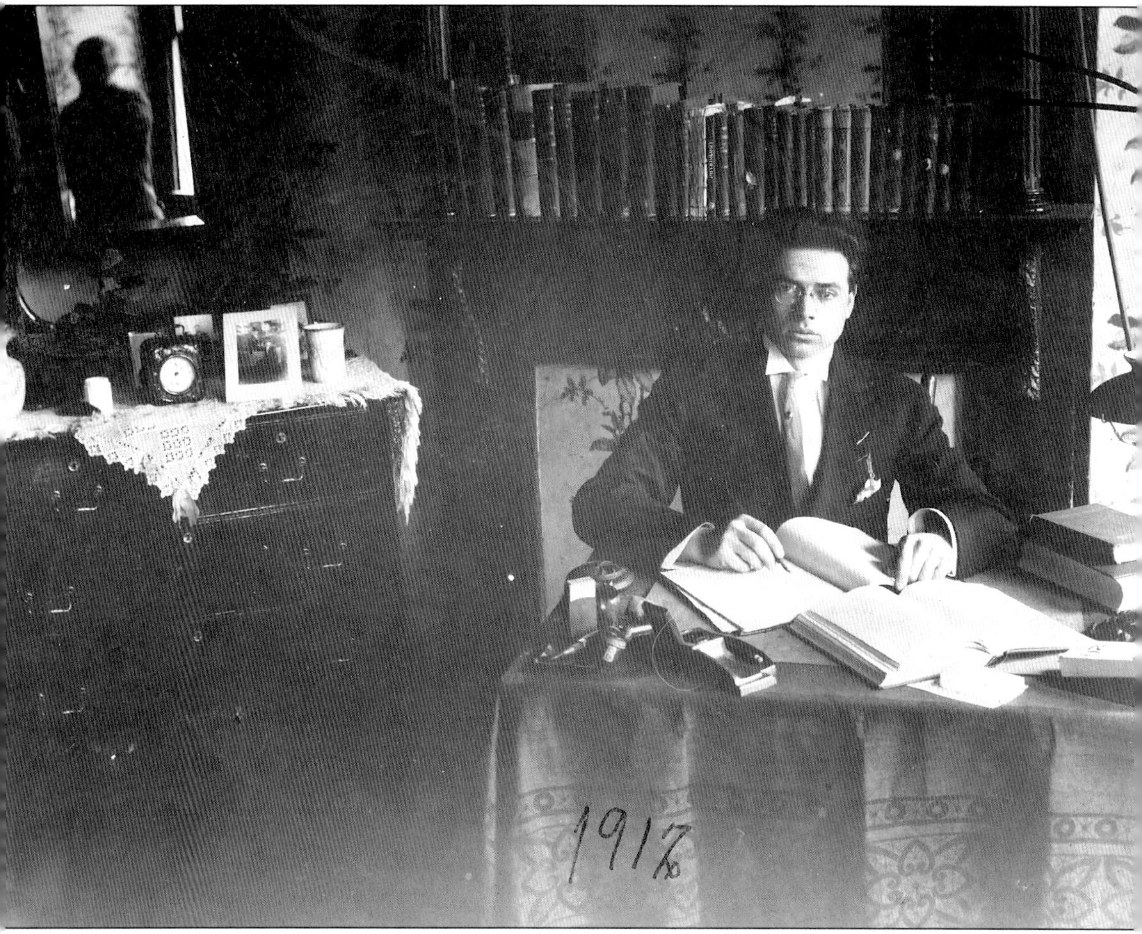


Dr. Morris Lebow, photographed at his office in 1917. Dr. Lebow was one of the first orthodontists in Rhode Island.

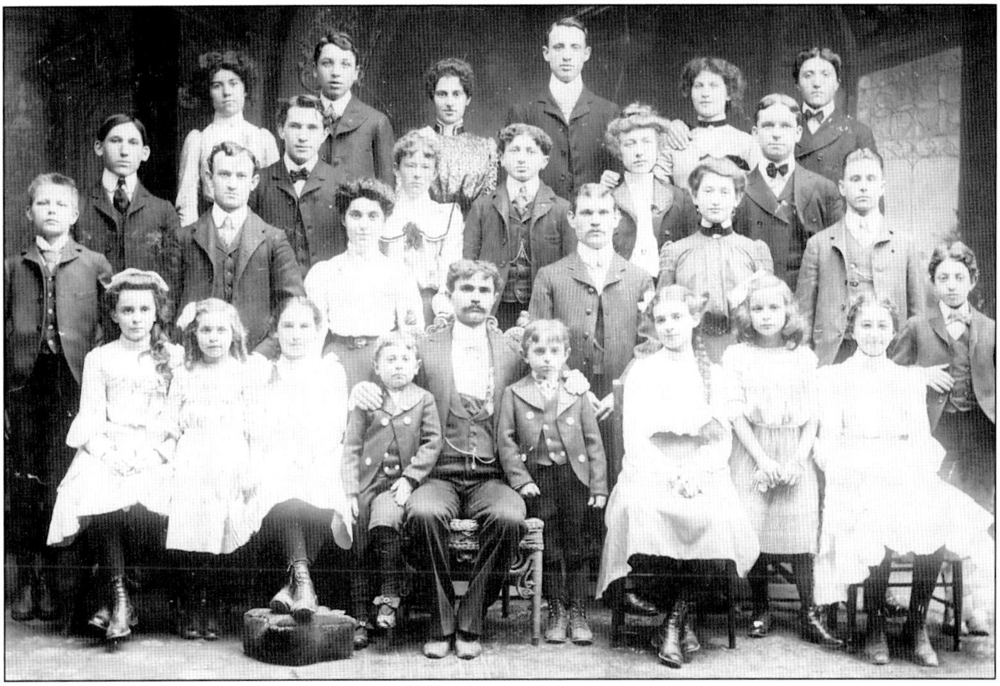

Sam Tatz (seated in front). Sam Tatz came to this country in the 1880s. He played the violin, was a dancing instructor, and was a collector for charitable causes.

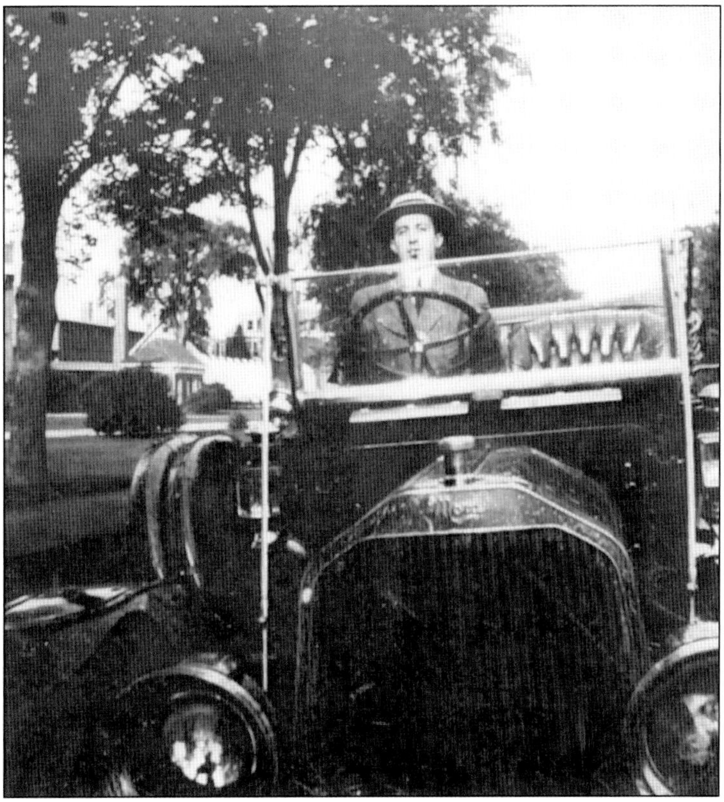

Dr. Samuel Starr, one of the early group of Jewish physicians practicing in Providence. He is shown at the wheel of his Morris touring car, c. 1912, perhaps on his way to a house call.

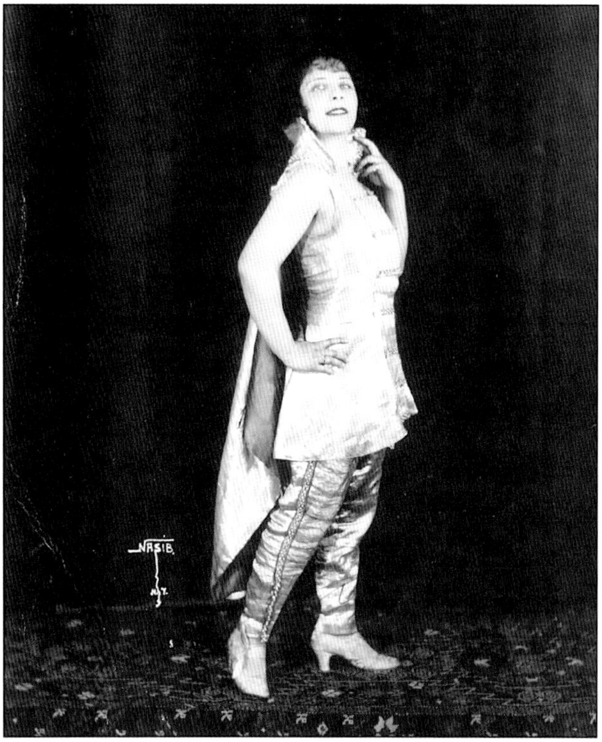


Thelma Winnerman (stage name, Billie Wynn). A vaudeville performer and musician, she played the trumpet in the 1920s.

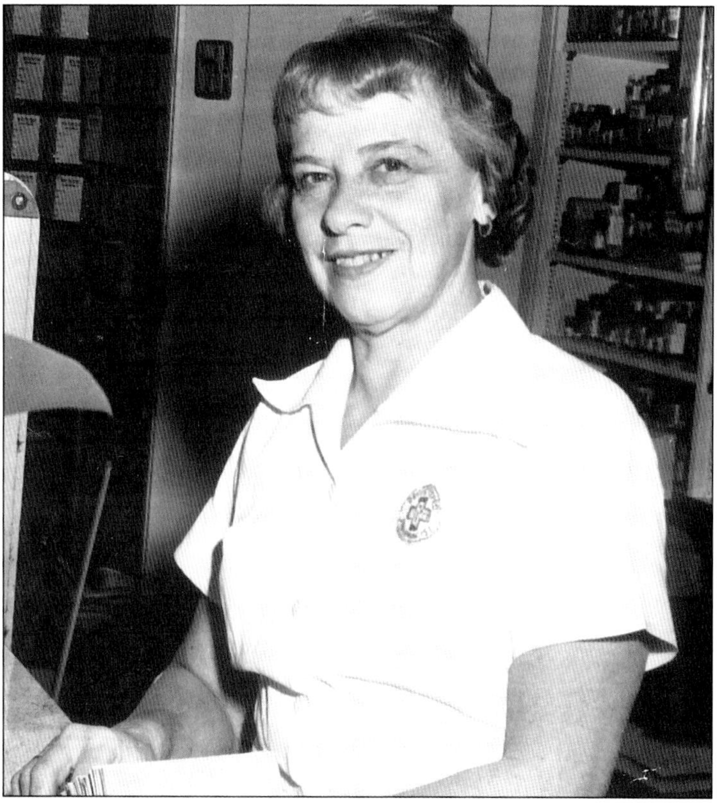

Rose Goldsmith Kunstler, pharmacist.

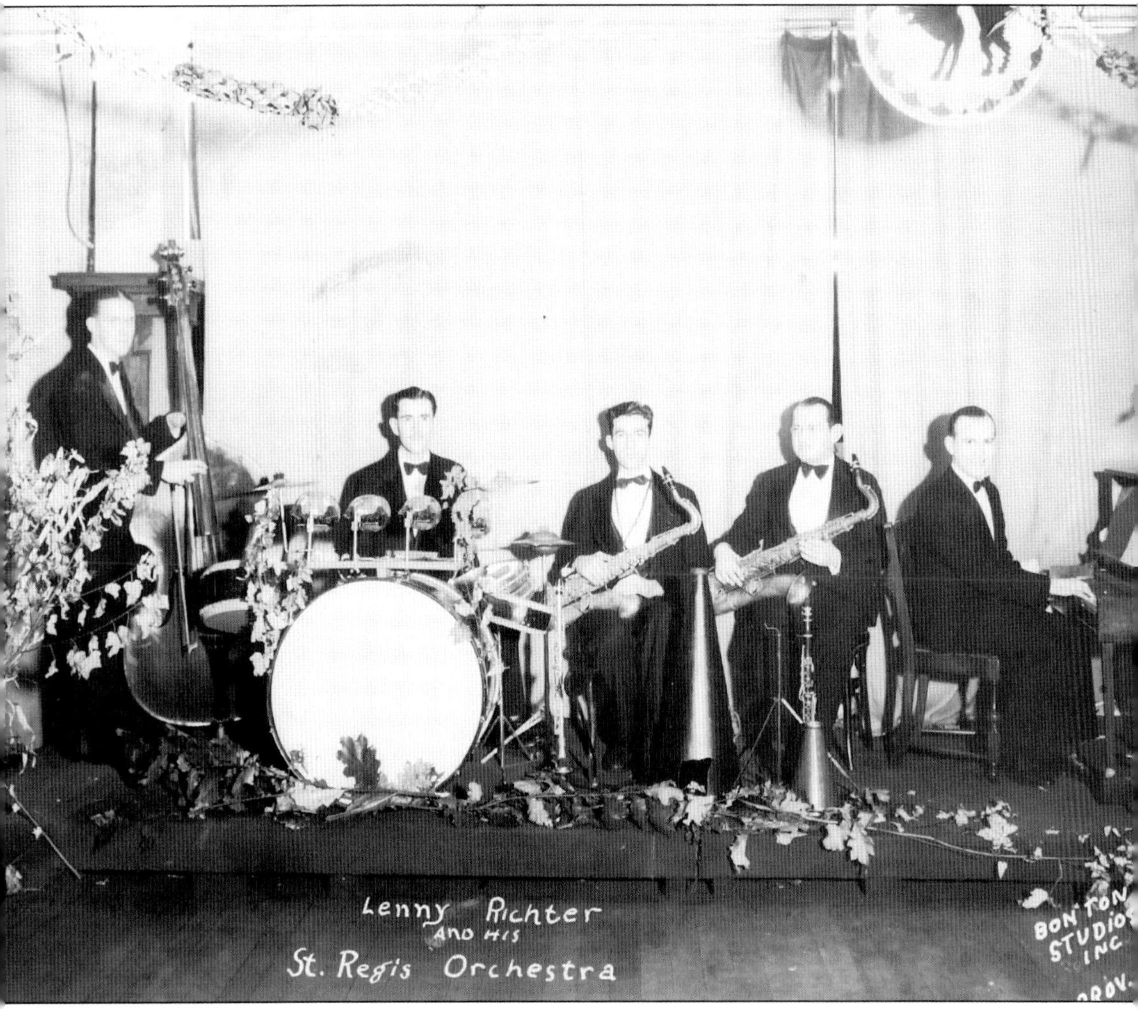

Lenny Richter, orchestra leader, and his St. Regis Orchestra, 1933.

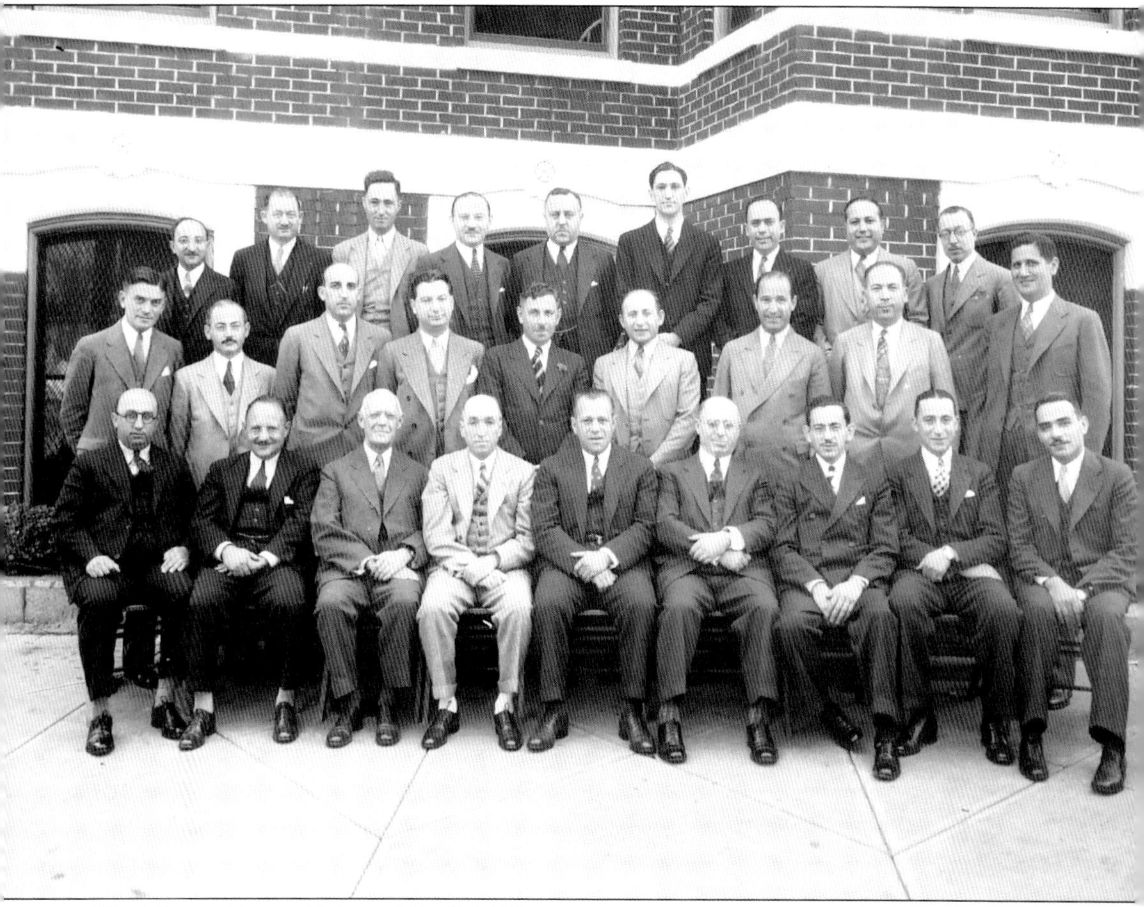

The Miriam Hospital Medical Staff, 1935.

Samuel Gereboff, an accountant with the firm Gereboff & Co., Providence. He practiced for more than 50 years.

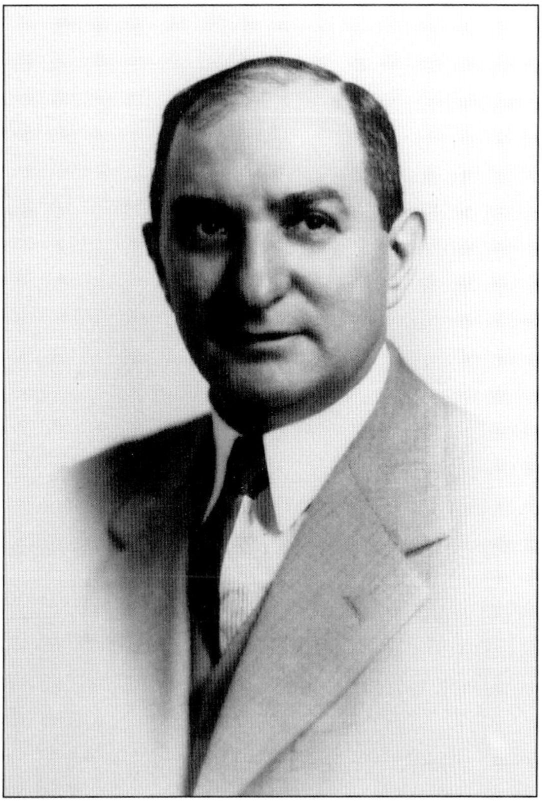

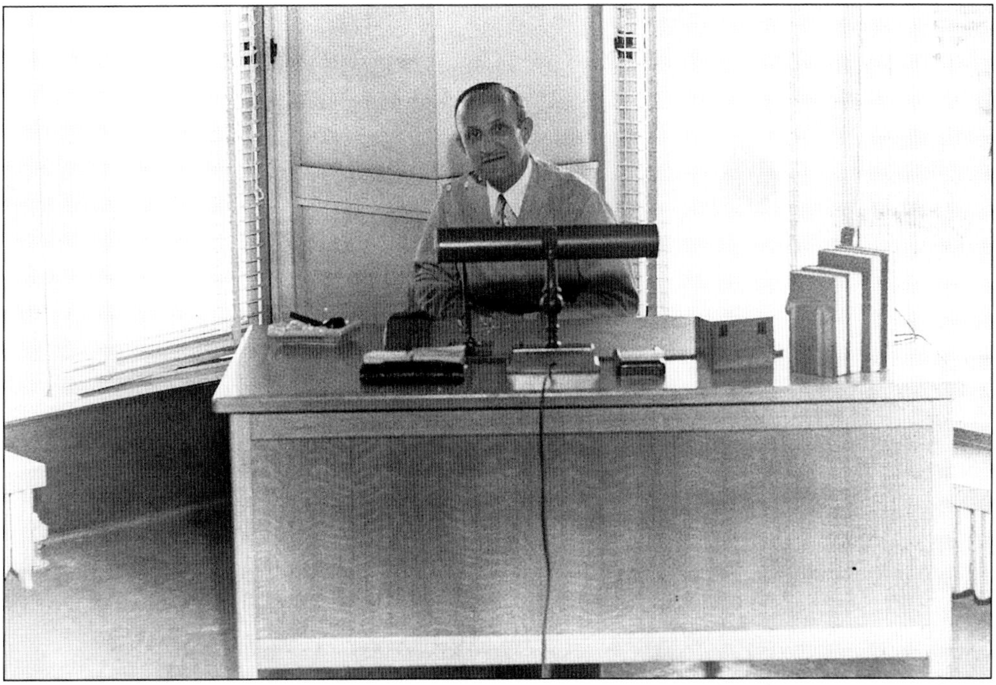

Dr. Carl Jagolinzer, optometrist. Dr. Jagolinzer's practice was located in downtown Providence for 59 years.

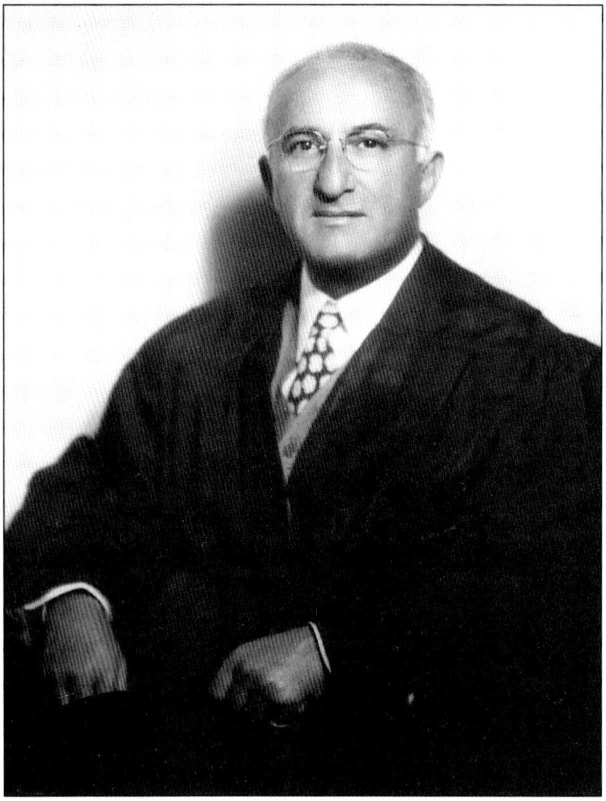

Judge Philip C. Joslin, Justice of the Superior Court from 1932 to 1958. Judge Joslin served with distinction. J. Jerome Hahn was the first Jewish Justice on the Superior and Supreme Courts.

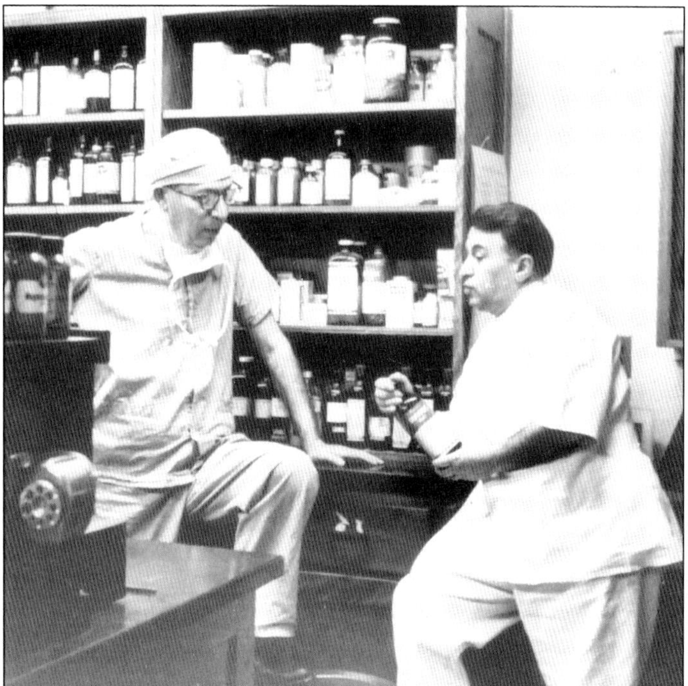

Dr. Joseph Webber, surgeon (left), and Beryl Segal, pharmacist, in the Miriam Hospital pharmacy.

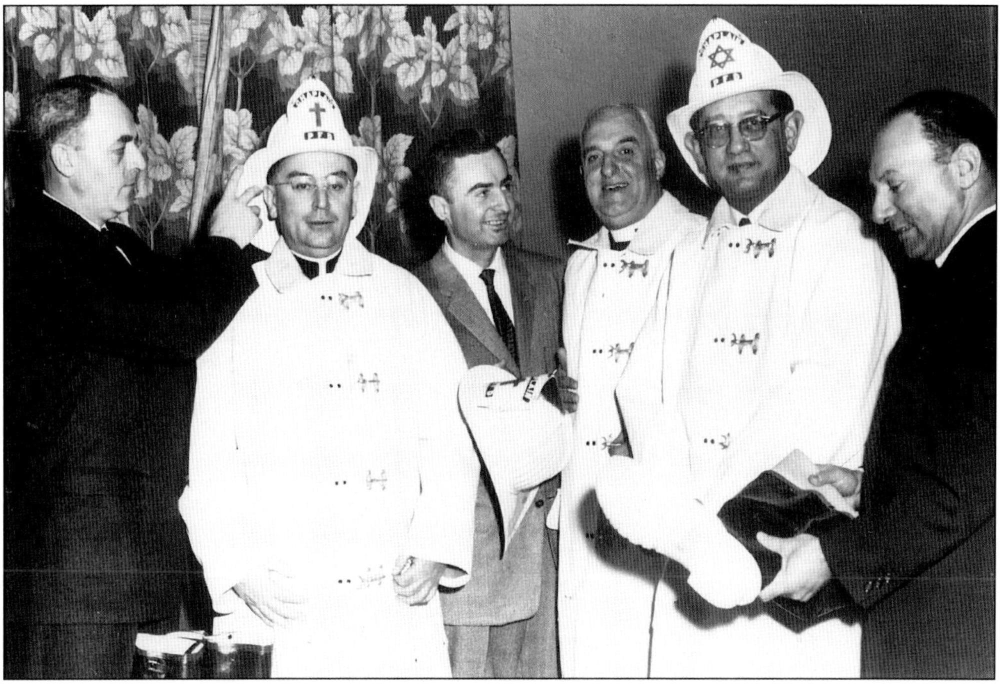

Louis Gorodetsky, private, a member of the Providence Fire Department. Louis Gorodetsky is believed to have been the first Jewish firefighter.

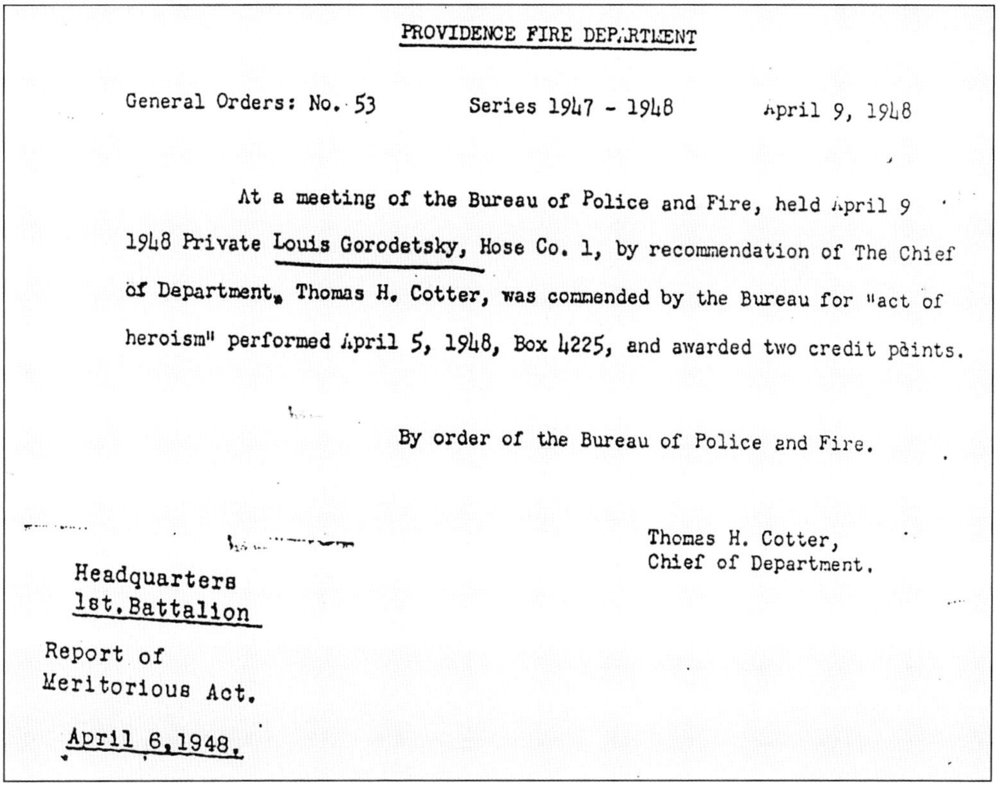

PROVIDENCE FIRE DEPARTMENT

General Orders: No. 53 Series 1947 - 1948 April 9, 1948

At a meeting of the Bureau of Police and Fire, held April 9 1948 Private Louis Gorodetsky, Hose Co. 1, by recommendation of The Chief of Department, Thomas H. Cotter, was commended by the Bureau for "act of heroism" performed April 5, 1948, Box 4225, and awarded two credit points.

By order of the Bureau of Police and Fire.

Thomas H. Cotter,
Chief of Department.

Headquarters
1st. Battalion

Report of
Meritorious Act.

April 6, 1948.

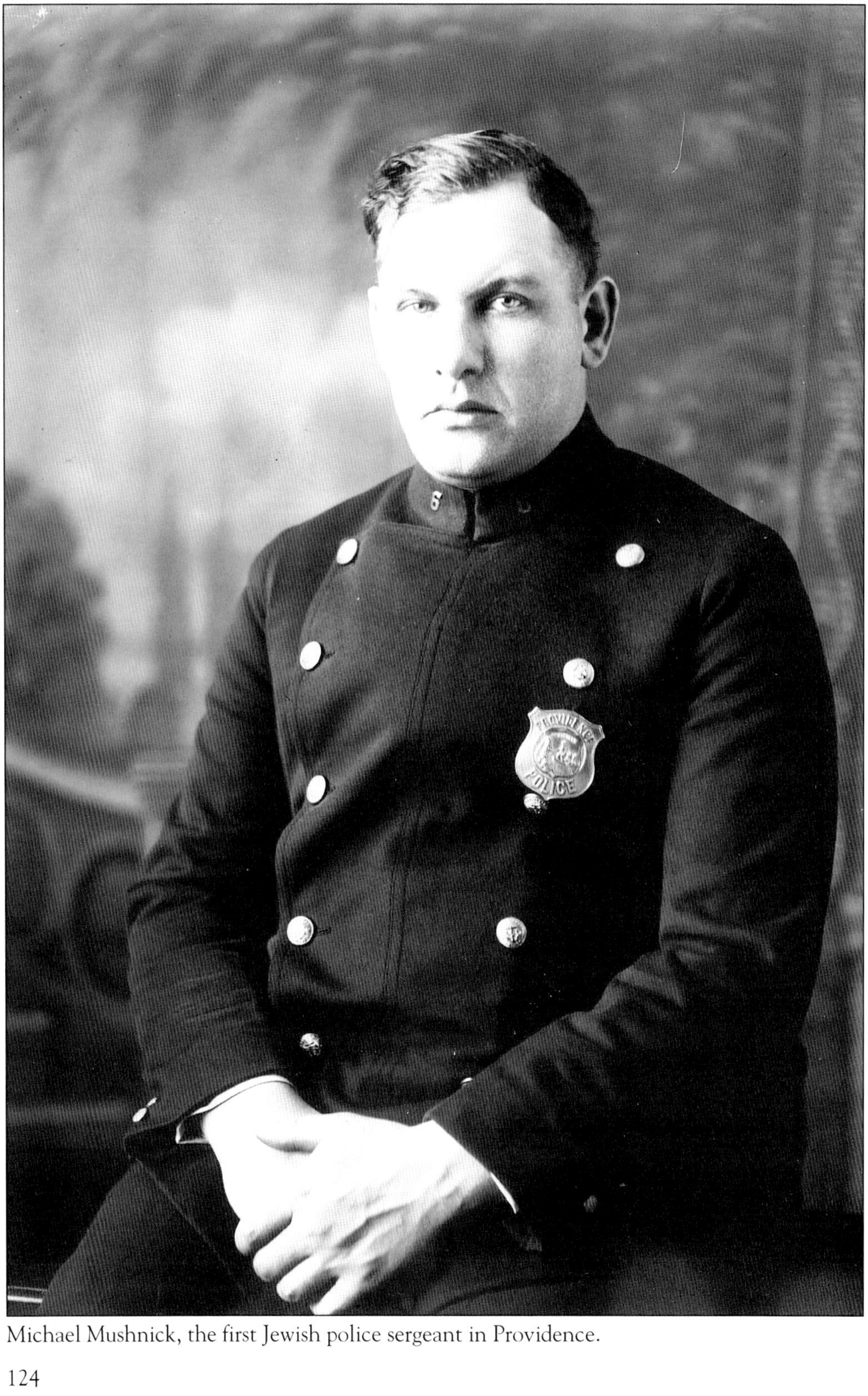

Michael Mushnick, the first Jewish police sergeant in Providence.

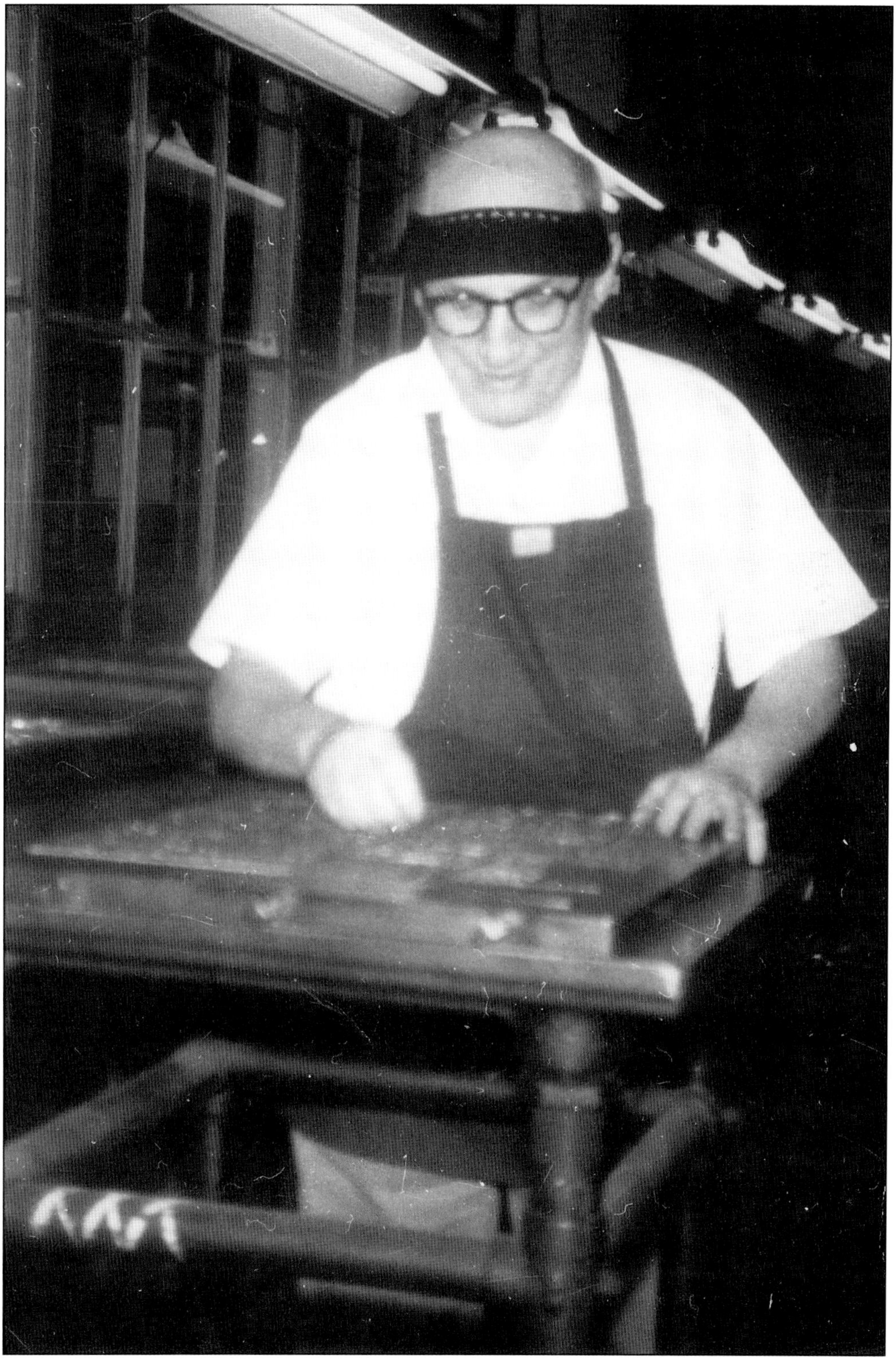

David S. Goldman, a typesetter at the *Providence Journal*, 1952.

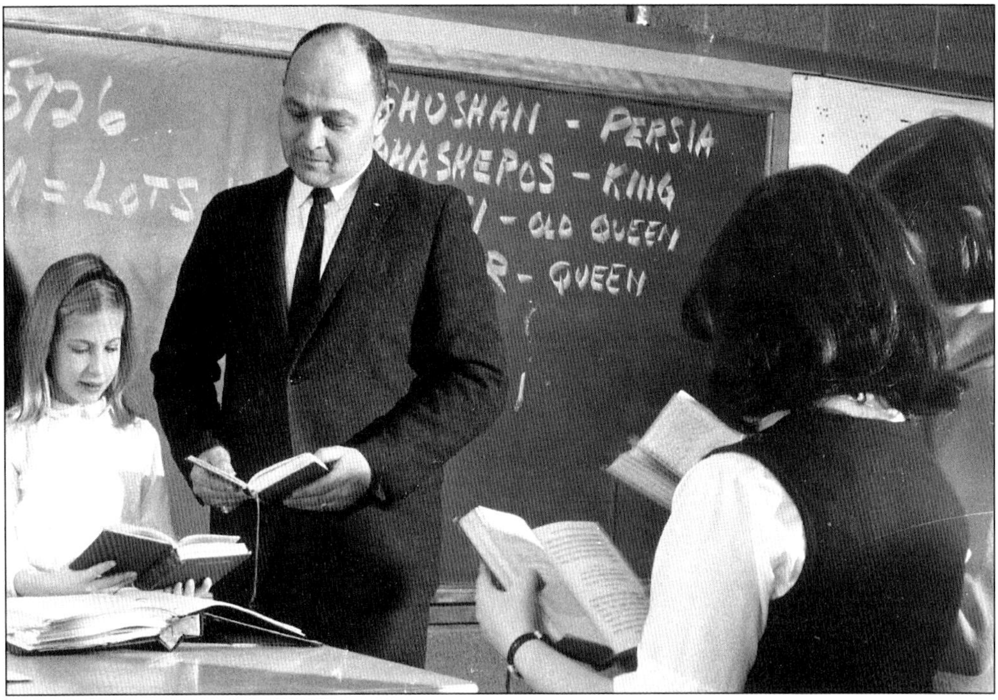


Samuel Stepak, a teacher at the Temple Beth El Religious School.

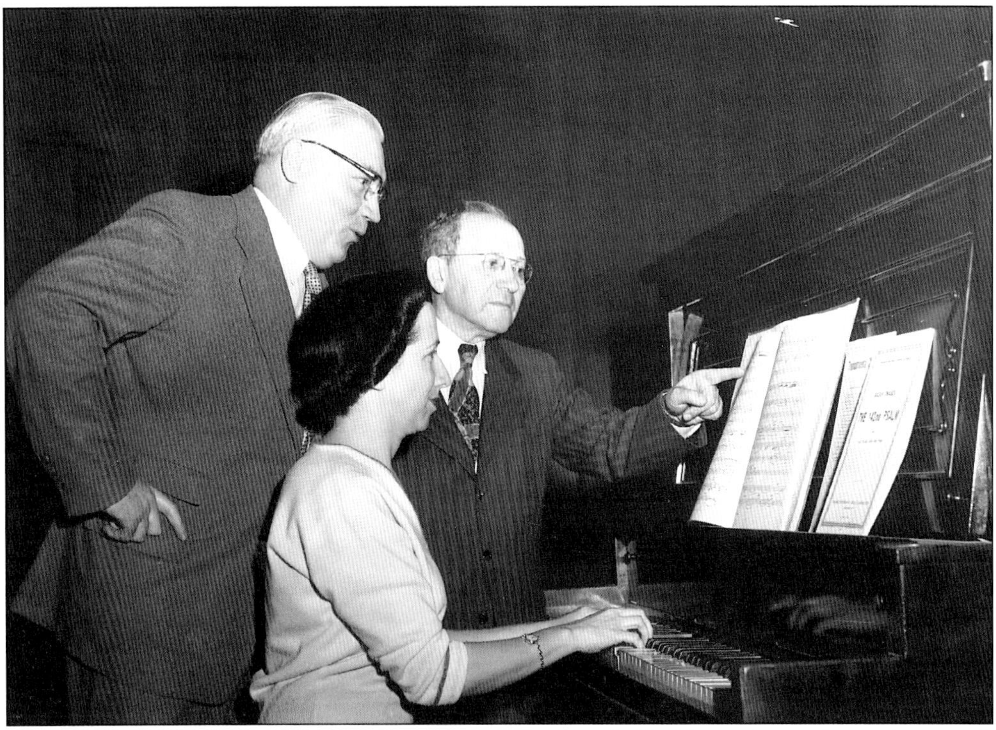

Cantor Jacob Hohenemser, cantor from 1940 to 1964 (left). He is shown here along with choirmaster, organist, and composer Arthur Einstein and pianist Muriel Port (Stevens), all from the Temple Emanu-El.

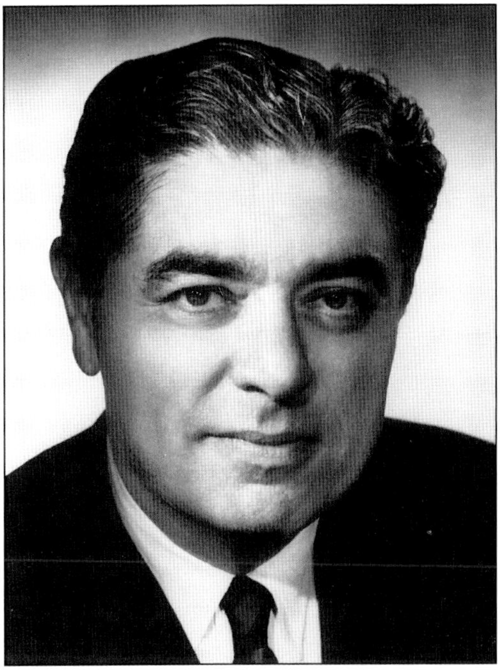
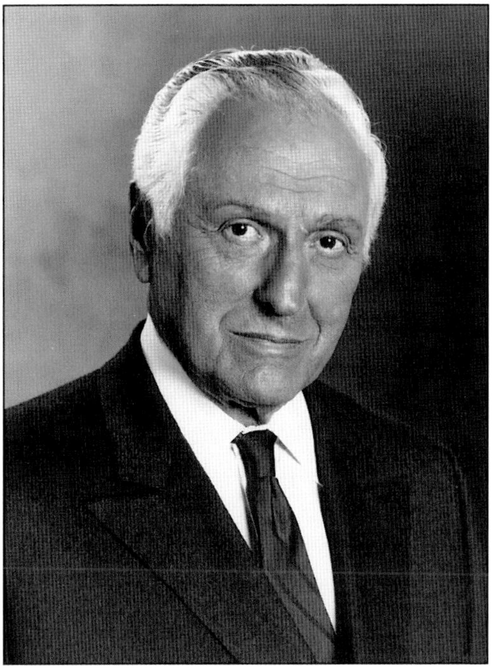

Former governors Frank Licht (left) and Bruce Sundlun (right). Jews came to many of the towns and villages of Rhode Island. Some tarried a while and then moved on. Many more remained, putting down roots often in places outside of urban centers. As others joined them, they formed communities with a synagogue as its heart. During the time of which we have written, the synagogue was their "associative center" where as part of a congregation they could worship, meet people, receive help, and, for newcomers, relieve their loneliness.

Future years brought many changes in the lives of these early settlers and their descendants. Their participation in the Rhode Island community included the election of two men who became the first Jewish governors of the State of Rhode Island. Governor Frank Licht (left), son of a Russian immigrant, served from 1969 to 1973. Governor Bruce Sundlun (right), the grandson of a man who immigrated from Lithuania, held the office of governor from 1991 to 1995.

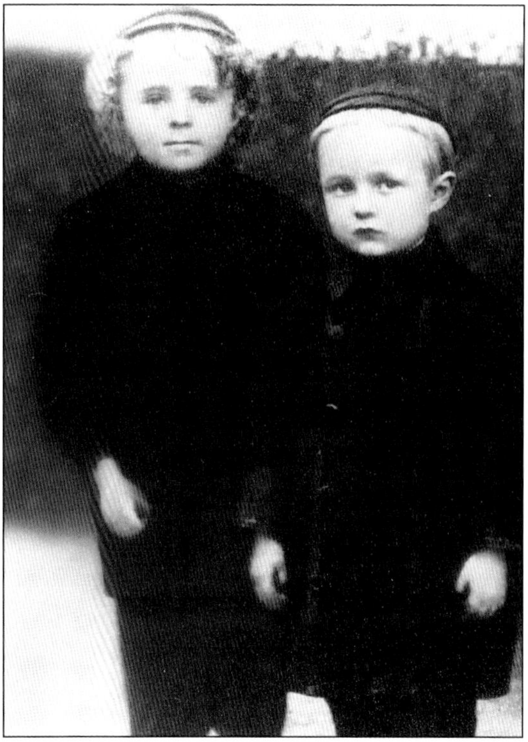

Joseph Goodman (left) and his brother Jacob, c. 1910.

# Acknowledgments

*The Jews of Rhode Island: 1658–1958* is a project of the Rhode Island Jewish Historical Association. All royalties accrued from its publication will go to the support of the Association and its activities.

Most of the images in this book are from the archives of the Rhode Island Jewish Historical Association.

Special thanks are due to Dr. Alene Silver, for her dedicated work in arranging photographs; and to Anne Sherman, Rhode Island Jewish Historical Association office manager, for assistance above and beyond the call of duty.

Thanks are also due Joyce Blackman, Aaron Cohen (president of the Rhode Island Jewish Historical Association), Maurice Cohen, Rabbi Leslie Y. Gutterman, Elizabeth J. Johnson, the Spaulding Research House Research Library, Sarah Leavitt (author of the Images of America book *Slater Mill*), the Rhode Island Historical Society for permission to use their photographs published previously in *Rhode Island Jewish Historical Notes*, Toby Rossner (director of Media Services of the Bureau of Jewish Education of Rhode Island), and Ellen Smith (curator of the American Jewish Historical Society).